southern
THEORY

Raewyn Connell

southern
THEORY

The global dynamics of knowledge
in social science

polity

Contents

Introduction

The purpose of this book is to propose a new path for social theory that will help social science to serve democratic purposes on a world scale. The dominant powers reshaping our world seek to close down, rather than open up, the self-knowledge of society. In such a world, social science has a vital democratic role to play.

But social science is, at best, ambiguously democratic. Its dominant genres picture the world as it is seen by men, by capitalists, by the educated and affluent. Most important, they picture the world as seen from the rich capital-exporting countries of Europe and North America—the global metropole. To ground knowledge of society in other experiences remains a fragile project. Yet only knowledge produced on a planetary scale is adequate to support the self-understanding of societies now being forcibly reshaped on a planetary scale. This book is concerned with how social science might operate democratically on such a scale.

The first section, 'Northern theory', examines how modern social science embeds the viewpoints, perspectives and problems of metropolitan society, while presenting itself as universal knowledge. I take the case of sociology, and first explore its history, starting with the great myth of the 'founding fathers'. Next I look at the genre of general theory, focusing on three extremely influential modern writers, and finally I examine the attempt of metropolitan sociologists to shake free from parochialism through theories of globalisation.

The second section, 'Looking South', explores what happened to the same social science in a colony of settlement, Australia. The intellectual relationship with the metropole has changed quite dramatically over the last century, without ever generating a distinctive point of view. I explore— with some autobiographical sadness—the ambivalences of social science in a situation of economic and cultural dependence.

The third and longest section, 'Southern theory', discusses social theorising that has arisen in four situations where dependence has been challenged: postcolonial Africa, modernising Iran, Latin America since World War II, and India since the Emergency of the 1970s. In each of these chapters, I try to follow the threads of local arguments wherever they lead. That is to say, I take them seriously as theory—as texts to learn *from*, not just *about*. I also explore what these debates reveal about the project of theorising in the global periphery, its intellectual and practical problems, and its differing forms.

In the final section, 'Antipodean reflections', I explore consequences of Southern perspectives for social science as a project on a world scale. One task is to rethink the role of the land in social structure and dynamics, an issue highlighted by Indigenous people's movements. Another is to rethink the character of social-scientific knowledge (epistemology, methods and forms of communication) in a context of respect for intellectual traditions from the global periphery. In the final chapter, I make some proposals about how to do this, and suggest how the task is connected with the project of democracy.

***

I use the name 'Southern theory' for several reasons. First, the phrase calls attention to periphery–centre relations in the realm of knowledge. The editors of the Indian periodical *Subaltern Studies* used the term 'subaltern' not so much to name a social category as to highlight relations of power (see Chapter 8). Similarly, I use the term 'Southern' not to name a sharply bounded category of states or societies, but to emphasise relations—

authority, exclusion and inclusion, hegemony, partnership, sponsorship, appropriation—between intellectuals and institutions in the metropole and those in the world periphery.

Second, the title emphasises that the majority world does produce *theory*. The Beninese philosopher Paulin Hountondji describes a pattern in colonial science, carried forward to the postcolonial world, where data-gathering and application happen in the colony, while theorising happens in the metropole (see Chapter 5). Most social science still follows this pattern. Yet theory does emerge from the social experience of the periphery, in many genres and styles.

Third, the title calls attention to the fact that social thought happens in particular places. I am writing this book in Australia, a country whose name, given by British colonisers in the early nineteenth century, means 'the south land'. Like Chileans, white Australians often think of themselves as living at the end of the earth, and their distance from the metropole produces odd effects in social science. But Australia also has an Indigenous population for whom this is not the end of the earth, but the centre. Australian Aboriginal civilisation is the oldest continuously existing culture in the world. Relationship to the land is a key theme in Aboriginal custom, politics and art, and this is the starting point for the discussion in Chapter 9.

***

The issues discussed in this book are not new. A generation ago they were debated in India, when the distinguished French anthropologist Louis Dumont made the classic pronouncement that the idea of a Hindu sociology was a contradiction in terms (Das 1995: 34). The idea of an economics for the developing countries, launched by the Argentinian Raúl Prebisch, was put down with equal bluntness by North American economists (see Chapter 7). In the 1980s, the International Sociological Association debated 'indigenous sociologies', with limited success (see Chapter 5).

Dumont's belief that social science can have only one, universal, body of concepts and methods, the one created in the global North, is still dominant. It remains the default assumption in every social science except, ironically, Dumont's own. In Chapter 2, I show this assumption at work in modern classics of sociological theory, and in Chapter 3—even more ironically—in recent sociologies of globalisation.

The power of this assumption can be seen in hundreds of forums, from research granting bodies to university curricula. A startling case is the Gulbenkian Foundation report *Open the Social Sciences* (1996). A distinguished international panel, chaired by Immanuel Wallerstein, met over a couple of years to ponder the past and future of social science. Something pathbreaking might have been expected. As it turned out, the history of social science the panel wrote was immaculately Eurocentric, and the viewpoint from which it discussed current problems was North American. Ideas from the rest of the world were treated as footnotes to 'the heritage' of Comte, Weber, Marx, Smith, Ranke and friends.

The idea of a universal science of human behaviour and society has a certain grandeur, and a certain usefulness. As Chilla Bulbeck (1998) shows in exploring world feminism, however carefully we acknowledge cultural and economic difference, universalist ideas such as rights and equality remain important for a democratic politics. But when the claim of universal knowledge or universal values is made from a position of privilege, it is likely to serve hegemony not liberation.

The social sciences took their modern institutional form in the second half of the nineteenth century, at the high tide of European imperialism. As Ashis Nandy has emphasised, the colonial connection worked both ways; the metropole too was profoundly affected (see Chapter 8). Imperialism had become the condition of existence of metropolitan society by the time the new sciences made 'society' an object of systematic theory.

This connection was quite plain to intellectuals in the nineteenth century. As I show in Chapter 1, in a distorted form it became the basis of sociology as an intellectual enterprise. But twentieth century sociology, rightly rejecting the muddy idea of 'social evolution', also rejected the sense of connection with the colonised world that had underpinned it. With anthropology now the designated intellectual container for primitive societies, the rest of social science formed itself on ethnocentric assumptions that amounted to a gigantic lie—that modernity created itself within the North Atlantic world, independent of the rest of humanity. Models constructed on the basis of that lie, such as functionalist sociology, modernisation theory and neoclassical economics, were then exported to the rest of the world with all the authority of the most advanced knowledge, and all the weight of First World wealth and power.

There have been attempts to correct this, thematising colonialism and world inequality within metropolitan social science. Among the attempts were underconsumptionist and Marxist theories of imperialism, from Hobson and Lenin onwards, and the 'world system' approach developed by Immanuel Wallerstein and his colleagues. In sharp-edged projects such as Georges Balandier's *Sociology of Black Africa* (1955), the political dilemmas involved in practising social science in the 'colonial situation' were squarely faced. Such work is inspiring, and will be discussed at various points in the book. But it has a profound problem: it works through categories produced in the metropole, and does not dialogue with the *ideas* produced by the colonised world.

Metropolitan sciences, continuously updated at home, continue to be exported. The trade now includes Foucault and Habermas, queer theory, economic modelling and evolutionary psychology. Metropolitan theory is distributed through a global network of institutions including universities, scientific organisations, journals and—as Arturo Escobar (1995) has eloquently shown—development institutions from the World Bank down.

The hegemony of metropolitan knowledge does not obliterate all others. Alternative ways of thinking about the world certainly persist. But they are readily marginalised, as African discussions of indigenous knowledge have shown—intellectually discredited, dropped from the curricula of schools and universities, or ripped off by corporations pursuing intellectual property rights (Odora Hoppers 2002). Veena Das (1995: 30) points to the particular way this disenfranchisement works for social theory. Under the hegemony of metropolitan theory, the Indian intellectual is forced to relegate local bodies of thought to the past—to treat them as 'traditions' of historical or ethnographic interest, but not as sources of intellectual authority in the present.

Therefore, it is futile to challenge metropolitan predominance by discovering alternative 'founding fathers' of the same social science—for instance, by claiming that Ibn Khaldun invented sociology back in the fourteenth century CE (Alatas 2006). This gives the same kind of rhetorical satisfaction as the idea that classical Greek culture had African roots (Bernal 1987), but does nothing to change the terms of intellectual production in the present. Such moves may even be counter-productive, placing the glories of Arab or African thought firmly in a distant past.

The claim made by this book is rather that colonised and peripheral societies produce social thought *about the modern world* which has as much intellectual power as metropolitan social thought, and more political relevance. Since the ground is different, the form of theorising is often different too. Work needs to be done to develop the connections, as well as the contrasts, between these bodies of thought and those of the metropole.

This book touches on issues discussed in 'postcolonial theory' in literary studies. Though I am happy to acknowledge the inspiration of Edward Said's *Orientalism* and other work in its genre, the central problems examined here are different. This book concerns research and theory about the social, and its focus is the construction and reconstruction of social science. Social science has to be understood in its cultural, political and economic contexts—but it does not reduce to any of those.

***

I have gone about the job by making a study of texts, and this needs some justification. Hountondji (1983), in his incisive *African Philosophy: Myth and Reality*, makes the crucial observation that philosophy is a text-based form of knowledge. This is true for social theory too. Many communities have social, moral and ontological outlooks richly expressed in oral, visual or ceremonial forms. (Chapter 9 touches on social knowledge embedded in such forms.) But it is only written texts that allow sustained argument and systematic critique. Oral knowledge can certainly cumulate, but only texts allow us to trace and reflect on the process. Further, it is only written texts that allow the communication of complex social knowledge across planetary distances.

I focus on a relatively small number of texts. There is a genre of writing where one skips lightly across a large number of sources. Chapters 1 and 4 do this, in an attempt to reconstruct the historical trajectory of sociology in the metropole and in Australia; Chapter 3 does it in an attempt to map the globalisation literature. For the rest of the book I work at closer focus. I have wanted to do reasonable justice to the theoretical projects of the authors I am discussing, whether in the metropole or in the periphery. That means settling down with specific texts and trying to understand, in some detail, how they work.

The texts partly chose themselves by being available in Australian libraries, or accessible to a traveller. I can read several languages, but only English with complete fluency, so I have depended a good deal on translations. Some are—as the Italian proverb '*traduttore, traditore*' says—treasons on the text. Yet most of the translations I have worked with seem honest attempts at the difficult task of communicating across languages, and I am deeply grateful to the translators for doing this work.

I have looked for influential statements of social thought, whatever their genre may be. They range from formal treatise to popular non-fiction, from academic journal article to sermon. In finding them I have taken advice from friends and colleagues in a number of countries.

The first half of the book focuses on sociology, the social science in which I have worked longest; I keep this focus in order to make the critique of Northern theory as precise as possible. When I turn to Southern theory in the second half, the scope widens. In disciplinary terms, these chapters move among anthropology, history, psychology, philosophy, economics and cultural studies as well as sociology; they also treat texts that are unclassifiable blends across the field.

Chapters 5 to 8 are *not* attempts to write histories of African, Iranian, Latin American or Indian social thought. I don't have the technical knowledge to do such a thing. Understanding a text certainly requires some background, and I hope readers unfamiliar with these literatures will pick up a little of the fascinating histories involved. But my central concern is with reading social theory, and that necessarily concerns the way texts communicate *beyond* their immediate contexts. Ultimately, it concerns the way they might enter a global communication of knowledge.

The second half of the book therefore records a series of encounters, between a certain reader and certain texts. They are encounters across distances, social and historical as well as geographical. For a person of my background to come to terms with, say, Ali Shariati's revolutionary Shi'ism (Chapter 6) or Raúl Prebisch's trade crisis economics (Chapter 7) is not simple. But it has to be *possible* if a global dialogue of social knowledge is to happen.

This is, frankly, an experiment. If it is not too presumptuous, I might call the book the story of my experiment with truth. It has certainly involved a long struggle for understanding, and a radical rethinking of positions from which I began many years ago.

***

Texts are written for publics. That is easily forgotten in metropolitan social science, where the 'public' is usually a taken-for-granted professional audience. It is impossible to forget with a text like Al-e Ahmad's *Gharbzadegi* ('Westoxication', 1982a), written in a highly personal style for an Iranian urban middle-class readership at a specific moment of cultural change. Yet *Gharbzadegi* is, as I argue in Chapter 6, important beyond that place and moment.

With Al-e Ahmad's writing, and with some other texts, I have a sense of the writing actually creating the public it addresses, assembling a readership that had not been assembled before. Assembling new publics across different regions of the world is a vital capacity for social science if it is to function as the self-knowledge of global society.

Social science's object of knowledge never stands still. Currently the social structures of every part of the world are being impacted by the market agenda of neoliberal politics and the widening reach of transnational business. The motivated self-ignorance of market society is both a puzzle and an obstacle for social science. Neoliberal transition has become a strong focus of social theory in Latin America, though not everywhere else (Chapter 7). In the long run, metropolitan social science too must be transformed.

In Chapter 10, I discuss the new configurations of knowledge that might result when Southern theory is everywhere respected, and differently formed theories speak together. This discussion is a shaky beginning at best. If I can convince readers it is a beginning that should be improved on, then the book is serving its purpose.

Acknowledgments

Several chapters of this book are based on previously published papers. I am grateful for permission to reprint material from: 'Why is Classical Theory Classical?' *American Journal of Sociology*, 1997, vol. 102, no. 6, 1511–57; 'Australia and World Sociology', in John Germov and Tara Renae McGee, (eds), *Histories of Australian Sociology*, Melbourne: Melbourne University Press, 2005, 3–27; 'Northern Theory: The Political Geography of General Social Theory', *Theory and Society*, 2006, vol. 35, 237–64; 'Conocimiento indígena y poder global: lecciones de los debates africanos', *Nómadas*, 2006, no. 25, 86–97; and 'Sociological theories of globalisation: the view from the global North', *Sociological Theory*, 2007, vol. 25, no. 4. I thank the readers and editors involved for their advice.

Intellectual work is always collective work. Though I am responsible for this text, it could not have been written without the help of others. The book was first suggested by my partner Pam Benton, whose inspiration remains in every part of it. The systematic work began in a 'classical theory' course at the University of California, Santa Cruz, and I am grateful to participants and colleagues including John Sanbonmatsu, Paul Lubeck and Terry Burke. Colleagues in Australia and overseas have helped with advice, reading lists, critical commentary on drafts, and models of relevant work. I especially thank Robert Morrell, Teresa Valdés, Radhika Chopra, Behrooz Ghamari, Frederic Vandenberghe, Chilla Bulbeck, Jane Kenway, Sandra Kessler, Barbara Leigh; members of the Sydney inter-university social theory group; and readers for my two publishers, Polity Press and Allen & Unwin Australia. The influence of Paulin Hountondji will be obvious in my text, which I hope may introduce his thought to new audiences.

Though this book has been written without the benefit of research grants, it does have a material base. This was provided by the University of Sydney and my colleagues in the Faculty of Education and Social Work, to whom I owe a great debt. Research assistants John Fisher and Molly Nicholson, and administrative assistant Deborah Young, have been important participants in this project.

There is also an emotional base to intellectual work, well known to writers though less known to neoliberal managers. I could not have finished this project without the continuing support of Patricia Selkirk, Toni Schofield, Helen Meekosha, Kirsten Gomard, Peta Tancred and Barrie Thorne. I have relied especially on the support of Kylie Benton-Connell, to whom I dedicate whatever is good here, confident that she and her generation will take it further.

PART I
Northern theory

1

Empire and the creation of a social science

If savage man has come out of an animal state (Homo descended from Pithecanthropus), if barbaric man has come from savage man, if half-civilized man has come from barbaric man, if civilized man has come from half-civilized man, if enlightened man has come from early civilized man, then there has in the long run always been progress in spite of the forms of degeneracy and all the rhythms to which this series of phenomena has been subjected.

—Lester F. Ward (1903)

An equally familiar fact is that the women, occupying a servile position, do all the unskilled labour and bear the burdens; with which may be joined the fact that not unfrequently during war they carry the supplies, as in Asia among the Bhils and Khonds, as in Polynesia among the New Caledonians and Sandwich Islanders, as in America among the Comanches, Mundrucus, Patagonians . . .

—Herbert Spencer (1879)

Origin stories

Open any introductory sociology textbook and you will probably find, in the first few pages, a discussion of founding fathers focused on Marx, Durkheim and Weber. The first chapter may also cite Comte, Spencer, Tönnies and Simmel, and perhaps a few others. In the view normally presented to students, these men created sociology in response to dramatic changes in European society: the Industrial Revolution, class conflict, secularisation, alienation and the modern state. This curriculum is backed by histories such as Alan Swingewood's (2000) *Short History of Sociological Thought*. This well-regarded British text presents a two-part narrative of 'Foundations: Classical Sociology' (centring on Durkheim, Weber and Marx), and 'Modern Sociology', tied together by the belief that 'Marx, Weber and Durkheim have remained at the core of modern sociology' (2000: x). Sociologists take this account of their origins seriously. Twenty years ago, a star-studded review of *Social Theory Today* began with a ringing declaration of 'the centrality of the classics' (Alexander 1987). In the new century, commentary on classical texts remains a significant genre of theoretical writing (Baehr 2002).

The idea of classical theory embodies a canon, in the sense of literary theory: a privileged set of texts, whose interpretation and reinterpretation defines a field (Seidman 1994). This particular canon embeds an internalist doctrine of sociology's history as a social science. The story consists of a foundational moment arising from the internal transformation of European society; classic discipline-defining texts written by a small group of brilliant authors; and a direct line of descent from them to us.

But sociologists in the classical period itself did not have this origin story. When Franklin Giddings (1896), the first professor of sociology at Columbia University, published *The Principles of Sociology*, he named as the founding father—Adam Smith. Victor Branford (1904), expounding 'the founders of sociology' to a meeting in London, named as the central figure—Condorcet.

Turn-of-the-century sociology had no list of classic texts in the modern sense. Writers expounding the new science would commonly refer to Comte as the inventor of the term, to Darwin as the key figure in the theory of evolution, and then to any of a wide range of figures in the landscape of evolutionary speculation. Witness the account of the discipline in the second edition of *Dynamic Sociology* (1897) by Lester Ward, later the founding president of the American Sociological Society. At the time of the first edition in 1883, Ward observed, the term 'sociology' had not been in popular use. However, in the intervening decade a series of brilliant scientific contributions had established sociology as a popular concept. There were now research journals, university courses, societies; and sociology 'bids fair to become the leading science of the twentieth century, as biology has been that of the nineteenth'. Ward listed 37 notable contributors to the new science. The list included Durkheim and Tönnies, but not Marx or Weber.

The list of notables became a common feature in the textbooks of sociology that multiplied in the United States from the 1890s, Giddings' *Principles* being one of the first. (Ward had included Giddings in his list, and Giddings politely included Ward in his.) The famous 'Green Bible' of the Chicago School, Park and Burgess's (1924) *Introduction to the Science of Sociology*, listed 23 'representative works in systematic sociology'. Simmel and Durkheim were among them, but not Marx, Weber or Pareto. Only one work by Weber was mentioned in this thousand-page volume, and then only in the notes.

As late as the 1920s, then, there was no sense that certain texts were discipline-defining classics demanding special study. Rather, there was a sense of a broad, almost impersonal advance of scientific knowledge, the notables being simply leading members of the pioneering crew. Sociologists accepted the view, articulated early in the history of the discipline by Charles Letourneau (1881: vi), who was to hold the first chair of sociology in the world, that: 'The commencement of any science, however simple, is always a collective work. It requires the constant labour of many patient workmen . . .'

We therefore have strong reasons to doubt the conventional picture of the creation of sociology. This is not just to question the influence of certain individuals. We must examine the history of sociology as a collective product—the shared concerns, assumptions and practices making up the discipline at various times, and the shape given that history by the changing social forces that constructed the new science.

Global difference and empire

Sociology as a teaching discipline and a public discourse was constructed during the final two decades of the nineteenth century and the first decade of the twentieth in the great cities and university towns of France, the United States, Britain, Germany and, a little later, Russia. The internalist foundation story interprets these places as the site of a process of modernisation, or capitalist industrialisation, with sociology seen as an attempt to interpret what was emerging here. 'It was above all a science of the new industrial society' (Bottomore 1987: 7).

The main difficulty with this view is that it does not square with the most relevant evidence—what sociologists at the time were writing. Most general textbooks of sociology, up to World War I, did not have a great deal to say about the modernisation of the society in which the authors lived. Giddings' *Readings in Descriptive and Historical Sociology* (1906), typical in this respect, ranged from polyandry in Ceylon via matrilineal survivals among the Tartars to the mining camps of California. It was so little focused on modernity that it took as its reading on 'sovereignty' a medieval rendering of the legend of King Arthur.

What is in college textbooks need not correspond to the research focus of sociology, but on this too we have abundant evidence. Between 1898 and 1913, Émile Durkheim and his hard-working collaborators produced twelve issues of *L'année sociologique*, an extraordinarily detailed international survey of each year's publications in, or relevant to, sociology. In these twelve issues, nearly 2400 reviews were published. (I have counted only the reviews in large type, whatever their length, not the brief notices in small type in the early issues, nor the listings of titles without reviews.) The reviews concerning Western/Northern Europe and modern North America increase with time: they average 24 per cent of all reviews in the first six issues, 28 per cent in the next five issues, and 32 per cent in the bumper issue of the year before the war.

Modern industrial society was certainly included: the journal published reviews about the American worker, the European middle class, technology in German industries, books by the Webbs and by Sombart, Booth on London poverty, even a work by Ramsay MacDonald, later Labour prime minister of Britain. But works focused on the recent or contemporary societies of Europe and North America made up only a fraction of the content of *L'année sociologique*: about 28 per cent of all reviews. Even fewer were focused on 'the new industrial society', since the reviews on Europe included treatises on peasant folk-tales, witchcraft in Scotland, crime in Asturias and the measurements of skulls.

Twice as many of the reviews concerned ancient and medieval societies, colonial or remote societies, or global surveys of human history. Studies of holy war in ancient Israel, Malay magic, Buddhist India, technical points of Roman law, medieval vengeance, Aboriginal kinship in central Australia and the legal systems of primitive societies were more characteristic of sociology as seen in *L'année sociologique* than studies of new technology or bureaucracy.

The enormous spectrum of human history that the sociologists took as their domain was organised by a central idea: difference between the civilisation of the metropole and other cultures whose main feature was their primitiveness. I will call this the idea of global difference. Presented in many different forms, this contrast pervades the sociology of the late nineteenth and early twentieth centuries.

The idea of global difference was often conveyed by a discussion of 'origins'. In this genre of writing, sociologists would posit an original state of society, then speculate on the process of evolution that must have led from then to now. The bulk of the three volumes of Herbert Spencer's *Principles of Sociology*, first issued in the 1870s, told such a story for every type of institution that Spencer could think of: domestic institutions, political institutions, ecclesiastical institutions, and so on. Spencer acted as if the proof of social evolution were not complete without an evolutionary narrative, from origins to the contemporary form, for each and every case.

The formula of development from a primitive origin to an advanced form was widespread in Victorian thought (Burrow 1966). Sociologists simply applied a logic that their audience would find familiar. The same architecture is found in works as well known as Durkheim's *Division of Labour in Society* (1893) and as obscure as Fairbanks' *Introduction to Sociology* (1896).

In none of these works was the idea of an origin taken as a concrete historical question. It could have been, because historians' knowledge of early societies was growing dramatically in these decades. Troy, Mycenae and Knossos were excavated by Schliemann and Evans. Flinders Petrie systematised the archaeology of Egypt, and the first evidence of Sumerian culture was uncovered at Lagash and Nippur (Stiebing 1993). But sociologists were not interested in where and when a particular originating event occurred, nor were they concerned about when the major changes actually happened. Time functioned in sociological thought mainly as a sign of global difference.

Durkheim did not have to find a precise time in the past for 'segmentary societies'; they existed in his own day. Durkheim used the example of the Kabyle of Algeria as well as the ancient Hebrews, and made no conceptual distinction between the two. He knew about the Hebrews because the ancient texts were in his library. How did he know about Kabylia? Because the French had conquered Algeria earlier in the century, and at the time Durkheim wrote, French colonists were evicting the local population from the best land (Bennoune 1988). Given the recent history of conquest, peasant rebellion and debate over colonisation, no French intellectual could fail to know something about the Kabyle. Indeed, the social life of France's North African subjects was being documented in great detail by a series of private and official enquiries (Burke 1980).

Algeria was not an isolated case. In the dozen years before *Division of Labour* was published, the armies of the French republic had moved out from Algeria to conquer Tunisia; had fought a war in Indo-China, conquered Annam and Tonkin (modern Vietnam) and seized control of Laos and Cambodia; and had established a protectorate over Madagascar. Under the Berlin Treaty of 1885, French trading posts in Central and Western Africa became the basis of a whole new empire. While Durkheim was writing and publishing the *Division of Labor* and the *Rules of Sociological Method* (1895), French colonial armies were engaged in a spectacular series of campaigns against the Muslim regimes of inland North and West Africa which produced vast conquests from the Atlantic almost to the Nile.

All this was part of a larger process. The British empire, also a maritime empire with a pre-industrial history, similarly gained a new dynamism and grew to a vast size in the nineteenth century (Cain and Hopkins 1993). The thirteen-colony United States became one of the most dynamic imperial powers of the nineteenth century, with about 80 years of overland conquest and settlement (the 'westward expansion'), followed by a shorter period of overseas conquest. The Tsarist overland conquests, begun in earlier centuries, were extended to North-east and Central Asia. In the later part of the nineteenth century, they were consolidated by Russian settlement. Prussia's expansion as an imperial power began with conquest within Europe—in the process, setting up a relationship between dominant and conquered races in the East which became the subject of young Max

Weber's (1894) first sociological research. German overseas colonies in Africa and the Pacific followed the formation of the Reich in 1871. By the time the system of rival empires reached its crisis in the Great War of 1914–18, the expansion of Western power to a global scale had reached its climax.

In this light, the making of sociology takes on a new significance. The places where the discipline was created were the urban and cultural centres of the major imperial powers at the high tide of modern imperialism. They were the 'metropole', in the useful French term, to the larger colonial world. The intellectuals who created sociology were very much aware of this.

Since Kiernan's (1969) remarkable survey *The Lords of Human Kind*, historians have begun to grasp the immense impact that the global expansion of North Atlantic power had on popular culture (MacDonald 1994) and intellectual life (Said 1993) in the metropole, as well as in the colonies. It would be astonishing if the new science of society had escaped the impact of the greatest social change in the world at the time. In fact, the relationship was intimate. Sociology was formed within the culture of imperialism, and embodied an intellectual response to the colonised world. This fact is crucial in understanding the content and method of sociology, as well as the discipline's wider cultural significance.

The content and method of sociology

As remarked by the civilised Arthur Todd (the first, and perhaps still the only, professor of sociology to introduce Japanese cherry-blossom paintings into a discussion of social theory): 'From Comte onward sociologists have pretty generally agreed that the only justification for a Science of Society is its contributions to a workable theory of progress' (Todd 1918: vii). John Stuart Mill, the sharpest mind among all whose idea of social science was shaped by Comte, had cautioned against equating historical change with improvement (Mill 1843: 596). Few of the sociologists took heed. Spencer's first attempt at social theory, in *Social Statics* (1850), made moral improvement the touchstone of analysis of 'the social state'. Discovering and expounding laws of progress was the core of what sociology meant for the next two generations.

In Auguste Comte's writings, the idea mostly had to do with the ancient–medieval–modern sequence in Europe. Critics in the later nineteenth century rejected the arbitrariness of Comte's system and demanded an empirical base for the concept of progress.

This was the common ground between Spencer and Letourneau, and it is a fact of the greatest significance that both of these authors turned to the ethnographical dividend of empire as their main source of sociological data. Spencer's *Principles of Sociology* documented its evolutionary stories from the writings of European travellers, missionaries, settlers and colonial officials, as well as historians. For instance, Spencer's reference list for his section on 'Political Institutions' ranged from the journals of the North American explorers Lewis and Clarke, through the *Journal of the Asiatic Society of Bengal* and *Thirty-three years in Tasmania and Victoria* to that riveting work, *A Phrenologist among the Todas*. Letourneau's *Sociology, Based Upon Ethnography* (1881), while setting the facts out in a finer grid, was very similar in its sources.

By the time sociology was institutionalised in the final decade of the century, the central proof of progress—and therefore the main intellectual ground on which the new science rested—was the contrast of metropolitan and colonised societies. Sociologists did not debate the importance of this contrast. Rather, they debated how it should be interpreted—whether through physical evolution from lower to higher human types, or an evolution of mind and social forms; whether competition or cooperation was the motor of progress. In this context, Durkheim's *Division of Labor* was no founding text. It was a late intervention in a long-running debate.

The concern with progress was not a 'value' separable from the science; it was constitutive of sociological knowledge. The arguments of Ward, Hobhouse, Durkheim, Spencer and Comte himself are absurd if one does not presuppose the *reality* of progress. It was as an account of progress that sociology spread beyond the metropole. Spencer's sociology, for instance, was being debated in India well before the turn of the century, and in translation became a significant influence on the intellectuals of Meiji Japan and the Chinese republican movement (Tominaga 1994; Grieder 1981).

The topics addressed by the new discipline are revealing. A social science based on the social relations of empire must deal with race, and a social science concerned with evolutionary progress and hierarchies of populations must deal with gender and sexuality. And in fact, race, gender and sexuality *were* core issues in early sociology. When Du Bois proposed in 1901 that the colour line was 'the problem of the twentieth century', he was saying nothing unusual for the time (Du Bois 1950: 281). Global difference was persistently interpreted in terms of race. Letourneau's 'ethnography' meant a science of racial differences, and his *Sociology* opened with an enumeration of the human races, with black, yellow and white distinguished by brain size. Ward (1897) was confident that global race conflict reflected the superiority of the European races, and that universal progress was dependent on their universal triumph.

Here sociology reflected, in the most direct way, the social relations of imperialism. This is not to say that all sociologists were outright racists, though some certainly were (see Crozier (1911) for a toxic example). Others, Du Bois and Durkheim among them, suffered the effects of racism. The point is rather that racial hierarchy on a world scale was a perception built into the concept of 'progress', and was a central part of what sociology was thought to be about.

Nor was there any question about the importance of gender and sexuality. Comte, in his *Système de politique positive*, gave considerable prominence to the social role of women, and his famous conflict with Mill included sharp differences over the subjection of women. When Spencer came to write the substantive part of *The Principles of Sociology*, the very first set of institutions he addressed was the 'Domestic'. By this he meant what we now call gender issues: kinship, family and the status of women. Letourneau treated marriage and the family before, and at greater length than, property. He dealt with sexuality ('the genesic need') near the start of *Sociology*, with an impressive absence of Victorian delicacy. Menstruation, infanticide, prostitution, promiscuity and sodomy were all on his agenda. In the next generation, Ward, Tönnies, Sumner and Thomas all continued the focus on sex and gender.

Some of this can be explained on internalist lines, through the influence of first-wave feminism (Paxton 1991). But the way gender and sexual issues were taken up in sociology was very much affected by evolutionary concerns and the issues of empire. In the imperial context, racial and sexual issues were not separate. In the later nineteenth century, the expansion of the North Atlantic powers was accompanied by a growing fear of miscegenation, a hardening colour line, the colonisers' growing contempt for the sexuality or masculinity of the colonised (Sinha 1995), and fears of racial swamping. Echoes are heard even in the most abstract metropolitan texts. Giddings (1896: xiii), expounding his theme of 'consciousness of kind', remarked that: 'Living creatures do not commonly mate with individuals of other than their own species.' His first example was: 'White men do not usually marry black women.'

The most striking feature of sociological method was its bold abstraction. Comte offered cultural 'laws' of vast scope; and the inaugural meeting of the American Sociological Society, 60 years later, was still celebrating tremendous 'laws' of social evolution. Durkheim (1895) argued convincingly that this approach was the basis of the whole enterprise: 'Comparative sociology is not a particular branch of sociology; it is sociology itself . . .' (1895: 139). The comparative method meant assembling examples of the particular social 'species' under study, and examining their variations.

This method rested on a one-way flow of information, a capacity to examine a range of societies from the outside, and an ability to move freely from one society to another—features which all map the relation of colonial domination. Letourneau (1881) expressed the sociological point of view in a striking image:

> Let us imagine an observer placed somewhere high up in air above our terrestrial equator, far enough from the globe on which we live to take in a whole hemisphere at one glance, and yet close enough to distinguish with the aid, if need be, of a magnifying-glass, the continents and the seas, the great ranges of mountains, the white frozen tops of the polar regions, etc. etc. (1881: 15).

The imperial gaze is particularly evident in broad surveys such as Spencer's *Descriptive Sociology* and the collective project of *L'année sociologique*. Perhaps the most striking example is Hobhouse, Wheeler and Ginsberg's *Material Culture and Social Institutions of the Simpler Peoples* (1915), a late attempt to overcome the unsystematic use of data in theories of social evolution by providing a statistical base for comparative sociology. Hobhouse and his colleagues surveyed the whole world, collecting information on more than 500 societies. They classified societies by grade of economic development, and tried to establish correlations of development with institutional patterns of law, government, family, war and social hierarchy.

These surveys are virtually forgotten now, but the imperial gaze can also be found in familiar texts such as William Graham Sumner's (1934) *Folkways*, first published in 1906. The whole world and the whole of history was the field of attention. Few cases delayed the author for more than two sentences. For Sumner, the force of the argument did not lie in the depth of his ethnographic understanding. It was provided by the assemblage itself, the synoptic view of human affairs from a great height.

The obvious risk here is incoherence. This problem could be overcome with a variant of the comparative method whose dramatic quality produced some of the best-remembered 'classical' texts. I call this approach grand ethnography, in contrast to the close-focus fieldwork of Franz Boas, W.E.B. Du Bois, or the French specialists on Algeria and Morocco. The usual style of grand ethnography was built on the idea of global difference, presenting holistic accounts of the societies found at the origin and the end of progress.

The famous contrast of *Gemeinschaft* with *Gesellschaft* is grand ethnography in this sense, identifying polar states of society. Durkheim's *Division of Labor* was a more rigorous grand ethnography, specifying the basis of the contrast in the division of labour. *L'année sociologique* took a persistent interest in attempts to distinguish primitive from modern law, in German theories of *Naturvölker* and their distinction from *Kulturvölker*, and in attempts to formulate the nature of primitive religion. Grand ethnography was the artistic climax of Comtean sociology, the literary form taken by the theory of progress as the rhetoric of the struggle for existence was bypassed.

Sociology in the political culture of empire

Late nineteenth and early twentieth century metropolitan society had several groups of intellectuals grappling with the analysis of society. The mobilisation of European and American workers had produced one intellectual ferment; the mobilisation of women produced another. The claim that Harriet Martineau was the 'first woman sociologist' (Hoecker-Drysdale 1992) is anachronistic, but the story of Martineau—novelist, political economist, translator of Comte, travel writer and reformer—should alert us to the complexity of the milieu in which sociology arose.

Beyond the metropole, there were many intellectuals in these decades who looked at modernity from the standpoint of non-European cultures, and at Europeans from the standpoint of the colonised. Changes in culture and social life were central issues to writers as diverse as al-Afghani in the Islamic Middle East (see Chapter 6), Chatterjee and Tagore in Bengal (see Chapter 8), and Sun Yat-sen (1927) in China.

From these groups, a range of discourses about society emerged, of which sociology was only one. The anarchist Bakunin (1873), criticising Comte on one side and Marx on the other, recognised astonishingly early that a 'science of society' might rationalise the interests of a particular social group. Following Bakunin's lead, we should consider the social location in which sociology developed, and the cultural issues to which it was a response.

Sociology developed in a specific social location: among the men of the metropolitan liberal bourgeoisie. Those who wrote sociology were a mixture of engineers and doctors, academics, journalists, clerics, and a few who (like Weber after his breakdown) could live on their family capital.

This is not to say that the sociologists were, generally speaking, either rich or apologists for the rich. Ross (1991) points to the social distance between the academic makers of American sociology and the capitalist entrepreneurs of American industrialisation. Weber was a fierce critic of the ruling class of the German Reich, and Durkheim was no friend of the French aristocracy. Nevertheless, they were beneficiaries of both class and gender hierarchies. Most lived modest bourgeois lives, supported by the domestic labor of women in patriarchal households. Their social interests were well captured by Comte's slogan 'Order and Progress'.

Men of this sort began to discuss 'the Social Science', as Mill called it, from the 1850s on, in a diffuse movement to apply scientific thinking to society and promote moral improvement. A successful Association for the Promotion of Social Science was set up in London as early as 1857 (Yeo 1966), and was soon copied in Boston. The same movement produced a heavily moralised 'social science' curriculum in North American colleges from the 1860s (Bernard and Bernard 1965). Individual attempts to synthesise the facts of primitive life and social progress, such as Edward Tylor's *Primitive Culture* (1873), counterpointed attempts to establish institutes to formulate a science of man. The latter, in France, gave rise to the first academic chair to be named 'sociology', to which Letourneau was appointed in 1885 (Clark 1973).

In the 1890s, the social science curriculum in the United States, already fissuring, began to be replaced by more self-consciously scientific courses called 'sociology'. Their claim to scientificity was closely connected with the shift to comparative method and imperial gaze discussed above. Hence the world-spanning content of the first generation of sociology textbooks. Named sociology departments were established, undergraduate courses multiplied, and a market for textbooks rapidly developed (Morgan 1983).

Europe was a little slower to set up departments of sociology, but quicker with associations and journals. By the outbreak of the Great War, sociological societies, journals of sociology and university courses in sociology were established institutions in most metropolitan countries. International links were built up—for instance, through Worms' *Institut International de Sociologie*, launched in 1893; through visits both ways across the North Atlantic; and through the journals. These provided a practical basis for sociology to develop as an international cultural formation. Historians who emphasise the distinctness of national traditions of sociology (e.g. Levine 1995) underestimate the extent to which scholars of the period saw themselves as part of an international academic milieu, and conceived of sociology as a universal science.

Overlapping the academic initiatives was a genre of popular sociological writing. A text like Benjamin Kidd's *Social Evolution* could be a considerable best-seller. Within four years of its publication in 1894, this book had gone through fourteen printings in England, and had American, German, Swedish, French, Russian and Italian editions.

Sociological thought first circulated as part of the uplifting and informative literature consumed by a new educated reading public who read novelists like Dickens and Eliot, cultural critics like Ruskin and Arnold, and scientists like Darwin and Huxley. Sociology circulated through the same channels as these writers. Thus Spencer's *The Study of Sociology* (1873) was first published in instalments in magazines: the *Contemporary Review* in Britain and the *Popular Science Monthly* in the United States. It was then issued in book form in a new popular education collection called the 'International Scientific Series'. Spencer's *Principles of Sociology*, an integral part of the vast survey of human knowledge which he called the 'Synthetic Philosophy', was first issued in instalments to subscribers, the first volume coming out in ten parts over three years, while Spencer was still writing it.

The relationship between writers and readers was thus far more intimate than professional sociological writing later became. Lepenies (1988) has suggested that European sociology was culturally positioned 'between literature and science', but that exaggerates the contrast. Science, too, was ethically and politically charged. Darwin, for instance, long hesitated to publish his work on evolution because he knew its religious and political consequences (Desmond and Moore 1992). Sociologists were expected, as scientists, to provide moral and political teaching. Their teaching especially addressed the dilemma that was inescapable for men of the liberal bourgeoisie: the tension between material privilege and reforming principle.

Nineteenth century liberalism was itself a complex movement. It was often at odds with radical and democratic movements. But in liberal struggles against the Ancien Régime, commitments were forged which L.T. Hobhouse, recently appointed to the first chair of sociology in England, rousingly declared in his *Liberalism* (1911): civil liberty and the rule of law, fiscal liberty, personal liberty, social liberty, economic liberty, domestic liberty, local, racial and national liberty, international liberty, political liberty and popular sovereignty. These remained culturally powerful beliefs in the public addressed by sociology.

These commitments were challenged by the class and gender inequalities of the metropole (Therborn 1976; Deegan 1988), and even more severely challenged by empire. As Ranajit Guha (1989: 277) observes, the universalising project of bourgeois culture reached its limit in colonialism. Concepts of liberty, rights and independence were plainly, repeatedly and brutally violated by what the North Atlantic states were doing all over the world to the colonised.

Sociology, the science of progress that claimed the world as its province and used so extensively the data of empire, was positioned squarely in this contradiction. And it offered a resolution. Sociology displaced imperial power over the colonised into an abstract space of difference. The comparative method and grand ethnography deleted the actual practice of colonialism from the intellectual world built on the gains of empire.

The relation between the imperial powers and the conquered was most directly addressed by the Darwinian wing of Comtean sociology (Spencer, Sumner, Ward, Hobhouse, Kidd, and fringe figures like Crozier). They addressed it by constructing a fiction of 'social evolution' which naturalised global difference. It is no wonder that Spencer became immensely popular in the colonies of settlement, where the idea of the evolutionary superiority of the settlers replaced missionary religion as the main justification of empire.

This was despite the fact that Spencer was personally opposed to imperial conquest. Spencer sharply denounced 'the diabolical cruelties committed by the invading Europeans' in America, the South Seas and elsewhere. Like Gladstone—with whom he discussed the question—Spencer saw forcible conquest as a sign of militarism. But he had no such objection to peaceable settlement and economic competition. In the same passages, it is clear he regarded the colonised as 'inferior races', likely to lose out in evolutionary competition (Spencer 1873: 212; Duncan 1908: 224). Even Hobhouse (1911: 43), in full flight expounding the principles of liberalism, blurred them in the case of empire by wondering whether the black races were capable of self-rule.

In other writers, there was no distance at all between naturalising progress and justifying empire. The climax of Kidd's *Social Evolution* was a justification for rule of the tropical regions of the world—now languishing under the maladministration of 'the black and coloured races'—by the more progressive peoples of European extraction. Kidd's reconciliation of imperial rule with his belief that natural selection tended towards more religious and ethical conduct epitomises the ideological work done by sociology.

The resolution which sociology offered to the dilemmas of liberalism claimed the status of science. Mill and Comte had insisted programmatically that sociology must promulgate 'laws'. This task was accepted by both academic and popular writers in sociology. Legitimacy for laws of progress was provided by the prestige of geology and evolutionary biology. Accordingly, treatises on sociology often expounded organic evolution, and might even start with the evolution of the stars and the solar system (e.g. Ward 1897).

This conception of laws of progress enabled sociology to conflate the problems of empire with the problems of the metropole. The 'social science' of the 1860s and 1870s embraced the social tensions of the metropole as ethical and practical problems. Questions of poverty, class struggle and social amelioration—'the social question' in the terminology of the day—also came on to the agenda of the sociological societies and journals in the 1890s and 1900s. In cities such as London, Chicago and Paris, there was significant contact and overlap between academic sociologists, Fabian socialists, feminists, progressive liberals, religious and ethical reformers, and social workers (Besnard 1983; Deegan 1988; Yeo 1996).

What 'social science' contributed to the 'social question' was an interpretation of metropolitan problems in the light of an over-arching theory of progress. A characteristic example was the discussion of socialism found in many treatises of sociology. The universal approach of sociologists was to evaluate the goals of the workers' movement in terms of their own model of evolutionary progress—whether the conclusion was endorsement of a mild ethical socialism (as by Hobhouse, Durkheim and Small) or robust rejection (as by Spencer and Sumner).

The crisis and remaking of sociology

In *Pure Sociology: A Treatise on the Origin and Spontaneous Development of Society*, Ward (1903: 450–1) offered as proof of progress the fact that atrocities were scarcely possible in modern society. Just thirteen years later, the British army lost 60 000 young men killed or wounded on a single day at the Battle of the Somme.

The Great War marked a crisis of the old imperialism and triggered major shifts in global power. The European empires began to fissure, with the independence of Ireland and the dismemberment of the Hapsburg empire. The French, British and American systems continued to expand by taking over former Ottoman and German territories and increasing their economic penetration of China and Latin America. The United States emerged as the leading industrial power. The 1940s saw a second crisis of imperialism, with the Japanese offensive against Western power in Asia, the independence of India from the British and Indonesia from the Dutch, and the Vietnamese war of liberation against the French. Soviet power reconstituted the old Tsarist empire but supported the break-up of other empires, and stood as a challenge to global capitalism. By mid-century, the nuclear-armed United States had become the leading international investor, the dominant military power, and the centre of mass communications and an emerging world commercial culture.

These changes altered the conditions of existence for sociology, beginning with the Great War itself. The war tore apart the intellectual community of sociologists that had been developing around the North

Atlantic. Some, like Hobhouse, were horrified by the fighting; others became belligerent. Small at Chicago broke with his German contacts, clashing with Simmel in particular (Bannister 1987). Weber went into the army, as did younger members of the *Année sociologique* group, some of whom were killed. The young German Sociological Society liquidated itself when war broke out, and donated its money to a fund for German war propaganda in neutral countries (Liebersohn 1988). This was exactly the work that Durkheim undertook on the other side.

The more important impact was at the level of ideas. Social evolution had generally been understood as the growth of reason and civilised conduct: 'Objectively viewed, progress is an increasing intercourse, a multiplication of relationships, an advance in material well-being, a growth of population, and an evolution of rational conduct. It is a final display in the grand metamorphosis of universal evolution' (Giddings 1896: 359). Such a view was always based on blindness towards the violence of colonialism. As the experience of the frontier came home to the metropole, the foundation of metropolitan sociology's world-view was ruptured. It was no longer possible to take progress as the reality to be studied, the object of knowledge. 'Cheap optimism', as Hobhouse (1915) realised during the war, was now forbidden by history. Comtean language was too well entrenched to be immediately abandoned, but in books written after the war, evocations of 'progress' tail off quite soon. When Vilfredo Pareto, in the *Treatise of General Sociology* (1916), denounced 'sentimental ethics' as a basis for sociology and demanded a harsher realism, he was distancing himself from what he already saw as the pseudo-science of Comte and Spencer, and from his own earlier liberalism.

If we see the decade around 1920 as the historical moment when the project of Comte, Spencer, Letourneau and their successors had irretrievably broken down, we can also see that there were several possible responses. The project could simply have been abandoned, as happened to some of the nineteenth century's new sciences—for instance, phrenology. Alternatively, sociology could have been merged into critical cultural movements. The possibility is suggested by Oswald Spengler's *Decline of the West* (1918–22), a book that had enormous influence in the 1920s. Spengler offered a scathing criticism of the Eurocentrism of European intellectuals and their view of human history. He saw European expansion as the 'murder' of other cultures, such as the Aztec/Maya culture in central America; and thus treated contemporary imperialism not as the triumph of light, but as a sign of the Last Days. The break with the framework of progress could hardly be more complete.

The project of a critical sociology of culture seemed for a while to flourish. In Weimar Germany, Scheler and Mannheim converged on a 'sociology of knowledge', the object of fierce controversy for a short period. Mannheim (1935) in exile, like the scholars of the Frankfurt School, began to develop a synthesis of Freudian psychoanalysis with structural sociology to explain the catastrophe of Fascism. A synthesis of phenomenology with sociology was proposed by Schutz (1932) in Austria; a social theory grounded in idealist philosophy was proposed by Gentile in Italy (Bellamy 1987).

Revolutionary movements also gave rise to possible sociologies. In Russia, the Bolshevik leader Bukharin (1925) produced 'a system of sociology' as ambitious as anything in the capitalist world at that time. Much better remembered are the social theories of the Italian revolutionary Gramsci. Du Bois (1968), having left academic sociology for civil rights activism, connected race issues in the metropole with movements in the colonial world and, increasingly, with the structure of global capitalism.

None of these initiatives, however, produced an institutionalised replacement for the old sociology. Most of the Europeans just mentioned were killed or driven into exile. Colonial dominance in Africa remained unshaken and Du Bois, returning to academia in the 1930s, found no audience for his internationalist views.

There was only one place where academic sociology flourished between 1920 and 1950: in the new world power, the United States. But here the discipline was transformed, in a change so fundamental that it can be regarded—to use Althusser's expression—as an epistemological break (Althusser and Balibar 1970).

The new object of knowledge was society, and especially social difference and social disorder, *within the metropole*. Familiar markers of this shift are the prominence of the Chicago School's urban research, and the growth of specialisations within sociology—many of them defined by a social problem or an administrative apparatus of metropolitan society.

In terms of method, where the old sociology had focused on difference between the metropole and the primitive, the new sociology focused on difference within metropolitan society. This can be seen clearly in statistical techniques, from early measures of correlation, through attitude scaling in the inter-war decades, to the formalisation of latent structure analysis by Lazarsfeld at the mid-century (Easthope 1974). The 1920s and 1930s saw a flowering of empirical research on the social life of American towns, cities and suburbs. There was great inventiveness in method, such as the first fusion of psychoanalysis with field sociology (Dollard 1937). The Chicago School did not just do urban ethnography. It set up a comprehensive system of surveillance for America's second largest, and at the time most turbulent, city (Smith and White 1929).

The rapid development of sociology in this direction was made possible by corporate and government funding, begun before the war but greatly accelerated in the 1920s. Ross (1991, p. 402) gives the impressive total of $41 million of Rockefeller money going to American social science and social work between 1922 and 1929. A high point was reached when the US national government set up a Committee on Recent Social Trends, with Ogburn, a president of the American Sociological Society and its leading advocate of empiricism, as director of research.

As research expertise rose, however, the concept of the discipline narrowed. The North American university provided an organisational definition that contradicted the Comtean vision. Sociology could survive here not as a meta-science, but as one department among a range of social science departments, distinguished from history, political science, economics and psychology only by its special focus of interest. The difficulty, for a discipline whose earlier claims had been so vast, was to define that special focus. 'Social relations' (MacIver 1937), 'groups', forms of association and human relations (Hiller 1933), 'the social process' (Reuter and Hart 1933)—no formulation was very convincing, and none became generally accepted.

Bannister's (1987) absorbing history of sociological scientism in the United States in this period shows that the empiricist triumph failed to produce an intellectual program for sociology. Pitirim Sorokin (1928: 757), an acid critic of the empiricists, remarked at the end of his survey of *Contemporary Sociological Theories* that: 'The whole field reminds one of a half-wild national forest rather than a carefully planned garden.' The new sociology started life as the old sociology had died, with a severe deficit of legitimacy.

The new concept of sociology and the new origin story

In this conceptual vacuum—as Hinkle (1994: 339) aptly describes the situation after the collapse of evolutionism—the formation of the classical canon began. A condition for this development was a change in sociology's audience. The late Victorian liberal reading public was no more. However, the enormous wealth being accumulated in the United States made possible for the first time in history a mass higher education system. Here sociology expanded tremendously in the three decades after World War II (Turner and Turner 1990). A mass audience of students required a teacher training program, which was provided by expanding sociology PhD programs. It was in this milieu, and at this moment, that the pedagogy of classical texts developed.

The crucial step was taken in Talcott Parsons' *The Structure of Social Action* (1937). Parsons was not the first North American theorist to address the intellectual disintegration of sociology (Turner and Turner 1990: 71ff), but there is no denying the genius of his solution. Parsons purged sociology's history, acknowledging the collapse of the Comtean agenda. He took the empirical problem of post-crisis sociology, difference and disorder in the metropole, and made it the theoretical centre of the discipline (the 'Hobbesian problem of order'). Parsons' later work, establishing the idea of a 'social system', provided a method for thinking the society of the metropole as a self-contained unit. Parsons was no historian, and did not claim to be writing the history of sociology. But his reconstruction of the 'emergence' of a social-action model in the theoretical logic of Marshall, Pareto, Weber and Durkheim was understandably read as an origin narrative, and this story created norms for the discipline (Camic 1989).

A canonical view still had to be established against other accounts of sociology. Parsons' vision, however, acquired powerful allies. In his very widely read *The Sociological Imagination*, C. Wright Mills (1959) constructed a composite image of 'the classic social analyst' which he held up as a model of how sociology ought to be done. 'Classical sociology', to Mills, was a style of work more than a period—though he conveyed a definite sense that it was more practised in the past, and included Marx, Weber and Durkheim among his examples. A canonical view was also reinforced by theorists wishing to establish a particular issue as significant. For instance, Merton's (1949) account of anomie helped establish Durkheim as classic.

The translation into English of the main European texts incorporated into the canon was accomplished between 1930 and 1950, and a literature of commentary appeared. Levine (1995, p. 63) aptly remarks of the 1960s and 1970s that 'fresh translations, editions, and secondary analyses of classic authors became one of the faster-growing industries within sociology'. Bendix's very widely read *Max Weber: An Intellectual Portrait* was issued in 1960. Coser's *Functions of Social Conflict* (1956) was in large part a commentary on Simmel. North American interest even helped to create a Weber revival in German sociology 'after a period of inattention to its classical past', as Lüschen (1994: 11) tactfully put it. German sociologists held a celebration of Weber at their national conference in 1964.

Platt (1995), in a brilliant study of the North American reception of Durkheim, rightly observes the complexity of influences behind the choice of founding fathers: broad historical circumstance, particular academic entrepreneurs or departments, affinity with current trends in the profession. These factors seem to have worked for Weber and Durkheim but against Parsons' other nominee, Pareto. Though Pareto was even more eligible as a systematic theorist, his irony and pessimism were perhaps too obtrusive for his texts to work as foundations for the revived discipline.

The changes are most dramatic in the case of Marx. To Parsons in *The Structure of Social Action*, he was part of the background—essentially a minor utilitarian. Some American textbooks of sociology in the 1940s and 1950s got along without any attention to Marx at all. But Marxism remained a force in global culture. It became, for instance, the key intellectual influence in African politics in the decades of decolonisation. A progressive American sociologist at this time could find an important resource here. In his best canon-making style, Mills issued a collection of Marxist texts, with commentary, in 1962.

However, Marx did not become a full-fledged Founding Father in sociology until the discipline's expansion in the 1960s and the radicalisation of metropolitan university students. The 'radical sociology' proposed by the US student movement centred on Marx and Marxists (Horowitz 1971), and academic sociology responded. In 1965 the American Sociological Association's annual meeting included a plenary session called 'A

Re-Evaluation of Karl Marx'. Marx now assumed a more prominent place in accounts of the history of sociological theory (Bottomore and Nisbet 1978), and appeared more often in textbooks for undergraduates. A sociological literature of commentary on Marx multiplied.

The trinity of Marx, Durkheim and Weber was thus a late development in the construction of the canon. Durkheim and Weber were the survivors of the canon-making enterprise of Parsons' generation; Marx was grafted on in the next generation; and other candidates fell by the wayside. The trio appears in the role of The Founding Fathers in elementary textbooks in the 1970s (e.g. McGee 1977). In theoretical sociology, a considerable effort of interpretation now tried to make sense of the Marx–Durkheim–Weber grouping as creators of a theory of modernity (e.g. Giddens 1971; Alexander 1982, 1983).

In most other countries that could afford to have sociology, the discipline was created or remade in the 1950s and 1960s on the basis of research techniques, research problems and theoretical languages, not to mention textbooks and instructors, imported from the United States. (For example, Japan: Tominaga 1994; Australia: Baldock and Lally 1974; Scandinavia: Allardt 1994.) With the reconstructed discipline came its reconstructed foundation story. Thus world sociology arrived at the situation described in the opening paragraphs of this chapter.

Reflection

I have argued that the classical canon in sociology was created, mainly in the United States, as part of an effort at reconstruction after the collapse of the first European-American project of sociology; that a new foundation story replaced earlier and very different accounts of the making of sociology; and that this whole course of events can only be understood in the framework of global history, especially the history of imperialism.

In one sense this does not matter; the retrospectively chosen classics actually have little to do with the creative impulses of recent sociology. But the symbolic power of 'classical sociology' remains, and generates distorted pictures of the history of sociology, and of the scope and value of sociology. Nisbet's (1967) list of the 'unit-ideas of sociology' (community, authority, status, the sacred, alienation) was a travesty of history, but had some plausibility as a map of the narrowed territory left after the canon-making was in full swing. Above all, the internalist story directs sociology's attention away from analyses of the social world that come from intellectuals beyond the metropole.

Better connections *have* been made. As Burke (1980) shows, at the very time Durkheim and his colleagues were building the imperial gaze into their sociology, other French social scientists engaged intellectuals of the Islamic world in dialogue about modernity, colonialism and culture. In the same generation, Du Bois moved from a focus on race relations within the United States to a strongly internationalist perspective, with particular attention to Africa. In the first half of the twentieth century, black African intellectuals such as Sol Plaatje and Jomo Kenyatta dialogued with the metropole through social science as well as political struggle (see Chapter 5). The mainstream of metropolitan sociology made little use of such contacts; but this other history is also real, and we need to build on it today.

2

Modern general theory and its hidden assumptions

But one should not lose sight of the real.

—Frantz Fanon (1952)

In this chapter, I examine the approach to the world found in the most prestigious genre of work in sociology, general theory. Admittedly, works of general theory are not everybody's bedtime reading. Yet they have a powerful influence in defining the issues with which a discipline should be concerned, and the concepts or methods it should use.

By general theory I mean theorising that tries to formulate a broad vision of the social, and offers concepts that apply beyond a particular society, place or time. Such texts make propositions or hypotheses that are relevant everywhere, or propose methods of analysis that will work under all conditions. This is very difficult to do well. Justifiably, credible works of general theory carry great weight.

Overwhelmingly, general theory is produced in the metropole. Does this matter? The sociology of knowledge would suggest that it does. On the other hand, the very generality of general theory, the aspiration to universal relevance, implies that this genre could escape from local determinations.

I propose to study this question through a close examination of key texts. I focus on three of the most influential sociological thinkers of the last generation: James S. Coleman, Anthony Giddens and Pierre Bourdieu. In each case, I focus on the text that most explicitly states a general perspective for social analysis. My goal is not to review these authors' whole oeuvres, though I will often refer to their other writings for context. My hope is rather, by examining the way these texts work, to tease out the geopolitical assumptions underlying general theory as such.

Of course, three texts cannot represent a whole field, but these seem a good place to start. They come from three countries influential in the history of sociology, and they represent contrasting styles of work—one building a tightly knit propositional system, the second an elaborate scheme of categories, and the third a practical toolkit for social analysis. Their authors all have reputations as major theorists. Their work is, for instance, prominent in Charles Camic and Neil Gross's (1998) survey of 'contemporary developments in sociological theory'. The *Web of Science* online database provides solid evidence that these particular books are widely known and used. In the last ten years, Giddens' *The Constitution of Society* has had 2279 citations recorded, Bourdieu's *The Logic of Practice* has had 1236, and Coleman's *Foundations of Social Theory* has had 1860.

Northern choosers: Coleman's *Foundations of Social Theory*

James S. Coleman's *Foundations of Social Theory* was published in 1990 as the summation of a very distinguished intellectual career. The author had been for three decades a leading figure in US sociology, working in fields as diverse as youth studies, quantitative methodology, educational inequality and rational choice theory. Famous far beyond sociology for the 'Coleman Report' on race and schooling, Coleman also had an agenda for the remaking of the discipline.

Across a thousand pages, *Foundations* makes a heroic traverse of sociological problems ranging from socialisation and the family to corporate management, the state and revolution. Coleman shows in every chapter how existing knowledge can be rewritten in a single language of choices and choosers. In the final section of the book, this rewriting evolves into a mathematical formalisation, presenting algebraic models of social processes, strongly influenced by game theory. The book was greeted by some reviewers as the most important piece of social theory since Parsons' *Structure of Social Action*, and Coleman as a 'master of social thought' on a par with Weber and Durkheim (Abell 1991; Fararo 1991; Hechter 1992).

Coleman's theoretical ambition is announced in his first sentence: 'A central problem in social science is that of accounting for the functioning of some kind of social system.' A social system is defined as a set of individuals linked by transactions, in which they must engage to satisfy their own interests because the other individuals have some control over the resources they need. The interplay between individual and system, the micro–macro link, becomes a formative problem in Coleman's theorising, and is generally a central problem in modern positivism.

Less readily noticed, because it is so common in sociological theorising, is Coleman's assumption that this language of individual and system, interest, control and resource, micro and macro, is of universal relevance. The concepts can be applied in any time and place. This is in accord with the epistemology of the positivist school from which Coleman comes. The attempt to make universal statements—'highly generalized propositions', in Marion Levy's (1970) phrase—able to be tested empirically was always their key strategy of theory-building.

Coleman is explicit about his starting-point: 'the individual', also called 'the person' or 'the natural person'. These are the 'elementary actors' of social theory, up to the point where 'corporate actors' are introduced. In one of the few passages where Coleman approaches eloquence, he insists that, even in the processes where sovereignty is transferred to collectivities, 'individual persons do have primacy' (Coleman 1990: 3, 32, 367, 493, 531).

Critics such as Neil Smelser (1990) have seen this as the central weakness of Coleman's work, a paradoxical attempt to construct a social science from individualist assumptions. The more important problem is what kind of individual is being brought into play. Coleman is sharply critical of the 'intellectual disarray' in sociology resulting from varying conceptions of the person:

> The correct path for social theory is a more difficult one: to maintain a single conception of what individuals are like and to generate the varying systemic functioning not from different kinds of creatures, but from different structures of relations within which these creatures find themselves (Coleman 1990: 197).

So what kind of creature does Coleman maintain? The 'natural persons' in his text pursue their own interests; they make calculations about costs and benefits; they bargain with others; they give up rights or receive rights; they engage in purposive actions towards a goal. In short, they behave like entrepreneurs in a market—all the time.

This is not surprising. It is, after all, the model of the individual in marginalist economics from which Coleman was borrowing. But this shows that Coleman is not quite accurate in claiming the individual as the starting point of his theory. Equally, his starting point is a concept of the market—the social structure that gives rise to that particular kind of individual. Coleman is more sociological in his underlying reasoning than he admits. His theorising is a grand generalisation of the vision of people and social relations characteristic of modern neoliberalism.

Coleman follows the time-honoured strategy of moving from (apparently) simple to (apparently) complex phenomena. Indeed, this provides the architecture of the book as a whole, as well as many moves within it—for example: 'Social relations between two persons are, of course, the building blocks of social organization' (1990: 43). This allows him to start with radical abstraction and simplification, construct a less-simple derivation, and then compare the product with some actual set of events. The theoretical strategy leads to a consistent disembedding of events from their historical contexts.

Coleman's actors move in an energetic dance, calculating, bargaining and exchanging on a featureless dance floor. It is not entirely accidental that his visual models of action systems resemble teaching diagrams for the foxtrot and the jazz waltz. The featurelessness of the dance floor follows from the ahistorical method. In each derivation, the same limited set of elements and possible relations is set in motion. The theoretical logic will not work, any more than one can dance a foxtrot, if the dance-floor is lumpy with footprints from previous dances or with the bodies of previous dancers.

To use another metaphor, Coleman's own: at each important step in the argument, Coleman has to imagine a space in which the building (he repeatedly invokes 'building blocks') of the social system can go ahead. His account presupposes the cleared space of the building site. His book has no name for this space, in which the 'set of independent individuals' that provide his 'theoretical foundation' can be conceived to exist. It is a significant silence. As I will show later, we can find and name this space.

The principle that the theory is universally relevant allows Coleman to dip into any period of history. He picks examples from modern US demography, a theatre fire, transnational corporations, US high schools, the South Sea bubble, a student demonstration, medieval European land tenure, the constitution of the Soviet Union, a printing union, and Eskimo polar bear hunts. In this respect, *Foundations of Social Theory* is strikingly traditional. This is the way evidence was deployed in Sumner's *Folkways* and other books of the pre-World War I era. Illustrations from any place, any time have the same relevance. Indeed, *imaginary* examples have the same standing for Coleman as real ones.

Most examples come from North America and Europe in the twentieth century. At a few points in the text, however, Coleman speaks of 'primitive' societies. Late in the book he gives, with an air of amusement, the example of a Bedouin husband riding while his wife carries a burden on foot—and an American wife takes the family car. Early in the book, two such cases pop up together: 'nomadic tribes of the Sahara' dividing rights to a camel, and 'Eskimos' dividing the carcass of a bear. It seems that there is a heartland of Coleman's sociology, and also an exotic periphery.

Well into the text, in Chapter 20, Coleman opens a discussion of 'modern society'. What is distinctive about the modern, Coleman proposes, is a predominance of 'purposively constructed' relationships over 'natural' ones, 'a long-term historical development in which the primordial, natural environment is replaced by a purposively constructed one. The change occurs in both the physical environment and the social environment' (Coleman 1990: 552). This means the predominance of 'the new, purposively constructed corporate actors' over 'primordial ties and the old corporate actors based on them (family, clan, ethnic group, and community)'.

Here Coleman is replaying the argument of an earlier book, *The Asymmetric Society* (1982). This thought is central to his agenda for sociology, since he sees the loss of 'primordial ties' as constituting a deep social crisis. His theory at this point depends on the very traditional figure of sociological thought that constructs a global difference between the modern and the primitive (see Chapter 1). This grand ethnography is reproduced even in Coleman's reply to critics of *Foundations*, where he evokes 'a fundamental structural difference between the societies now emerging and all those that have gone before' (Coleman 1992: 268). Coleman does not speak of 'capitalism' because he has no theory of accumulation. He generally lumps the state and corporations together, on one side of the divide that has the family on the other. Modernity is both the creation of the new and the dissolution of the old. This yields a fluid world of 'freestanding' corporate actors 'without a fixed relation either to natural persons or to other corporate actors'—in fact, market society.

The exotic examples now fall into place. The primitive tribes who hunt bears, cut up camels and make their wives walk are beyond the edge of the modern. At a couple of points in the text, this edge is almost in view. One is the discussion of the Palestinian revolt (1992: 484–6). The Palestinians are being drawn into 'prosperity' by the Israeli economy, yet turn against it, and start throwing rocks and committing arson. Coleman's interest is not in how this conflict arose; it is in how well the course of events matches general theories of frustration and revolution.

Though his account of the constitution of a social system is overwhelmingly a consensus theory (drawing on social contract models with a whiff of Parsons), Coleman acknowledges that some systems are coercive. He calls the very coercive ones 'disjoint constitutions', where one set of actors creates arrangements that 'impose constraints and demands on a different set of actors'. That might sound like the definition of an empire, or perhaps the structural adjustment policies imposed on Latin America by US banks and the IMF. But Coleman's principal example (1992: 327–8) is Stalinist paper constitutions that defined the workers as beneficiaries and other classes as targets.

Coleman ignores the whole historical experience of empire and global domination. He never mentions colonies. He treats slavery briefly, in terms of the intellectual problem it creates for an exchange theory of society. (His memorable solution is that it is rational for the slave to accept enslavement if the alternative is death.) Despite the universal ambitions of the theory, then, *Foundations* misses or misrepresents vast tracts of human history, and ignores the social experience of the majority world now.

Agents of the gavotte: Giddens' *Constitution of Society*

In 1984 Anthony Giddens published *The Constitution of Society*, with the subtitle 'Outline of the Theory of Structuration'. This too was the culmination of a long project. His approach can be seen developing through *New Rules of Sociological Method* (1976), which gave an account of practical action, *Central Problems in Social Theory* (1979), which expanded on the relation between action and structure, and *A Contemporary Critique of Historical Materialism* (1981), which criticised Marx's view of world history and proposed an alternative.

The task Giddens set himself in this series of books was a reformulation of social theory as a whole, the reconciliation of conflicting intellectual traditions, and the creation of a consistent conceptual framework for social research and social critique. This magnificent project involved an enormous effort of synthesis, on a scale hardly matched in modern social thought except by Habermas. In the *Constitution*, Giddens incorporates research ranging from psychoanalytic accounts of the development of trust to Goffman's anatomies of encounters, debates on the origins of the state, innovative work in geography, and the empirical sociology of education, taking in Parsons, Blau and Foucault along the way.

This tremendous range of reference makes sense because the object of knowledge is so broad. Giddens says at the start:

> The basic domain of study of the social sciences, according to the theory of structuration, is neither the experience of the individual actor, nor the existence of any form of societal totality, but social practices ordered across space and time. Human social activities, like some self-reproducing items in nature, are recursive . . . To be a human being is to be a purposive agent, who both has reasons for his or her activities and is able, if asked, to elaborate discursively upon those reasons (Giddens 1984: 35).

The field of theory, then, is unbounded. It concerns social practices and human beings *in general.* The theory of structuration embraces all social relations, all social structures and all societies. So Giddens dips into the stories of neo-Confucian China, ancient China, the financial moguls of the City of London, a car factory, a concentration camp. Since the theory concerns all possible social relations, Giddens—like Coleman—has no hesitation in analysing imaginary examples as well.

Like Coleman, however, he draws almost no examples from the colonised world. A striking example is his discussion of the development of autonomy. Giddens makes effective use of Erik Erikson's psychoanalytic model of human development. But he makes no use of Erikson's famous cross-cultural analysis in the very book, *Childhood and Society*, that is being quoted. The result is a universalised, completely abstracted, account of human development—very much at odds with the diversity revealed in the modern sociology of childhood (Erikson 1950; Orellana et al. 2001).

Giddens frames his task in terms of the history of social theory and philosophy—for instance, coming to terms with the 'linguistic turn'. He repeatedly rewrites familiar sociological or psychological concepts in the language of structuration, much as Coleman rewrites in the language of markets and choice.

Giddens also undertakes to transcend dichotomies in existing theory. By far the most important is the dichotomy between objectivism and subjectivism. Transcending this one leads to Giddens' basic principle of the 'duality of structure', whose child is structuration itself, 'the structuring of social relations across time and space, in virtue of the duality of structure'. The fundamental concept in Giddens' theory thus arises from reflection on the internal antinomies of a European/North American intellectual tradition.

The text of *Constitution* alternates between critical commentary on existing literature, and frequent bursts of definition and concept-elaboration. Even a favourable reviewer such as Jonathan Turner (1986) was moved to remark on the 'definitional texture' of the book. This is the opposite of Coleman's strategy of taking the smallest set of categories for the longest possible walk. Giddens' work reads as if the vastness of the field creates vacuums which theory must expand to fill. The result is often both enthusiastic and banal—as we see in a model of social change so generalised that it covers every episode in the history of the world, yet says almost nothing about them (1984: 244ff).

Where Giddens is in no degree banal—where he has a strong line and argues eloquently for it—is in the theory of the agent. Giddens' agent is not only active, as with Coleman and Bourdieu, but also knowledgeable:

> The knowledge of social conventions, of oneself and of other human beings, presumed in being able to 'go on' in the diversity of contexts of social life is detailed and dazzling. All competent members of society are vastly skilled in the practical accomplishments of social activities and are expert 'sociologists'. The knowledge they possess is not incidental to the persistent patterning of social life but is integral to it ... Human agents always know what they are doing on the level of discursive consciousness ... (Giddens 1984: 26).

Agency is understood in terms of the universal requirements of the duality of structure. Consider, for instance, Giddens' strong argument against the positivist search for laws in social science, which 'produces a form of reified discourse not true to the real characteristics of human agents'. The 'real characteristics' are the competencies that allow actors to constitute and reconstitute social systems through their routine activities and interactions. To Giddens, these capacities appear the same in all times and places, because what the agent is required for, in the theory, is always the same.

But where Coleman's and Bourdieu's agents are tacticians and bargainers, always with a sharp eye out for a deal, Giddens' agents are much more subdued and orderly. Giddens does not, in fact, have a market model of the person. His accounts of agency emphasise routine, trust and coordination, the interlocking of activities between different agents. If Coleman's tacticians seem to be weaving across the floor in a foxtrot, Giddens' diagrams seem to be maps of a stately gavotte, executed by a ballroom full of well-trained dancers.

The agent may be an individual, but Giddens is emphatic that his theorising does not start with the individual. To him, society is equally real. Indeed, Giddens' concept of agency depends on a notion of the social order. But so does his concept of the social depend on the notion of agency. The principle of the 'duality of structure' locks the two levels together *logically*.

Giddens theorises the social in two divergent ways. In the first mode he is concerned with how society is possible, how organised social existence can occur and persist. As John Urry (1986) puts it, much of *Constitution* is 'principally concerned with constituting an ontology of the social'. Concepts such as 'structuration' relate to these questions, and their extreme abstraction results from Giddens trying to give answers that will be valid for any known, or any possible, form of human social existence. Hence such enormous categories as 'reciprocity between actors in contexts of co-presence' (English translation: 'people doing things together face to face').

Yet Giddens is also aware of the glorious diversity of human social experience. He has read widely, and is interested in history. So he has a second mode of theorising, in which he elaborates categories of social situations and processes: types of time, types of regionalisation, types of context, types of constraint, types of society, types of resources, and so forth.

These categories, too, are abstract, but in a different way. They are meant to catch the ways in which situations differ, rather than what is necessary to all social processes. Nigel Thrift (1985) has suggested that the nub of Giddens' whole argument is that 'social theory must become more contextual'. These are the categories that allow him to map the diversity of social action's contexts.

With Giddens' enthusiasm for definition and his fertility in elaborating concepts, they add up to a tremendous grid, through which one can gaze on human history from a great height, seeing where each episode fits in an intelligible scheme. This view-from-above on the whole story of human civilisation gives a grandeur to *Constitution* more reminiscent of Spencer and Comte than of Giddens' contemporaries in the social theory trade.

The most important part of this grid defines types of society. Giddens' grand ethnography is a threefold scheme distinguishing:

1   tribal society;
2   class-divided society (roughly, with cities but without factories); and
3   class society, or capitalism.

This is obviously intended as a historical order, the latter arising after the former, though Giddens insists it is not an 'evolutionary scheme'. The different types of society are distinguished by different 'structural principles' and are marked by different 'contradictions'. The traditional character of Giddens' thinking is especially clear in relation to his first category. Tribal societies are closer to nature; they are 'cold'—that is, not adapted to change; they are dominated by kinship and tradition; they are segmented, and so on (1984: 182, 193ff).

How are these types of society related to each other? To Giddens, the most important point is that they are logically distinct. If a society is one, it is not the other. However, once the later forms come into being, different types of society can coexist within an inter-societal system. Giddens invents the term 'time–space edge' to define where one structuring principle gives way to another. The relationship across a time–space edge may be one of domination or of symbiosis. Thus Giddens arrives at a way of referring to matters that other people discuss under the name of empire.

The relationship that *Constitution* does not theorise is colonisation; the structuring principle it does not explicitly name is imperialism; and the type of society that never enters its classifications is the colony. ('Colonisation' appears once in the book's index—as a reference to Goffman's research on asylums.) For a world-spanning book of general social theory, written in the heartland of the greatest imperial power the world had ever seen, this is interesting. The struggle for de-colonisation was certainly one of the most dramatic and important changes, on a world scale, in Giddens' lifetime. What the theory of structuration says about it is that: 'What is a "liberation movement" from one perspective might be a "terrorist organization" from another' (Giddens 1984: 337). That quotation is anti-colonial movements, decolonisation, neo-colonialism and post-independence struggles, as far as *Constitution* is concerned.

The problem is not just the absence of factual detail about the majority world. The grid of types of society—that is, the part of his theory where Giddens is the most traditional sociologist—leads to a doctrine that systematically downplays the significance of imperialism and the experience of colonised societies. In a crucial passage of *Constitution*, Giddens explains that modern capitalism—the third type of society—is not like the others, and did not evolve out of them. Rather, it resulted from 'massive discontinuities':

> introduced by the intertwining of political and industrial revolutions from the eighteenth century onwards. The distinctive structural principle of the class societies of modern capitalism is to be found in the disembedding, yet interconnecting, of state and economic institutions. The tremendous economic power generated by the harnessing of allocative resources to a generic tendency towards technical improvement is matched by an enormous expansion in the administrative 'reach' of the state . . . (Giddens 1984: 183)

That is to say, Giddens sees modernity as an endogenous change within Europe (or 'the West'), producing a pattern which is *afterwards* exported to the rest of the world. This is, of course, the standard social-scientific view of the origins of modernity, encapsulated in the idea of the 'Industrial Revolution'. It stands in contrast to the world-systems approach in which capitalism involved from the start a colonial economy. In Wallerstein's (1979) account, conquest and core–periphery relations are not a by-product; they are constitutive of modern capitalism as a system.

This is a very loaded difference. Giddens implies that the West is dominant not because it conquered the rest of the world, but because of its 'temporal precedence'. The West industrialised and modernised first. Other social orders are passing away not because Europeans with guns came and shattered them, but because modernity is irresistible. On this point, Giddens remained entirely consistent, because this was to be the core of his model of globalisation too.

Southern tacticians: Bourdieu's *Logic of Practice*

Pierre Bourdieu's *The Logic of Practice* also had a long gestation. Its first form as an *Outline of a Theory of Practice* (*Esquisse*, which can also mean a sketch or draft) was published in French in 1972; a revision was made for the English translation in 1977; a further revision, meant to be definitive, hit print in 1980 as *Le sens pratique*, and was in turn translated into English in 1990. All this was only the later stage of an enterprise that began in Algeria in the 1950s, as a study of Berber-speaking farming communities in Kabylia (Bourdieu 2002; Yacine 2003, 2005). A large part of the *Logic* (and the *Outline*) describes the daily lives of these communities, in dense ethnographic text interspersed with methodological comments.

Here the focus is on the global South. Nor was this an arbitrary choice of subject-matter. Bourdieu's Algerian experience was, on his own account, formative in his 'conversion' from philosopher to social scientist and in shaping his distinctive approach to social science. The young Bourdieu became a field researcher in close collaboration with Algerian students and colleagues such as Abdelmalak Sayad.

This did not make Bourdieu an anthropologist in the conventional sense. As early as 1958, Bourdieu—as Sayad (1996) remarks, a 'véritable entrepreneur scientifique'—had published *Sociologie de l'Algérie*. Fourteen years later, when the *Esquisse* came out, Bourdieu had also published influential work in the sociology of education and culture. By the time *Le sens pratique* came out, he had also published *Distinction*, on class hierarchies. By the time the *Logic* appeared in English, Bourdieu held the most prestigious academic chair of sociology in France. Bourdieu constantly—and rightly—subverted the division of labour by which anthropology studied the primitive and sociology the advanced.

The Logic of Practice is an attempt to develop a credible basis for social-scientific knowledge, in the form of an analytic strategy and conceptual language, and to show this approach at work. Bourdieu thinks his project has cultural, political, and philosophical importance. As he says in characteristic rhetoric at the end of the Preface:

> By forcing one to discover externality at the heart of internality, banality in the illusion of rarity, the common in the pursuit of the unique, sociology does more than denounce all the impostures of

egoistic narcissism; it offers perhaps the only means of contributing, if only through awareness of determinations, to the construction, otherwise abandoned to the forces of the world, of something like a subject (Bourdieu 1990: 21).

To get to the place where 'something like a subject' will come into view, Bourdieu has to deal with existing accounts of the social and subjectivity. His opening chapters therefore critique both 'objectivism', as represented by structural linguistics, Lévi-Strauss, and structuralist Marxism, and (more summarily and angrily) 'subjectivism', as represented by Sartre and rational choice theory. He rejects structuralism because it takes a god-like view of social reality. The theorists are not present in the world being theorised; therefore, they cannot learn from analysing their own social practice. On the other hand Bourdieu rejects subjectivism because it refuses to recognise the constraints on social action, thinking that practice can be understood purely from the viewpoint of decisions of the will.

Universal social laws might be fetishes, but Bourdieu certainly works on an assumption of the *methodological* homogeneity of human history. His theoretical toolkit is intended to work anywhere and everywhere. Rogers Brubaker (1993) nicely captures this by suggesting that what Bourdieu offers is not a fixed propositional scheme but a theoretical habitus, a well-defined manner of *doing* the job of theorising.

Bourdieu lays out the toolkit twice in *Logic*: briefly in the Preface, and more extensively in Chapters 3, 7 and 8. These are the now familiar concepts of practice and structure, strategy, social reproduction, habitus, field, symbolic capital and domination. The concepts of symbolic violence and the cultural arbitrary, central to Bourdieu's sociology of education, are not much in evidence in the *Logic*, but the rest of his contribution to modern sociological thought is in view.

My purpose here is not to criticise these concepts; I did this a couple of decades ago, and many others have done so since (Connell 1983; Calhoun et al. 1993; Robbins 2000; Swartz and Zolberg 2004). Rather, as with Coleman's and Giddens' concepts, I want to ask what view of the world and its inhabitants is at work in them. At one level, there is a striking similarity to Coleman's theorising and a contrast with Giddens'. The agent in Bourdieu's world—the person who engages in practice, uses practical logic, and is the bearer of the *habitus*—is very much a tactician, man-oeuvring for advantage in a world where he confronts other tacticians, who are also manoeuvring.

'Even when they give every appearance of disinterestedness,' Bourdieu remarks towards the end of his exposition, 'practices never cease to comply with an economic logic.' Strategies are always seeking 'profit' of one kind or another. Bourdieu's peasant is a more sophisticated bargainer than Coleman's rational chooser, manoeuvring simultaneously in several dimensions of social reality, and letting some strategies unfold over long periods. Bourdieu energetically extends the market vision into apparently non-market fields of social life, including cases where the market logic is systematically denied by the people themselves. This gives Bourdieu's sociology a strongly ironic flavour.

However, Bourdieu's agent goes bargaining in a lumpier world than Coleman's. Here the debt to Lévi-Strauss and Marxism is clear. There is no cleared space; the social world is already shaped by structures, especially those of class and kinship. It is these structures that give rise to the *habitus*, the internalised principles of action. These structures are regenerated through the deal-making of the agents, who manoeuvre always within limits set by the *habitus*. Thus Bourdieu's theory of practice becomes, systematically, a theory of social reproduction.

A society or social formation, then, is at one level a self-regenerating set of structures, at another level a set of agents engaged in an endless dance of strategising, bargaining and exchange. Through this dance, whose rules are set by the structures, the structures reproduce themselves. The ironic effects of the *habitus* constantly bend events back into their former patterns. Bourdieu is well aware that in real life things do change, and the good old *habitus* becomes awkward in new circumstances. But structural change is not what his theorising explains.

The dance of practice, then, is a *danse macabre*, in which the ghostly emissaries of the structures perform their semi-scripted revels, and at the end of each cycle of practice sink back into their graves—that is, their places in the structures. Time is of the essence in the steps of the dance. But at the level of the whole, history is frozen.

To make the rough social psychology of the *habitus* work as a mechanism of reproduction, Bourdieu has to make a strong assumption of cultural homogeneity. This may sound strange in the sociologist who made differences in cultural capital so central to the sociology of education. Yet in the *Logic* Bourdieu constantly presents the social order as culturally homogeneous, and Margaret Archer (1983) has shown that a similar assumption underpins Bourdieu's educational sociology. In the *Logic*, there seem to be no debates among the Kabyle, no religious tensions, no radical movements.

This is very marked in relation to gender, an issue to which Bourdieu gives a lot of attention in the *Logic*. He draws an absolute dichotomy between the man's world and the woman's world, making clear that his energetic bargaining 'agent' is a man. The gender system is mapped as a simple dichotomy and a simple hierarchy. In a vivid passage, where Bourdieu is explaining how the *habitus* is built into the body, he describes the stances of the manly man (upright, alert, etc.) and the well-brought-up woman (stooped, eyes downcast, etc.).

This schematic model was worked out for Kabylia, but Bourdieu clearly thought it was not confined there. In *Masculine Domination* (2001), he presented the same idea as a general model of patriarchy, ignoring a whole generation of feminist research. Because of Bourdieu's fame as a theorist, this badly outdated formulation is now having a considerable influence in some areas of gender studies.

In most of the text, Bourdieu treats the world of the Kabyle, the world of metropolitan France and other milieux as methodologically continuous. This does not mean that he thinks all societies are of the same type. In several passages of the *Logic*, Bourdieu discusses the 'pre-capitalist economy'. In the chapter on 'modes of domination' especially, Bourdieu dichotomises in a very traditional sociological manner.

This consists of presenting opposing pictures of the modern and the pre-modern as types of society. In Bourdieu's pre-modern, the material economy and the symbolic economy are inextricably mixed. In the modern, after 'the disenchanting of the natural world reduced to its economic dimension alone', they are separated into distinct fields. In the pre-modern, social advantage must be continuously recreated by personal attention and effort. In the modern, this is accomplished by institutionalisation.

In his preface to the *Logic* (1990: 3), Bourdieu tells a memorable story. He was admiring some photographs of storage jars he had taken during his old fieldwork. The photographs were so good because the roof of the house where he found them was missing. The roof was missing because it had been destroyed by the French army when it expelled the occupants. This passage is, I think, the only mention in the *Logic* that a war—indeed, an exceptionally bitter war—of colonial repression and liberation was raging in Algeria during the time Bourdieu was doing his research.

This is remarkable. How could such an event as the Franco-Algerian war *not* seem relevant to the analysis of practice, when fine details of parallel-cousin marriage do? Bourdieu certainly knew the story. He had been sent to Algeria to do his military service, stayed to research and teach in a hostile environment, eventually left Algeria under the threat of violence from colonialist diehards. He worked with Algerian colleagues, did some research under the eyes of the military in 'relocation camps', and did other fieldwork among peasants carrying weapons. In texts of the late 1950s and early 1960s, Bourdieu had written about the disintegrating effects of colonialism and the colonial war, and in the *Logic* he proposed an ethic of human solidarity. But still Bourdieu did not see the anti-colonial struggle as essential material for his own statement of general theory or social-scientific method.

The most famous theorist of this struggle was Frantz Fanon, who not only overlapped Bourdieu's time in Algeria but also made research trips to Kabylia, before leaving the country to work openly for the Algerian FLN (National Liberation Front). Fanon's *L'an V de la révolution algérienne* appeared in 1959; *The Wretched of the Earth* (with a famous preface by Sartre) in 1961, while Bourdieu was still engaged with Algerian issues. These books deal directly with the practice that was transforming the society Bourdieu wrote about, yet they are never mentioned in *The Logic of Practice*. No other participants in the Algerian struggle have their ideas considered in the *Logic*, either. Bourdieu had long been contemptuous of the schematic theories of revolution that circulated on the French left. He regarded Fanon and Sartre as purveyors of myth; he supported the colonised but wished to distance himself from the doctrine of the FLN. He seems to have considered his own early sociology as a cold dose of facts needed to educate people on both sides of the Algerian struggle (Bourdieu 1979).

Nevertheless, at the deepest level it is not Bourdieu's political history but his conception of theory that makes the anti-colonial struggle irrelevant. To arrive at 'something like a subject', the European conceptual framing is self-sufficient. In the centre of this debate, as Bourdieu knew it from his early studies in philosophy onwards, there were no voices from Africa.

Bourdieu's own project of creating a universally applicable toolkit gave him no reason to search out colonial voices, because it made irrelevant the specific history of the societies through which the tools are illustrated. Nor did his toolkit require him to address a liberation struggle as a social process.

The result, in the *Logic*, is a text with a structure Bourdieu doubtless did not intend, but which is all too familiar in European writings about the majority world. Knowledge about a colonised society is acquired by an author from the metropole and deployed in a metropolitan debate. Debates among the colonised are ignored, the intellectuals of colonised societies are unreferenced, and social process is analysed in an ethnographic time-warp. The possibilities for a different structure of knowledge that undoubtedly existed in Bourdieu's early research are never realised in the later theorising.

The Northernness of general theory

It is now time to reflect on the geopolitical assumptions of the genre. This argument draws on the cases just discussed, but also attempts to move beyond them. The consequences of metropolitan geo-political location can be seen, I suggest, in four characteristic textual moves: the claim of universality; reading from the centre; gestures of exclusion; and grand erasure.

The claim of universality

In each of the texts just discussed, there is a strong and repeated claim to universal relevance. To these authors, and to many others, the very idea of theory involves talking in universals. It is assumed that all societies are knowable, and they are knowable in the same way and from the same point of view.

That this point of view originates in the metropole is not explicit. Indeed, this has to remain tacit—for if it were made explicit, universal relevance would immediately be called into question. Intellectuals in the periphery cannot universalise a locally generated perspective because its specificity is immediately obvious. It attracts a name such as 'African philosophy' or 'Latin American dependency theory', and the first question that gets asked is 'how far is this relevant to other situations?'

The claim of universality can also be made through method. An example is the rewriting of other social scientists' work in one's own conceptual language, as both Coleman and Giddens do. This rewriting is never just a translation: it is a subsumption, in which the universal relevance of the preferred theory is implicitly claimed.

Reading from the centre

Contributions to general theory are often presented as resolutions of some antinomy, problem or weakness in previous theory. All three of our texts present themselves in this way. It is a professional requirement—one must relate one's work to the literature. But whose literature? The three texts just discussed address problems that arise in a metropolitan theoretical literature, and this is usual in the genre.

For instance, Giddens and Bourdieu both focus on the antinomy of objectivism versus subjectivism. This is a classic problem for European cultural and social sciences. But it is *not* a central problem for colonial intelligentsias. The reason is apparent when we look at what objectivism and subjectivism share. They are alternative ways of picturing oneself at the centre of a world, alternative models of actions or systems with no external determinations. A general social theory shaped around the objectivism/subjectivism problem necessarily constructs a social world read through the metropole—not read through the metropole's action on the rest of the world.

A very important case of reading from the centre concerns time. On the small scale, the time the three theories suppose is generally abstract—that is, date-free—and continuous. On the large scale, the grand ethnographies offer the world-time of an intelligible historic succession (pre-modern to modern, pre-capitalist to capitalist, etc.). This is time as experienced in the metropole. In colonised and settler societies, time involves fundamental discontinuity and unintelligible succession.

Let me give one example, from many that could be given. In the early nineteenth century, the British imperial state took over from the Dutch in South Africa, and soon stepped up the level of violence, burning and killing in Xhosa settlements. A historian describes the Xhosa experience: 'Total war was a new and shattering experience for the Xhosa ... The havoc wrought by the colonial forces was not only cruel but incomprehensible ... Now that this foreign entity had crystallized as a threat there was no telling where it would all end' (Peires 1979: 53–4). For colonised cultures, conquest is not evolution, rationalisation or transformation, but catastrophe. Colonisation introduces fundamental disjunctions into social experience that simply cannot be represented in metropolitan theory's models of change through time.

Gestures of exclusion

The theorist's reading list is always an interesting document. I have noted the significant absence of the Algerian liberation movement from Bourdieu's exposition. Theorists from the colonised world are very rarely cited in metropolitan texts of general theory. There is a notable absence of reference to Islamic thought, given the wealth of Islamic discussions of modernity.

At times, texts of general theory include exotic items from the non-metropolitan world, but they do not introduce *ideas* from the periphery that have to be considered as part of the dialogue of theory. The formulae I have termed grand ethnography, emphasising the modern/pre-modern distinction, also render the social thought of colonised cultures irrelevant to the main theoretical conversation. That thought is treated as belonging to a world that has been surpassed.

Grand erasure

Social theory is built in a dialogue with empirical knowledge—sometimes derived from the theorist's own research, more often other people's. When that empirical knowledge derives wholly or mainly from the metropole, and where the theorist's concerns arise from the problems of metropolitan society, the effect is erasure of the experience of the majority of human kind from the foundations of social thought.

Erasure may also operate in the *way* experiences from the global South are referenced. Thus Bourdieu's *Logic* dwells on kinship strategies but erases the historical experience of colonial war. Colonial relationships as a social structure are erased by using the ethnographic present. The inherently divided culture of colonialism cannot be modelled in Coleman's derivations nor in Bourdieu's reproductionism. Nor, for that matter, can it be modelled in ethnomethodology's notion of the competent member of a culture. The politics of colonial and post-colonial society cannot be modelled by the depoliticised notions of power in Giddens and Coleman. The impossibility is sufficiently indicated by Coleman's ludicrous attempt to theorise slavery within rational choice theory, where the slave is supposed to have bought his right to stay alive.

Something worse can happen. In discussing Coleman's text, I noted how his account of social system-building presupposes a featureless, cleared space, and I suggested we could discover where that space is. It is certainly not in Europe. But it does exist in the neighbourhood of Chicago and Sydney.

Chicago was an exemplary new town in a colony of settlement, where space was cleared by the 'westward expansion' of the United States. This was a process of eliminating the societies, and most of the people, who had been there before. Sydney was also a new town, the main port of entry for the British conquest of Australia. To the British, Australia was understood as *terra nullius*, 'land belonging to nobody'. An entire continent was claimed for the Crown and distributed at the colonial government's pleasure. The deep connection that the existing population had to the land was obliterated.

Terra nullius, the coloniser's dream, is a sinister presupposition for social science. It is invoked every time we try to theorise the formation of social institutions and systems from scratch, in a blank space. Whenever we see the words 'building block' in a treatise of social theory, we should be asking who used to occupy the land.

***

Can we have social theory that does not claim universality for a metropolitan point of view, does not read from only one direction, does not exclude the experience and social thought of most of humanity, and is not constructed on *terra nullius*?

I believe we can. In fact, we have a good deal of it already, as the second half of this book will show. There are even moments in familiar texts that suggest new possibilities, moments when the edge of the metropole flickers into view, when light comes through the roof.

The extreme abstraction of the three texts examined in this chapter suggests another line of thought. Creating a separate domain of general theory is not the only way to conceptualise in social science. In Chapter 9, I explore the idea of a stronger—indeed, a literal—grounding of social thought.

Other paths for theory therefore exist. In following them, a number of problems arise. Do non-metropolitan intellectuals also write Northern theory? Certainly. I can speak with some authority here, as I have done it myself in *Gender and Power* (Connell 1987). When social scientists in the periphery write as if from the metropole, they meet difficulties of perspective and even identity, as I will show in Chapter 4. On the other hand, can metropolitan intellectuals escape the effects explored in this chapter? I believe they can, but they too face professional and cultural costs. (Some prospects are considered in Chapter 10.)

Therefore we should not underestimate the difficulties of a more inclusive theoretical project. But do we have any choice? It seems to me that the project of metropolitan social theory, in which the works of Giddens, Bourdieu and Coleman represent genuine pinnacles of achievement, is now exhausted. The problems mapped in this chapter cannot be overcome within this tradition of thought. We really have no choice but to face the difficulties of doing theory in a globally inclusive way.

3
Imagining globalisation

All remaining 'Chinese walls' the world over are being battered down. In this process, those cultural and political institutions that fettered capitalism are swept aside . . .

—William I. Robinson (2001)

In the new global electronic economy, fund managers, banks, corporations, as well as millions of individual investors, can transfer vast amounts of capital from one side of the world to another at the click of a mouse.

—Anthony Giddens (2002)

It is no longer possible to demarcate large geographical zones as center and periphery, North and South. In geographical regions such as the Southern Cone of Latin America or Southeast Asia, all levels of production can exist simultaneously and side by side . . . In the metropolises, too, labor spans the continuum from the heights to the depths of capitalist production: the sweatshops of New York and Paris can rival those of Hong Kong and Manila.

—Michael Hardt and Antonio Negri (2000)

Most theoretical texts in the social sciences are written in the global North, and most proceed on the assumption that this does not matter. But, as Chapter 2 showed for general theory and as Jennifer Robinson (2006) has recently shown for urban theory, 'where' does matter. With few exceptions, mainstream social theory sees and speaks from the global North.

Theories of globalisation therefore have a special significance. Globalisation theories name the world-as-a-whole as their object of knowledge. In principle, they include the global South, and thus offer a way for social theory to overcome its most devastating historic limitation.

Has this possibility been realised? In this chapter, I look at English-language sociological texts centered on the concept of globalisation, examining their methods for constructing a concept of global society, their antinomies, and their language and performative effectiveness. I begin by glancing at the circumstances from which recent globalisation theory emerged.

Sociology's encounters with the global

When sociology was first constructed, the whole inhabited world and the whole of human history were the new science's objects of knowledge. This is amply demonstrated by the detail of books such as Spencer's *Principles*, Sumner's *Folkways* and Tönnies' *Gemeinschaft und Gesellschaft*; by the first generation of teaching textbooks in sociology; and by Durkheim's fabulous attempt to survey all current sociological knowledge, the *Année sociologique*. As Chapter 1 showed, information from the colonial frontier played a key role in early sociological theorising.

The global scope of sociology was lost when the evolutionary framework collapsed. During the 1920s and 1930s, a very different enterprise took shape in the intellectual space still called 'sociology'. Its focus was social differentiation and social problems within the society of the metropole. This was the heyday of the Chicago School and the quantifiers who invented modern survey methods. Theoretical change soon followed—in particular, theories that encouraged the discipline to understand 'a society' as a self-contained system. It was, appropriately, Talcott Parsons (1937: 3) who celebrated the sea change with the famous gibe 'Spencer is dead'.

From the 1940s to the 1970s, it was common to take the boundaries of a nation-state as the boundaries of 'a society'. For instance, the first textbook of sociology written in Australia, when the new discipline was being installed here, was simply called *Australian Society* (Davies and Encel 1965). 'Development' was typically formulated as a comparative sociology of national societies. Sociology took one step beyond, in theories that addressed the cluster of nation-states that represented 'industrial society' and 'post-industrial society'. A few years later, the same territory was disputed in debates on postmodernity, 'risk society', 'reflexive modernisation', and so on (Touraine 1971; Crook et al. 1992; Seidman 1994; Beck 1992; Giddens 1990).

Most participants in these debates took no notice of the fact that the main cluster of 'industrial', 'postindustrial', 'modern' or 'postmodern' countries also constituted the global metropole. This was pointed out by Wallerstein (1974) and others building on the concept of imperialism (Amin 1974). Their arguments had little impact on mainstream sociology at the time.

But with the crisis of the metropolitan welfare state, the rise of neo-liberalism and worldwide economic restructuring, the conditions of existence for sociology changed. By the 1980s, sociology seemed to be entering its own crisis of relevance.

During the 1980s, the term 'globalisation' became popular among business journalists and management theorists, and began to generate a research literature in economics. The word described the strategies of large corporations based in Japan, the United States and Europe, but operating internationally—'multinational corporations' as they were called at the time. These strategies included international marketing campaigns, global sourcing by manufacturing firms, and shifting investment, employment and profit around different countries. More generally, 'globalisation' in business journalism and economics referred to the integration of capital markets that was part effect, part condition of those corporate strategies. Hence early articles about globalisation appeared in the financial rather than the general sections of newspapers (Fiss and Hirsch 2005: 39). Economic change was easily linked to other developments on the world scene: the breakdown of Soviet communism in the 1980s, the rise of neo-liberal politics, and the growth of cross-national institutions from the European Union to the transnational corporations.

Around 1990, the term 'globalisation' was picked up by a group of sociological theorists, mainly in the United Kingdom and United States.

A remarkable burst of writing re-established the contemporary relevance of sociology by making 'globalisation' one of its central topics. Suddenly Spencer had come back to life, and sociology was speaking once more about the world as a whole.

Sociologists could respond to this issue in two ways. One was to start from the new trends in international economic organisation and inquire into their social conditions and consequences. This was the approach taken in Saskia Sassen's (1991) sombre masterpiece *Global Cities*. She took the control needs of global businesses as a point of departure, examined the growth of new service markets and elite workforces, and studied the consequences for urban inequality.

Most sociologists of globalisation, however, followed a second path. In a constitutive act of reification, the idea of globalisation as an economic strategy was replaced by the idea of globalisation as *a new form of society*. As Ulrich Beck rather excitedly declared:

> A new kind of capitalism, a new kind of economy, a new kind of global order, a new kind of society and a new kind of personal life are coming into being, all of which differ from earlier phases of social development. Thus, sociologically and politically, we need a paradigm-shift, a new frame of reference (1999: 2).

Theories of globalisation offered varying answers to the resulting question: how should we understand this 'new kind of society'?

There is now a huge polemical and empirical literature on the topic; *Sociological Abstracts* currently lists more than 7000 texts which have 'globalisation' as a descriptor. My focus is much more specific. As Gane (2001) argues, this period has seen the emergence of 'a sociological *theory* of globalisation'. My focus is on English-language texts that offer a general conceptualisation of globalisation, rather than studies of particular processes or effects. I will explore how this theory is constructed, in its characteristic texts, and the ways in which that construction is related to its metropolitan base.

Global society and abstract linkage

The basis of most sociological thinking about globalisation, from the first wave of theoretical work, was the idea of global society (Turner 1989;

Smart 1994). Martin Albrow put the core idea very clearly: 'The real break, rupture with the modern, shift to a new epoch, comes not with the victory of the irrational over the rational, but *when the social takes on a meaning outside the frame of reference set by the nation-state*' (Albrow 1996: 58, my italics).

The concept of global society was built on the idea that boundaries were rapidly breaking down and there was a new intensity of links across distance among people, social entities or regions. Declarations of this idea, which we might call the concept of abstract linkage, are highly characteristic of the 'globalisation' literature in sociology. They are found in texts of all political outlooks:

> ... the rapidly increasing compression of the entire world into a single, global field (Robertson 1992: 174).
> ... a process leading to greater interdependence and mutual awareness (reflexivity) among economic, political and social units in the world, and among actors in general (Guillén 2001a: 236).
> Globalization ... is unifying the world into a single mode of production and a single global system and bringing about the organic integration of different countries and regions into a global economy (Robinson 2001: 159).

The concept of abstract linkage was often combined with a critique of the 'methodological nationalism' (Beck and Sznaider 2006) of sociological writing in the previous generation. The underlying idea of globalisation thus involved a concept that is, from a Parsonian point of view, a paradox—a system without a boundary. The first task of globalisation theorists, then, was to show how the new unbounded social system could be specified.

Given sociology's long-standing concern with transitions to modernity, a simple way of specifying 'global society' is to understand it as modernity spreading across the world. Beck (1999), in a classic statement of this view, presents a straightforward progression: once there was 'risk society'; now there is 'world risk society'. Beck acknowledges an evolution from calculable external risks to 'self-generated manufactured uncertainties', but substantially his picture is about the familiar politics of risk being played out on a larger geographical stage.

The same idea is found in Anthony Giddens' (2002) popular account of globalisation, *Runaway World*. This book paints a picture of global society that emphasises the politics of risk, the breakdown of tradition, the decline of family forms, the emergence of the pure relationship, the spreading of democracy and the rise of active citizenries and civil society. To readers of Giddens' other books since the mid-1980s, this list is very familiar. It summarises his account of modernity in *metropolitan* society.

The idea of modernity spreading from its heartland in Europe and North America to cover the whole world is probably the most widespread of all views of global society. It is close to neo-liberal ideology, with its concept of the universal market. It is flexible enough to admit diversity. Peter Berger (1997), for instance, sees four Western-derived subcultures (managerial, intellectual, commercial and religious) spreading out to form 'global culture'. The approach does not necessarily imply metropolitan domination, because theorists usually see the uptake as voluntary, attributing agency to the many 'eager participants in the formation of universalized global culture' (Meyer 2000: 240). As a sociological concept, it matches some popular ideas about development, such as the Chinese expression 'linking up with the tracks of the world'—that is, participating in capitalist modernity (Zhang 2001).

However, from the early days of sociological writing on the topic, this interpretation has been contested (Robertson 1992; Albrow 1996). Mike Featherstone, among the most sophisticated theorists of cultural studies, sharply criticised the idea of globalisation as generalised modernity:

> The process of globalization, then, does not seem to be producing cultural uniformity; rather it makes us aware of new levels of diversity. If there is a global culture it would be better to conceive of it not as a common culture, but as a field in which differences, power struggles and cultural prestige contests are played out (Featherstone 1995: 13–14).

In the context of theoretical debates in sociology in the 1980s and 1990s, this led to an alternative account of globalisation, which is vividly presented in Zygmunt Bauman's (1998) *Globalization: The Human Consequences*. In this text, Bauman describes an increase in social diversity, growing difficulty in forming social norms, the impossibility of rational planning, the predominance of consumption over production, and the transformation of politics into spectacle and media manipulation. These themes also are familiar. They can be found in Bauman's earlier writings about Europe, and in the broader literature on postmodernity as a condition of the 'advanced' societies (Crook et al. 1992).

There is, then, a second view of global society, as constituted by the condition of postmodernity on a world scale. The complexity and difference that Featherstone perceived in global culture, had already been perceived by him in the metropole, in analyses of consumer culture and the critique of integrationist sociology (Featherstone 1995: 80).

A third approach characterises global society not in terms of its traits, but in terms of its constitutive dynamic. This is a more interesting theoretical strategy, but its content is very familiar, since most such arguments are built on a Marxist concept of exploitation and accumulation. Teresa Brennan (2003) regards globalisation as driven by capitalism's inherent need to occupy more space, speed up production and circulation, and exploit nature as well as labour more intensively. William Robinson (2001) presupposes the political economy and focuses on the way the global interests of capital drive the making of a transnational state.

With Michael Hardt and Antonio Negri (2000), what is operating on a world scale is capital's response to the destructuring effect of proletarian struggle—a faithful translation of a model of capitalist dynamics in Italy worked out long before. Douglas Kellner's (2002) model of 'techno-capitalism' sees the interweaving of capitalist restructuring with scientific and technical development as the core process in globalisation. Leslie Sklair (2002) traces the institutional restructuring in greater detail, but shares the view of globalisation as driven by the search for corporate profit, requiring wider markets and labour forces.

These three approaches share an intellectual strategy. They leap straight to the level of the global, where they reify perceived trends as the nature of global society. The trends thus reified are based on concepts that have previously been worked out, not for speaking about colonies, empires or world affairs, but for speaking about *metropolitan societies*—that is, the cluster of modern, industrial, postmodern or postindustrial countries that had been the focus of theoretical debates in sociology for decades before.

The globalisation literature is not entirely defined by these three strategies of reification. Sklair, while presuming a dynamic of capitalist accumulation, also takes the view that global society can only be understood by examining the actual links between the parts. He argues (2001: 4) that a global system must be constructed by 'transnational practices', and this implies a research agenda tracing such practices.

Tracing transnational practices has proved to be a very fruitful research strategy, one not confined to the corporate world. Another important practical link, as Sassen notes, is population movements. Ulrike Schuerkens (2005: 549) speaks of 'a global world linked by transnational migrants'. Feminist theorists now often argue that globalisation is a gendered phenomenon (Chow 2003: 446; Acker 2004). But feminism has learnt a certain scepticism about world-spanning generalisations from the metropole (Mohanty, Russo and Torres 1991). So the focus has been on using empirical research techniques to document actual links: the creation of international networks of women's movements (Moghadam 2000), gender relations that involve transnational movement or pressures (Marchand and Runyan 2000) and emerging gender forms in global arenas (Hooper 2001).

Linkage approaches show that problems of globalisation can be treated in a less reified way. They have not, however, had the broad impact of the ideas of global society as global modernity or postmodernity, or as produced by an over-arching dynamic. These are the debates that have so far defined the sociological theory of globalisation.

The antinomies of globalisation theory

Argument in this field takes a characteristic form, which is revealed in attempts to classify the themes of the literature (Therborn 2000; Guillén 2001a). Having constructed a reified concept of global society, the mainstream sociological theory of globalisation is led into a series of antinomies from which it cannot escape. I will discuss the three most prominent.

Global versus local

From the first moments of sociological writing about globalisation, the global was seen in opposition to the local. The dichotomy was drawn from business literature, and so was a popular way of resolving it. The term 'glocalisation' was translated from Japanese business jargon (Robertson 1995) to refer to amalgams of local and global forces, such as the distinctive local marketing strategies of transnational advertisers.

To speak of 'glocalisation' is to resolve nothing. It is to assert both terms of a static polarity at once. The local/global opposition has not been conceptually resolved. In various forms—local/global, national/global—it continues to structure both debate and research (Therborn 2000; Sassen 2000; Schuerkens 2003). In an attempt to make the idea more dialectical, a well-known sociologist invented the even more appalling word 'grobalisation' to represent the forces that attempt to expand beyond the local (Ritzer 2003). But that restates the opposition; it does not transcend it.

From the turn of the century, sociologists began to take more notice of anti-globalisation resistance movements (Mann 2001; Eckstein 2002; Appelbaum and Robinson 2005)—a trend also seen in media discussions of globalisation (Fiss and Hirsch 2005). Such movements were typically seen as a reassertion of the local–or at least of local mediations of the global (Auyero 2001). But anti-globalisation movements themselves have strongly insisted on the systematic character of global power, so the dichotomy tends to be reinstalled. This is particularly clear in the work of Hardt and Negri (2004: 129). They proclaim 'an open network of singularities' as the essence of the forces of resistance. But the core of their model of global society is a concept of worldwide capitalist domination. Their whole picture of contemporary history is based on an absolute alterity between two constitutive forces, multitude and empire (Connell 2005b).

Homogeneity versus difference

The discourse of globalisation, with its themes of boundarylessness, common fate and growing integration, constantly hovers on the edge of assertions of global homogeneity, especially in culture. We all use the same technology, we have common consumption styles, we follow the same best practice, and so on. As Mauro Guillén (2001b: 3) notes, this emphasis reflects the concept's origins in management and business literature. In neoliberal theory and practice, the project of linking national markets was driven forward to create homogeneous business environments.

Yet sociological theorists have also been sharply aware of difference. Roland Robertson (1992: 172) emphasised that 'diversity is a basic aspect of globalization'. Guillén has argued for the significance of institutional diversity, but the more popular theme is cultural diversity. In the 1990s, sociologists generally set their faces against the thesis of Western cultural domination, the idea of the 'McDonaldisation' of the world. Instead, most adopted the theme of cultural mixing, mosaics and hybridity (Tomlinson 1999; Nederveen Pieterse 2004: 69).

Theorists with a background in ethnography have been especially prone to think that diversity is the heart of the matter. For instance, Arjun Appadurai's (1990) neologisms 'ethnoscapes', 'technoscapes', 'mediascapes' and 'ideoscapes' (alongside 'financescapes') offer names for the irregular configurations of cultural mixing and disjunction on a world scale. The trope of 'network' and an emphasis on diversity, difference and coalition has reappeared in recent discussions of resistance—for instance, discussions of the Seattle protest, the World Social Forum and 'internetworked' social movements (Mittelman 2004; Langman 2005). Some recent writers, however, have turned back. Kellner (2002: 292), for instance, muses on the 'strange amalgam' of homogenising forces and heterogeneity that constitutes globalisation; and Guillén's recent research suggests there is life in the convergence thesis yet (Henisz, Zelner and Guillén 2005; Polillo and Guillén 2005).

Dispersed versus concentrated power

The business discourse of globalisation began with claims about the declining power of the national state and the rising power of the market. A vigorous debate has continued among economists and political scientists (Kalb 2004; Mittelman 2004); it is not surprising that sociologists have also addressed this question.

They have not found agreement about the answer. Bauman accepts the thesis of states in decline, unable to regulate an international economy that is now effectively out of control. Arrighi suggests that many states in the world system have never had much power, the general view in world-systems analysis. Therborn thinks that states are still powerful in most parts of the world, and Guillén agrees, emphasising that they can choose different development paths. Evans considers the fate of the state contingent, not settled, while Mann emphasises the diversity of forms of power. To Sklair, the international economy has grown in importance compared with the national state, but there is nothing fragmented about it. Robinson agrees and sees business power materialised in a transnational state. Meyer denies that any such thing exists. Sassen sees business power reflected in some deterritorialisation of sovereignty. Giddens and Beck, while agreeing that the economy is moving out of control, are optimistic about the power of the state to control events—if the state's will is stiffened by an extra dose of democracy and civil society. Albrow sees a global state already emerging, not from capital but from the activities of citizens oriented to the common interests of world society.

Such spectacular disagreement about the locus of social power—an issue with which sociology as a discipline has a great deal of experience—strongly suggests an underlying problem. This is best analysed by thinking about these three debates together. All three difficulties arise from the project of constructing a model of the world from the perspective of the metropole, while imagining one is taking a global perspective.

As the global/local debate shows, globalisation theory is marked by a persisting polarity between system and singularity. It is clear that such concepts must coexist within any reified model of 'global society'. For the idea of the global is constituted by the idea of abstract linkage (i.e. 'compression', 'connectivity', 'network', 'reach'), as was shown in the set of definitions quoted above. The ground on which these concepts are defined, the difference that makes the definition of the global, is an equally abstract idea of non-linkage. This constitutes the concept of the local, the singular, and as a concept it has no meaning other than being the non-global. Its empirical content, in different authors' arguments, varies wildly.

Unless the whole analysis is constituted in another way, the polarity cannot be overcome. It sits in globalisation theory, not as the basis of a dynamic but as an antinomy. Theorists may choose to emphasise one pole or the other, or proffer some mixture of the two (glocalisation), but all such choices are conceptually arbitrary.

A similar difficulty afflicts the homogeneity/heterogeneity debate. Jonathan Friedman (1994) has criticised the 'cultural mixing' view of globalisation in scathing terms, and he is surely right. The only way in which a model of hybridisation can be sustained is by a prior reification of culture. The idea of 'a culture' as a thing, available to be mixed or inserted in a mosaic, breaks down precisely when a culture is treated as an actor among others in a global arena. On the other hand, the notion that a generalised 'global culture' exists, or is even being constituted, involves a startling exercise in synecdoche—taking the cellular phone plus the *anime* movie for the kind of working social order of which classical ethnography spoke.

The homogeneity/heterogeneity debate is undecidable. This antinomy does not arise from a conflict of evidence, but from the presuppositions at work in the concept of global society. The key presupposition concerns a process of integration that is both boundaryless and formless. This supposes an endless series of differences being overcome. The process will appear as homogeneity whenever the observer focuses on the overcoming, heterogeneity whenever the observer focuses on the differences. Again, the choice is conceptually arbitrary.

The spectacular disagreement over the locus of power in globalisation provides a way of understanding what is happening in all these debates. Metropolitan sociology in the 1990s constructed its narratives of global society mostly by scaling up its existing conceptual tools, rather than by launching a fresh research agenda on a global scale.

This scaling-up was structured by a prior concern—to avoid the main existing theories that understood power on a world scale as worldwide domination. This is quite logical, as the concept of abstract linkage is not compatible with the experience of being colonised. The sociological discourse of globalisation, as it emerged in the early 1990s, explicitly distanced itself from theories of imperialism and neocolonialism, and had at best an embarrassed relationship with world-systems analysis. There was a widespread refusal, in the literature based on a concept of abstract linkage, of any analysis that *named the metropole* as the centre of power, as the agent of cultural domination, or as the site of accumulation. Writers such as Bauman and Beck could certainly *recognise* differences between the global rich and the global poor, but the concept of globalisation gave them no coherent way of *explaining* these differences.

Thus sociological globalisation theory, produced in the metropole, was constituted in a way that—as Gyorgy Lukács (1971) long ago showed for European bourgeois thought—concealed the conditions of its own existence and set internal limits to its own development. The limits to thought in sociological globalisation theory sometimes appear as antinomies, sometimes as massive uncertainties.

Not all writings about globalisation are trapped in these problems. There are certain treatments of the concept that are geopolitically reflexive (notably Martin and Beittel 1998; and Appadurai 2001). But there is not much sociological writing at a conceptual level that does 'name the metropole'.

Rhetoric and performativity in globalisation theory

Some of the literature on globalisation is written in the good grey prose of sociology journals, and is remarkable only for its tacit claim to scientificity. Another part is written in a declamatory style with a colourful use of images and figures of speech. For instance, the idea that globalisation involves a weakening of boundaries and a multiplication of links is often conveyed by panoramic gestures (Spann 1966) like this:

> One can watch CNN in an African safari lodge. German investors converse in English with Chinese apparatchiks. Peruvian social workers spout the rhetoric of American feminism. Protestant preachers are active in India, while missionaries of the Hare Krishna movement return the compliment in Middle America (Berger 1997: 23).

Such passages work by emblematic instances rather than by considered evidence, and there are many, many other examples in the globalisation literature. Emblematic images convey the idea that we are all in the same boat, no matter where our bodies are located. We are all impacted by electronic technology, we all face global risks, and so on.

And there is no captain on board. Bauman (1998: 58) puts the point in italics: '*no one seems now to be in control*'. 'The world society is a stateless polity,' says John Meyer (2000: 236). Even William Robinson, who is pretty sure that a transnational state does exist, says there is no 'single headquarters for world capitalism' (Robinson 2001: 160). 'Out of control' may also mean unstoppable. '*The new globality cannot be reversed*,' says Beck (2000: 11) in italics. Sociological writing on globalisation does not generally share business journalism's imagery of a tidal wave of change, but some texts come close to that, and most share this language of irreversibility.

The popularity of emblematic instances and panoramic gestures suggests considerable under-determination by evidence. In other fields of sociology, such texts might be cause for scepticism; here, they almost define the field. Is globalisation theory, then, mainly trying to analyse something, or to accomplish something? In a perceptive paper, Jens Bartelson (2000) argues that the theorising of globalisation to some degree constitutes the fact. A startling confirmation is provided by Ian Roxborough (2002), who shows that the sociology of globalisation was picked up by the US military in working out its post-Cold War strategic doctrine, now at work in Iraq.

But the intended audience for most of this writing is a professional or 'educated general reader' audience. The texts themselves imply that this audience is metropolitan. They highlight metropolitan experience, and engage metropolitan debates and anxieties. Sociologists writing in professional journals are also, by default, addressing the metropole, since that is where the vast majority of the world's professional social scientists are concentrated.

J.L. Austin (1961), who invented the concept of performative utterance, famously remarked that the statement 'I do', uttered at the appropriate moment, does not so much report on a marriage as indulge in one. Many globalisation texts have a performative role in this sense. Such texts put a metaphorical arm around the reader's shoulder and speak confidentially about the problems 'we' now face: '. . . we all live more and more in a 'glocal' manner . . . The global does not lurk and threaten out there as the Great All-Encompassing; it noisily fills the innermost space of our own lives. Our own life is the locus of the glocal' (Beck 2000: 73–4; compare Bauman 1998: 77–8, Tomlinson 1999: 108).

The performative unity of writer and reader accounts for much of the declamatory style in globalisation texts. It implies a shared knowledge that can simply be recalled by panoramic gestures and emblematic instances. There is little need for laborious examination of evidence when the reader already has the news. What the reader may need is names for the news items, and sociological texts have been fertile in neologisms: 'Global Age', 'glocalization', 'world risk society', 'technoscapes', 'hybridity', and more.

The texts performatively construct a political agency. The 'we' in Beck's writing stands for cosmopolitan citizenship, civil society, oppositional groups and defence of the welfare state. Albrow, Brennan, Giddens, Therborn, Kellner, Mann and Evans in different styles all project a citizenry filled with a new consciousness, 'people of good will' engaging in 'performative citizenship', global 'norm formation', or more modest local improvements informed by global awareness. Though most think this agency is worldwide (Evans being an exception), and though Beck has even written a 'Cosmopolitan Manifesto' for it, the substance remains metropolitan. It is not really surprising that Beck's (2000: 129ff) account of 'responses to globalization' is almost entirely about Europe.

The shared experiences of metropolitan theorists and metropolitan readers do not include much of the sharp end of global social processes. The result is sociological texts that persistently underplay systemic violence. Little of the writing of the 1990s suggested the eruptions of transnational violence that were soon to follow. Beck's *What is Globalization?*, first published in 1997, hardly mentions violence; nor does Guillén's (2001a) survey of the globalisation literature of the 1990s; nor do Giddens' Reith Lectures first published in 1999. After the 9/11 Al Qaeda attack, Giddens (2002: xvi), obviously shocked, reached for the *Star Wars* image of the 'dark side' of globalisation to discuss crime and terrorism. He still missed the escalation of violence by metropolitan states—which, we should not forget, had been covertly bombing Iraq right through the 1990s.

This does not imply that sociological theory must be complicit with neoliberal globalisation. A good many texts (Kellner 2002; Robinson 2001; Sklair 2001; Chase-Dunn 2002) are openly oppositional. Indeed, the genre's main tendency has been to question the pure market agenda in the name of an extended concept of the social—thus reasserting the importance of sociology as a specific form of knowledge (Albrow 1996; Connell 2000). But it does not challenge the way that knowledge of the social is constituted.

The Northernness of globalisation theory

At this point, the answer to the question with which I opened this chapter is reasonably clear. Sociological theorising about globalisation embeds a view of the world from the global North, and therefore has not opened a fresh path for sociology. The main mechanisms by which a Northern viewpoint is embedded in these texts are closely related to the mechanisms discussed in Chapter 2.

The simplest mechanism is the exclusion of other viewpoints. Neither Bauman nor Beck, nor Robinson nor Kellner nor Sassen, refers to non-metropolitan social thought when presenting theories of globalisation. Nor does Robertson, despite his career in development studies. Peter Evans' (1997) review of the state under globalisation uses metropolitan sources with hardly an exception; so does Guillén's (2001a) survey of the sociology of globalisation. In Alberto Martinelli's (2003) introduction to the presidential session papers on globalisation from an International Sociological Association congress, every citation is Northern. At the end of *Runaway World*, Giddens helps the reader with an annotated reading list of two journal articles and 51 books. All 51 books are published in the metropole. Of the 51, just one centrally concerns a non-metropolitan point of view, and not even this one presents non-metropolitan social thought about globalisation.

This body of writing, while insisting on the global scope of social processes and the irreversible interplay of cultures, *almost never* cites non-metropolitan thinkers and *almost never* builds on social theory formulated outside the metropole. A body of writing about the global in which Weber is a major point of reference, while al-Afghani is not, defines itself as profoundly limited.

Lacking intellectual sources from the non-metropolitan world, it has been common to create a picture of global society by projecting traits already recognised in metropolitan society. The three strategies of reification discussed above are, in essence, three projections—of modernity, postmodernity, and socioeconomic dynamics respectively. Even the accounts of forces of resistance have a familiar ring to them.

Some globalisation theorists do go out to the periphery and conduct or supervise research there. This leads to another characteristic literature about globalisation: the comparative study of effects and strategies. Admirable examples are Evans' (1995) *Embedded Autonomy*, on the role of the state in industrial development in Korea, Brazil and India; Guillén's (2001b) *The Limits of Convergence*, on institutional patterns in economic development in Argentina, Korea and Spain; and Sassen's (2002) *Global Networks, Linked Cities*, an edited collection focusing on cities such as São Paulo, Shanghai and Mexico. What we see in this literature is a methodological projection. Data from the periphery are framed by concepts, debates and research strategies from the metropole. There is no reference to the *social thought* of the periphery in these texts.

There are good institutional reasons for this. Such projects are mainly organised through US universities and funded by US foundations. Guillén, with unusual candour, informs us that the research for *The Limits of Convergence* cost more than a quarter of a million US dollars. The authors and editors are professionally responsible to peers and institutions in the metropole—however much their hearts may be with communities in the periphery.

The social experiences generated in the majority world are rarely a major basis of globalisation theorists' arguments. We may speak, therefore, of an erasure of non-metropolitan experience in this literature too. The most important erasure in globalisation theory concerns colonialism. The fact that the majority world has deep prior experience of subjection to globalising powers is surely known to all the theorists. But this experience of subjection does not surface as a central issue in *any* of the theories of globalisation considered here. Some theorists explicitly deny that the old imperialism has relevance to the present; on this point, if no other, Giddens is at one with Hardt and Negri.

There are exceptions. Göran Therborn (2000: 161) acknowledges the 'full-scale disaster' that colonial penetration represented for societies in Africa and America. Yet Therborn does not follow the point through when discussing the later waves of globalisation. Discussions of 'hybridity' in cultural globalisation sometimes draw on postcolonial theory, but remain mostly a celebration of diversity. They make little reference to the devastating colonial histories of forced disruption (Bitterli 1989), nor to the continuing effects of this disruption shown, for instance, in the *Bringing Them Home* report on the Aboriginal children of the stolen generations in Australia (National Inquiry 1997).

The performative unity of writer and reader constructed by many of the globalisation texts also erases non-metropolitan experience. Perhaps the most remarkable example is in Beck's *What is Globalization?*, which ends with a short essay on 'The Brazilianization of Europe' (Beck 2000: 161–3). This does not discuss Brazil at all, but uses the name to evoke a horror scene of social fragmentation, violence and selfishness which the European readers surely do not want. The remarkable social and educational reconstruction efforts undertaken *by the Brazilians*, in the aftermath of a violent military dictatorship and in the teeth of corporate power, does not enter Beck's argument.

Science about the South

Metropolitan social science has a number of mechanisms for studying the non-metropolitan world, and has constituted several disciplines or sub-disciplines for the purpose. The most important are: Anthropology, the home of ethnographic description of non-industrial societies; Development Economics, which flourished during the Cold War, faltered, and is perhaps reviving as an alternative to neoliberalism; Area Studies (e.g. African Studies, Pacific Studies), most commonly an amalgam of history, political science and language study about a particular region; International Relations, traditionally concerned with diplomacy and war which, since decolonisation, has studied non-metropolitan countries in the Western interstate system; and Political Economy, which underpinned Marxist theories of imperialism and Wallerstein's 'world-system' approach.

Seen in this context, the northernness of the sociology of globalisation is not surprising, since a common logic has structured all these fields. This has gradually become clear since the critique of anthropology opened the issue of the geopolitics of knowledge a generation ago (Asad 1973). The common logic is that a system of categories is created by metropolitan intellectuals and read outwards to societies in the periphery, where the categories are filled in empirically. Put so bluntly, the operation sounds crude—yet it can be done with respect and may be intellectually important. Let me offer two examples.

The first is one of the great works of twentieth century social science. Claude Lévi-Strauss's (1949) *The Elementary Structures of Kinship* is based on vast learning about non-Western societies, patient attention to the detail of their social structures, and an attitude that validates them as equal members of a spectrum of social forms. This is a marked change from the outlook of Spencer, Durkheim and Sumner. As we discover in his autobiographical *Tristes Tropiques* (1955), Lévi-Strauss's ethnography was based on a deep humanism that recognised the common experience in very different cultures. It is not surprising that Lévi-Strauss's work was used by the United Nations, in the aftermath of World War II, to help build an international consensus against racism.

Yet there is no question that *The Elementary Structures of Kinship*, like the rest of Lévi-Strauss's structural anthropology, is a metropolitan intellectual project. The societies of the periphery, however respectfully studied, function as sources of data to be fitted into a system. The intellectual procedures of structuralism, as I noted in Chapter 2, contain in their core logic a metropolitan view of the world. The transformation of colonised societies under the impact of imperialism is methodologically excluded from Lévi-Strauss's theorising. Even the application of the foundational concept of a kinship system involves a conceptual disruption of local social realities that may disadvantage indigenous communities— for instance by suppressing the issue of their relation to the land (see Chapter 9). The embedding of anthropology in colonial structures is a long-established fact (Asad 1973), and for all his humanism Lévi-Strauss does not escape it.

Immanuel Wallerstein's world-system approach operates at another level, offering a macro-sociology of the world order. For a generation, world-system researchers provided the main alternative to sociology's focus on the metropole, and more recently have provided an alternative to the popular view of globalisation. Their approach allows us to see globalisation not as a 'new kind of society', but as a historically specific *project* coming out of a long history. For instance, from a background in world-system research, Philip McMichael in *Development and Social Change* (2000) treats 'the globalisation project' as a successor to the development project, a strategy developed by a new generation of capitalist leadership to get past welfare-state restraints on corporate power and the debt crisis of development.

As with structural anthropology, there is much to admire in the world-system approach. Not only does it name the metropole, it has studied patterns of metropole–periphery relations and their long-term changes. Wallerstein's research project, elaborated in his very influential *The Modern World-System* (1974a) and in the collaboration of a growing number of colleagues (Chase-Dunn 1995), yielded a detailed history of capitalism as a transnational system based on divisions of labour between core and periphery.

The building of this model, however, has revealed two major difficulties. First, the researchers' toolkit is drawn from Marxist political economy, so the basic categories are classes, states, exploitation and capital accumulation (see the crystal-clear summary by Hopkins 1979). World-system research is certainly a very creative application of this toolkit, but it shares the intellectual closures of political economy itself. This is seen in the short list of social actors recognised in world-system analyses: bourgeoisies, proletariats, intermediate classes, state elites, and not much more. The difficulty this framework has in dealing with issues of gender and race—constitutive structures of colonialism, on other reckonings—is familiar.

The second problem arises from another closure. Wallerstein made a great contribution when he took capitalism offshore, showing that it involved from the start a differentiated multistate economy. In building this argument, however, Wallerstein worked in the way globalisation theorists later did, generalising an analytic model already developed for the metropole. His argument generalised the concept of a social *system*, as is clear in the early statements of the approach (Wallerstein 1974b). This idea attracted other concepts of systems analysis—a boundary, internal differentiation of functions, subsystems, and so on.

This powerful tendency to reification led one current of world-system research to devise models of the pulsations within a capitalist world-economy, and led another into a trawl through history for world-systems great and small (Chase-Dunn and Grimes 1995). It led quite early to the idea that the future could be inferred from world-systems' laws of motion. In the later writing of Wallerstein (1999) and Chase-Dunn (2002), the once-fruitful research paradigm has turned into portentous speculation.

The underlying problem of the social-scientific approaches considered in this chapter is their geopolitical logic. They rely exclusively on the metropole for their intellectual tools and assumptions, and therefore treat the majority world as object. This closes off the possibility of social science working as a shared learning process, a dialogue, at the level of theory.

Inhabitants of the majority world are not just the objects of theory, the data mine for social science. They are also the subjects—the *producers* of theory about the social world and their own place in it.

We see this in works specifically about globalisation, such as Néstor García Canclini's *La globalización imaginada* (1999), Milton Santos's (2000) *Por uma outra globalização*, and Vinay Lal's *Empire of Knowledge* (2002), three recent contributions that move beyond the parameters of the metropolitan literature. Lal, for instance, gives a central role to systemic violence in creating and maintaining global inequalities, and argues the systemic significance of non-violent strategies of change.

We also see this more generally. Every colonised culture produces interpretations of imperialism. Intellectuals in the majority world have been studying empire, colonisation and globalisation processes as long as intellectuals in the metropole have. This represents a huge resource for learning, which metropolitan social science currently discards. Because of the metropole's hegemonic position in the global organisation of social science (as Sonntag (1999) shows for sociology), this waste is difficult to contest. Just how difficult can be seen in rich peripheral countries, which have the economic resources to produce alternatives, but not necessarily the desire. In the next chapter I take up this problem in the case I know best, Australia.

PART II
Looking south

4

The discovery of Australia

Australia is an English colony. Its cultural pattern is based on that fact of history—or, more precisely, on that pair of facts. Direct English inheritance determines the general design of our living and its detail, ranging from our enthusiasm for cricket to our indifference to the admirable wines which we produce. But the fact of our colonialism has a pervasive psychological effect, setting up a relationship as intimate and uneasy as that between an adolescent and his parent.

—A. A. Phillips (1953)

Two centuries ago, having lost thirteen colonies in North America, the British state planted a new one, a penal settlement, as far away as it was possible to sail. Both the memoirs of officials and surviving narratives from the convicts reveal how strange the new environment was felt to be: birds that laughed instead of singing, animals that hopped instead of running, Christmas in summer, and a native population for whom no place could be found in the European social order.

A ruthless expansion into this alien world followed, and through the nineteenth century fortunes were made in pastoralism, mining and trade. Wool, gold, wheat, meat and silver were shipped out to Europe (and more recently, coal and iron ore to East Asia). For a couple of generations, import-substitution industrialisation planted factories in the cities and manufacturers became prominent in the local ruling class; a witty economist wrote a book calling Australia 'a small rich industrial country' (Arndt 1968). Rich it remains, but it is now deindustrialised: the twenty-first century economy centres on services and mining. Under the 'White Australia' policy, official until the 1960s, a workforce was imported from Europe while immigration from Asia was forbidden. Diversity has grown but the large majority are still of European descent. Politicians still proclaim Australia's affiliation with the metropole: formerly with the British Empire, now with Western civilisation and the American Alliance.

This history produced cultural dilemmas that are bitterly contested. A small European community parked on the edge of Asia harbours racial anxieties which are still capable of turning elections. The relation between settler and Indigenous people has become an inflamed, unresolved issue (see Chapter 9). Identification with the metropole plus geographical remoteness plus economic dependence have led to chronic difficulties about identity. The prevailing attitude, which the literary critic A.A. Phillips famously dubbed 'the cultural cringe', is contested by outbursts of nationalism and searches for local grounding that have inspired some of the best Australian literature and art. But Australian nationalism, once socially radical, has gradually been captured by the political right—itself committed to dependence on metropolitan power and international capitalism.

In this contradictory world of settler colonialism, what happens to the social sciences? The relationship between colony and metropole remains crucial, and the broader cultural problems are reflected within social science disciplines. But the shape of these problems changes. In this chapter, I focus again on the case of sociology, and analyse colony–metropole relations in two historical moments: the Australian colonies' role in the making of sociology in the second half of the nineteenth century; and the forming of an academic discipline of sociology in Australian universities from the 1950s to the 1970s. Recent years have produced other possibilities, which I consider at the end of the chapter.

Australia's place in the making of sociology

During the second half of the nineteenth century, metropolitan texts—especially the writings of Comte and Spencer—circulated far beyond the metropole. Spencer had a considerable impact in Japan and India; Comte was read in Iran and had a powerful influence in Brazil. Such an impact depended on the existence of a local intelligentsia prepared to work with these ideas. The creation of a higher education system in Australia exactly coincided with the invention of sociology in the metropole. Comte's *System of Positive Polity*, subtitled *Treatise of Sociology*, was published between 1851 and 1854 in the early days of Louis Bonaparte's regime, the subject of Marx's *Eighteenth Brumaire*; the University of Sydney opened for business in 1852 and the University of Melbourne very soon after.

The colonial universities' curriculum was originally a stodgy amalgam of classics and technical training, but it gradually broadened, and as it did so it was possible for themes from 'the social science' to be included. Colonial newspapers—more diverse and intellectually substantial then than now—provided another arena in which 'the social question', relations between races, the status of women and other sociological themes were debated.

In the second half of the nineteenth century, these debates developed actively in Melbourne, then one of the largest cities in the world of settler colonialism, with a diverse and radical intelligentsia and a surprisingly open-minded university. A notable product of this milieu was the work of W.E. Hearn, an Irish classicist who became professor at the University of Melbourne in the 1850s and produced an impressive series of books over the next 30 years (La Nauze 1949). The unstructured state of the social sciences at the time is illustrated by the fact that Hearn was professor of history, literature, logic, political economy and law—most of them at the same time. His book *Plutology*, published in Melbourne in 1863, was arguably the first important text of economics to be written in Australia, and *The Aryan Household*, published in 1878, was the first important text of sociology.

The Aryan Household is recognisably part of the genre of studies of social progress, in broad comparative style, that were undertaken in the 1870s and 1880s by Tylor and Spencer in Britain, Letourneau in France, Ward in the United States and Tönnies in Germany. Hearn explained his purpose clearly in the introduction:

> I propose to describe the rise and the progress of the principal institutions that are common to the nations of the Aryan race. I shall endeavour to illustrate the social organization under which our remote forefathers lived. I shall, so far as I am able, trace the modes of thought and of feeling which, in their mutual relations, influenced their conduct. I shall indicate the germs of those institutions which have now attained so high a development; and I shall attempt to show the circumstances in which political society took its rise, and the steps by which, in Western Europe, it supplanted its ancient rival. (Hearn 1878: 2)

Several things are interesting about this passage. The tone is sober—this is intended as a technical contribution to science, not a popularisation. Hearn makes a simple identification with Europeans ('our remote forefathers'), reflecting the idea of Australian colonists as transplanted Britons. There is a clear presupposition of progress ('so high a development'). Notable also is Hearn's opening of a contrast between two types of society. This is an early example of the technique of grand ethnography (Chapter 1), which soon became central to metropolitan sociologists' representations of time and progress. A few pages later, Hearn gives a very clear summary of this way of representing change:

> In all its leading characteristics—political, legal, religious, economic— archaic society presents a complete contrast to that in which we live . . . no central government . . . no national church . . . few contracts . . . Men lived according to their customs . . . They were protected, or, if need were, avenged, by the help of their kinsmen. There was, in short, neither individual nor State. The clan, or some

association founded upon the model of the clan, and its subdivisions, filled the whole of our forefathers' social life (Hearn 1878: 4–5).

The rest of the book fills out this contrast. It traverses a range of sociological themes: the nature of custom, the position of women, the social organisation of the household, types of association, types of power, and the relationship between the state and civil society. But there is one oddity. Hearn, although he lived in a colony, found his examples rigorously in the early history of the 'Aryan' nations of Europe and their supposed ancestors.

It may partly be for that reason that Hearn's brilliant beginning found few Australian followers; he created no local school of sociological research. His text was, rather, a contribution from the colonies to the *metropolitan* literature of speculation about social progress. There was no institutionalisation of 'sociology' in the colonial universities, any more than there was at Oxford or Cambridge. When in the 1880s the University of Sydney began to modernise its badly outdated Arts curriculum, it developed modern history, philosophy and political economy, but did not try to develop sociology (Turney, Bygott and Chippendale 1991: 271 ff.).

That development occurred shortly afterwards in North American universities. The explosion of undergraduate sociology courses, textbooks, professional organisations and research output in American colleges met with an upsurge of interest in sociology across the North Atlantic, including the first chair of sociology in Britain in 1907.

It was these events that Francis Anderson, appointed to a chair of philosophy during the University of Sydney renovation of Arts, had in mind when he delivered the 1911 lecture that is often taken as the starting point of Australian sociology. *Sociology in Australia: A Plea for its Teaching*, published the next year as an eleven-page pamphlet, was not a work of sociology, nor was Anderson in any sense a sociologist. He was a professional philosopher who held a Comtean view of the structure of science. In this view, sociology was the 'mother science' that stated the broad principles of which specific sciences such as economics were examples. Sociology's task was 'to ascertain the natural laws which are manifested in social growth' (Anderson 1912: 10). Anderson seized upon the recent expansion of economics and commerce teaching at the University of Sydney to argue that the mother science should also be taught.

Anderson's view of sociology was, in 1912, already a little dated. Within ten years, the whole system of evolutionary social science and its laws of progress would be plunged into terminal crisis. Nothing like Anderson's program could possibly be implemented. His lecture marks the end of an era rather than the beginning: Comtean theory never got established here. But there was another feature of colonial reality that did make Australia important for sociology in the nineteenth century.

As I showed in Chapter 1, reports from the colonised world became a major data source for evolutionary social science. In the preface to his great work *Primitive Culture*, Edward Tylor (1873) made a 'general acknowledgment of obligations to writers on ethnography and kindred sciences, as well as to historians, travellers, and missionaries' (1873: I, vi). Such observers provided sociologists with rich documentation of the primitive which their grand ethnography sought to contrast with the advanced society of the metropole.

The British conquest of Australia was no exception. The first colonial governor was instructed to make contact with the natives and take them under his protection, which he dutifully attempted to do. His reports launched British colonial administration on a see-saw of conciliation, coercion and hand-wringing over the growing frontier violence between settlers and Aborigines. This lasted until the white colonists had seized the richest land in eastern Australia and persuaded Whitehall to grant them control of the rest, in the form of responsible government—in other words, quasi-independence. Accounts of this process, with descriptions of the Aboriginal communities to whom it was applied, flowed back to Britain.

A notable example comes from one of the great scientific documents of the age. Charles Darwin's *Journal of Researches* (better known as *The Voyage of the Beagle*) contains a chapter about his visit to Sydney and trip over the Blue Mountains, and then short visits to Van Diemen's Land (now Tasmania) and King George's Sound (now Western Australia). Here he witnessed a 'corrobery' of the White Cockatoo people. His description ends:

> When both tribes mingled in the dance, the ground trembled with the heaviness of their steps, and the air resounded with their wild cries. Every one appeared in high spirits, and the group of nearly

naked figures, viewed by the light of the blazing fires, all moving in hideous harmony, formed a perfect display of a festival amongst the lowest barbarians (Darwin 1839: 426).

Despite the pejoratives, Darwin was not hostile to the Australian Aboriginal groups he met. He admired their bushcraft and hunting skills, sympathised with their vulnerability to imported diseases, and did not blame them for the frontier violence. But he did regard the Australian Aborigines as a more primitive people than the British; he expected their extinction, and he saw this as an unavoidable consequence of a stronger variety of man meeting a weaker: 'Wherever the European has trod, death seems to pursue the aboriginal' (Darwin 1839: 411).

Hundreds of such accounts of native life in Australia—some much more substantial than Darwin's—came back to the metropole and became part of the raw material from which evolutionary social science was built. I could give examples from very well-known writers including Tylor himself and William Graham Sumner, but will quote just one, the progressive liberal Lester Ward. Surveying the races of mankind in his *Dynamic Sociology*, Ward (1897) declared:

> Among other very low savage races may be mentioned the Fuegians, who, though of rather large stature, are mentally little superior to animals; the aboriginal Australians of the interior, who, along with other simian characteristics, are nearly destitute of the fleshy muscles constituting the calf of the leg (*gastrocnemius* and *soleus*) ... Many of these tribes and races live almost entirely after the manner of wild beasts, having nothing that can be called government, religion, or society (1897: II, 418).

None of these theorists had visited Australia or met an Australian Aboriginal person, and none made any attempt to verify their startling (and, in Ward's and Sumner's cases, undoubtedly false) claims. Australian Aborigines had no human reality for them. They were simply tokens in the construction of a scientific fantasy of the primitive, which in turn validated a doctrine of social evolution.

Australia's role in the making of sociology, like that of the rest of the colonised world, was to be a data mine, a source of ethnographic examples of the primitive. Within the colonised world, Australia had the distinction of being *the most primitive of all*, illustrating the extremity of degradation or backwardness.

This was certainly the assumption behind the most famous appearance of Australia in the texts of 'classical' sociology. In the last decades of the nineteenth century, deliberate ethnographic observation was replacing 'historians, travellers and missionaries' as the key source of information about non-European peoples in the intellectual shift that produced modern social anthropology. Some of this pioneering work was done in Australia, and among the most influential was research conducted in the 1890s, in the central desert around Alice Springs, by Baldwin Spencer and F.J. Gillen.

Back in Paris, Spencer and Gillen's well-illustrated report *The Native Tribes of Central Australia* was read with enthusiasm by Durkheim and his colleagues. It was warmly reviewed in *L'année sociologique*, and a decade later became the main empirical basis for Durkheim's last book, *The Elementary Forms of Religious Life*, published in 1912.

In this book, the customs and mythology of the Arrernte people as they stood in the late nineteenth century became the basis for a general sociology of religion. Durkheim, like most sociologists who wrote about 'Australians', understood little of the diversity or dynamism of Indigenous cultures in Australia. Durkheim knew there were different communities, but believed they were 'perfectly homogeneous' because their societies 'all belong to one common type' (Durkheim 1912: 95). The Arrernte were used for one reason. Durkheim thought he had found, in Spencer and Gillen's ethnography, a detailed description of the most primitive form of religion, and he thought that by studying the most primitive form, he could reveal the most fundamental truths about religion. There is no ambiguity about this. Durkheim says exactly:

> In this book we propose to study the most primitive and simple religion which is actually known ... A religious system may be said to be the most primitive ... in the first place when it is found in a society whose organization is surpassed by no others in simplicity; and secondly when it is possible to explain it without making use of any element borrowed from a previous religion (Durkheim 1912: 1).

'Australian totemism' fitted the bill, because Australian Aborigines had the most primitive documented society. Here the crude racism of a Ward or Sumner is transcended—up to a point. Durkheim's prejudice takes a very sophisticated form; his sociology embeds a deeply ethnocentric viewpoint nonetheless. And it conceals a radical misunderstanding of Australian Indigenous cultures.

This was already knowable in Durkheim's day. In a biting review of *The Elementary Forms* published the following year, the anthropologist van Gennep (celebrated for his work on 'rites of passage') pointed out that the book was riddled with doubtful factual claims. But, more importantly, it was based on a monumental conceptual error—an error, I would say, that infected the whole enterprise of evolutionary sociology:

> The idea he [Durkheim] has derived from them [the ethnographic documents] of a primitive man . . . and of 'simple' societies is entirely erroneous. The more one knows of the Australians and the less one identifies the stage of their material civilization with that of their social organization, one discovers that the Australian societies are very complex, very far from the simple and the primitive, but very far advanced along their own paths of development (Van Gennep in 1913, quoted in Lukes 1985: 525).

The creation of Australian academic sociology

In the four decades that followed Anderson's appeal and Durkheim's great fantasy, while metropolitan sociology changed profoundly (see Chapter 1), little happened organisationally in Australia. Bits of the new welfare-state sociology popped up in odd contexts—the Workers' Education Association, university philosophy courses, political speculation by progressive liberals, or surveys of educational inequalities. But there was nothing like the Chicago School, let alone an Australian Parsons, to pull them together.

Australia's most brilliant social scientist, Vere Gordon Childe, left the country in 1921, dismayed at the Labor Party's betrayal of the workers, and went off to Europe to invent scientific prehistory. For the next generation his astonishing creativity was practically ignored in Australia, where it was known that he was a communist (Gathercole, Irving and Melleuish 1995). Other talented social researchers also left the country, such as Elton Mayo who became a founder of industrial sociology in the United States.

When research programs within the new sociological episteme finally appeared in Australia, they were outgrowths from social anthropology and social psychology. The professor of anthropology at the University of Sydney, A.P. Elkin, famous for his work on Aboriginal cultures, began in the early 1940s to direct some of his students towards ethnographic studies of 'our own society'—that is, white settler society. He also undertook a study of wartime social integration based on survey data. The notable products of this initiative were a well-observed, though modestly presented, ethnography of a mining town by Alan Walker (1945), and an even better ethnography of rural kinship and family life by Jean Craig (1957), later known to every sociologist in Australia as Jean Martin.

In the late 1940s, the new professor of psychology at the University of Melbourne, Oscar Oeser, launched a research program on 'social behaviour' which also drifted into the territory of the new sociology. His research team conducted elaborate observational and interview studies in a Victorian country town, in suburbs of Melbourne, and in seven factories. The topics included class-consciousness, job satisfaction, industrial relations and family life. This style of social-realist field observation was soon dropped by Australian psychology, which fell under the spell of behaviourism. But the three volumes of the *Social Structure and Personality* series (Oeser and Hammond 1954; Oeser and Emery 1954; Lafitte 1958) provided key empirical material for the first university courses in sociology, which were launched almost immediately after these books were published.

During the 1950s, the idea of social surveys on the white community became familiar. An Australian market research firm, Roy Morgan Research, started sample surveys using its 'Gallup Poll' in the 1940s. The poll findings, presented by Morgan as scientific measures of opinion, were reported in the press and increasingly noticed by politicians. University- and welfare-based surveys appeared, describing specific social groups and their problems. They included the aged in Victoria, surveyed by a University of Melbourne group (Hutchinson 1954); the young in Sydney, surveyed by a University of Sydney group (Connell, Francis and Skilbeck 1957); and the leisure problems of a Melbourne suburban estate, surveyed by the Brotherhood of St Laurence (Scott and U'ren 1962). Academic researchers also began to see the national census as a source of data for social analysis. George Zubrzycki (1960) thus conducted 'a demographic survey' of immigrants in Australia.

This generation of social researchers forged a new relationship with metropolitan sociology. Australia ceased to be a data mine, an economy exporting facts (or imagined facts). Most of these studies were published in Australia and remained unknown in the metropole. However, the new generation of researchers adopted the new American definition of the subject-matter of sociology, and they adopted the methods of metropolitan researchers.

Walker's *Coaltown*, for instance, mentioned no theory and did not compare its findings with any other research. But it was clearly modelled on community studies such as the Lynds' *Middletown* and Warner's 'Yankee City' series. The Sydney educationists' *Growing Up in an Australian City* was more explictly connected with models in the American sociology of youth. For *Old People in a Modern Australian Community*, the academic and business sponsors actually imported from Britain 'an experienced investigator of social problems' to run the study (Hutchinson 1954: v).

This stance was familiar in Australian intellectual life at the time. A.A. Phillips (1953: 85) diagnosed 'the persistence of the colonial surrender in the Australian mind' as a major problem for literature too. So it was easy for Australian sociology to constitute itself as a branch office of metropolitan sociology, importing metropolitan methods and topics in order to address a local audience about local versions of social problems.

The commonest title of an Australian sociological report, for the 30 years from 1950, was *X in Australia*—where *X* was a phenomenon already defined in the metropole and for which metropolitan paradigms of research were available. *X* might be 'religion', 'status and prestige', 'social stratification', 'divorce', 'marriage and the family', 'urbanization', 'prostitution', 'political leadership', 'women', 'mass media', 'immigrants' or 'sociology' itself. (These are all actual titles from the period.) The task of the Australian sociologist was to apply the metropolitan research technique, demonstrate that the phenomenon also existed in Australia, and say empirically what form it took here. In some of this writing there was a faint missionary flavour, as if the sociologists were bringing new light to the unsophisticated locals.

These metropolitan-style studies of 'our own society' were the knowledge base on which an academic discipline called 'sociology' was installed in Australia's expanding university system. The action was very fast. A half-dozen years, from 1959 to 1965, saw the first named chair of sociology, the first sociology teaching programs, the first textbook, the foundation of a professional association, and the first issues of its academic journal. This brief period even saw the first pop sociology best-seller, *The Lucky Country*, written by a journalist (Horne 1964). In the following decade, another ten departments of sociology sprang up around the country.

But a collection of social surveys was not enough to claim space in the universities as a new discipline. There also needed to be ideas, as Davies and Encel observed in the first edition of their textbook *Australian Society* (1965). In a vigorously argued paper on 'The Scope and Purpose of Sociology', Harold Fallding (1962) insisted that sociology was now an established discipline in terms of its object of knowledge—systems of social action—and its theoretical logic. Since no sociological theory was being produced in Australia, this too had to be imported from the metropole. Fallding's solution was to import Parsonian functionalism in a lump. Others imported empiricism, Weberianism, interpretive sociology and, a little later, neo-Marxism.

The result was a hybrid structure of knowledge in the new discipline, where Australian sociologists combined metropolitan theory and methodology with local data and audiences. A notable example was Sol Encel's (1970) monograph *Equality and Authority*. Encel's book traversed the metropolitan (mainly British and US) controversies about class and stratification, adopted a modified Weberian position, and then reported seriatim the author's impressive compilations of data about Australian elites. Another example, I have to confess, was Connell and Irving's *Class Structure in Australian History* (1980). We started with a chapter debating metropolitan theories of class before settling into an exposition of Australian empirical material.

Along with metropolitan theory—though this was hardly noticed at the time—came a metropolitan vision of what society was and how we should talk about it. 'Australian society' was simply presumed to be *the same kind of thing*, for which the same conceptual categories were unproblematically appropriate.

The rising quality of Australian research entrenched this pattern. As Australian sociologists became more sophisticated in using the metropolitan tools, they began to publish in metropolitan journals. There were good reasons: as well as the desire to find a wider audience, the prestige attached to international publication greatly helped promotion in Australian universities. However, to publish in those forums, Australians had to write in forms familiar to metropolitan editors: to use metropolitan concepts, address metropolitan literatures, and offer credible interventions in metropolitan debates. Australian sociology was thus produced as a professional account of Australian society as seen through metropolitan eyes.

The construction of Australian sociology as an academic discipline in the decades 1950–80 thus completely reversed the relationship between Australia and metropolitan sociology that had existed a hundred years earlier. Then Australia was treated as the site of difference—in fact, extreme difference—from the advanced society of the metropole. Now Australia was treated as the site of similarity.

Of course, this involved a shift of empirical interest from Aboriginal to settler society. But Australian society was not theorised in the new discipline as a settler society; it was simply regarded as part of modernity. Indigenous cultures were now regarded as the business of anthropology—which was, in Australian universities, the older and more prestigious discipline. This was a boundary the sociologists did not yet challenge. The *relationship* between Indigenous society and settler/modern society that had been so important for evolutionary sociology simply vanished as an intellectual theme.

Aboriginal *people* did concern sociologists, but in a new way: as the subjects of social processes characteristic of modernity. They could be seen as a disadvantaged group in a system of social stratification (Ancich et al. 1969). More commonly, they were classified under the North American rubric of 'ethnic minority'. This is how they were treated, for instance, in Baldock and Lally's (1974) survey of *Sociology in Australia and New Zealand*. In this book Aboriginal people appeared in a chapter on 'studies of ethnic minorities' whose primary focus was postwar non-British immigration. The ironic result of the new structure of sociological knowledge was that Indigenous groups were understood as being the same kind of group as the most recent settlers.

With local sociology wholly dependent on metropolitan concepts and methods, people began to wonder about the identity puzzle. What was specifically Australian about this? Australian sociology had, perhaps, a characteristic empirical focus—for instance, on migration. Indeed, Jean Martin, George Zubrzycki and other sociologists were prominent in constructing the discourse of multiculturalism that framed Australian policy on ethnicity and immigration until the 1990s revival of racism.

Alternatively, Australian sociology had a characteristic irony, because sociologists' documentation of stratification, elites and exclusions ran counter to Australian egalitarianism. Busting 'myths' about Australia became a favoured trope in Australian sociological writing in the 1960s (e.g. Taft 1962). But it was hard to see a distinctive cultural formation in the sociological books published in Australia, or in the papers in the *Australian and New Zealand Journal of Sociology*. A definition of the identity of Australian sociology thus proved very elusive, even in the period when the discipline was growing most vigorously.

New possibilities

The relationship between colony and metropole has been formative for Australian sociology, though the terms of that relationship have changed. Can the terms change again?

Much of Australian sociology continues on the path already mapped out. Metropolitan theory remains hegemonic. Parsonianism and Weberianism were displaced by structuralist Marxism, and that in turn by a strong wave of post-structuralism. In the twenty-first century, Foucauldians and Bourdieuvians frolic where functionalists once safely grazed.

Theories are certainly deployed with more sophistication and skill, and it is possible for Australian sociologists to do work that is path-breaking in international terms. John Braithwaite's (1989) criminological work on reintegration comes to mind, as does Michael Pusey's *Economic Rationalism in Canberra* (1991). Combining survey data on federal civil servants, analysis of political and institutional change, and a social vision influenced by Habermas, Pusey created a pioneering sociology of neoliberalism which has very wide implications.

Australians have also done work in sociological theory, not as peripheral consumers of the metropole's output but as participants in metropolitan debates. Notable examples are Clare Burton's (1985) synthesis of feminism and social theory; Jack Barbalet's (1998) work on the macro-sociology of emotions; and Pauline Johnson's (2006) study of the changing idea of the public realm in the thought of Jürgen Habermas. This work is often published in the metropole and, whether or not it uses any Australian research or experience, the focus is on a metropolitan literature. In effect, these authors have followed the same strategy as W.E. Hearn, doing Northern theory in new conditions and abandoning the identity problem.

But in a changed cultural and political environment, an opposite strategy was also possible: focusing on the specificity of Australia as a product of settler colonialism. Interest in the relationship between indigenous and settler society was revived by historians of frontier conflict, by anthropologists' rethinking of their own connection with colonialism, and above all by the Aboriginal Land Rights movement (see Chapter 9). A sociologist such as Vivien Johnson (1996) could become deeply interested in the Aboriginal art movement, considering not only the body of artistic work but also the ways in which it is appropriated by the dominant culture—including widespread commercial exploitation and copyright violation. In her *Radio Birdman*, Johnson (1990) turned the intellectual relationships around, using some Aboriginal social concepts for analysing that most metropolitan of social phenomena: a new wave rock band.

It was also now possible to think, from an Australian starting point, about global structures and connections. This was done by Chilla Bulbeck in *One World Women's Movement* (1988), written before globalisation had become a popular sociological theme. This book took up the problems raised by the United Nations Decade for Women (1975–85), discussing whether it was possible to have a united international feminism, given the different situations of women in different countries, and resistance to the dominance of white Western feminism. In the sequel *Re-orienting Western Feminisms* (1998), Bulbeck looked more deeply at the problems of universalism and cultural difference, and offered a complex relativism as a basis for political cooperation among women's movements. Few have gone as far down this track as Bulbeck. Nevertheless, in the 1990s it became more common for Australian sociologists to set their analyses in a broader international context, or within a wider understanding of colonialism (e.g. Bottomley (1992) on migration and culture; Gilding (1997) on the family; Connell (1993) on gender).

None of this defines a distinctive Australian school of sociology. What it does mean is that Australian sociologists have recognised a wider spectrum of *possibilities* inherent in the geopolitical situation of a rich peripheral country and the history of settler colonialism. Recognising these possibilities, Australian sociology may contribute to much more important goals than the creation of a local ethos. For the first time, as Bulbeck's work clearly shows, it is possible to move beyond the traditional link with the metropole to link with the intellectual projects of other regions of the periphery.

PART III
Southern theory

5

Indigenous knowledge and African Renaissance

As social scientists, we have to leave the campus and talk to the people face-to-face. This is perhaps even more imperative for African social scientists. For they will only find listeners in their own countries if they adapt to their language. On the other hand, it is only through contact with local knowledge that they can acquire the insights which are today of prime importance for the questions of developmental politics.

—Mamadou Diawara (2000)

From Yoruba oral poetry to sociological theory

In 1986 the new journal *International Sociology* published a paper by the Nigerian sociologist Akinsola Akiwowo called 'Contributions to the Sociology of Knowledge from an African Oral Poetry'. It was one of the most striking contributions to a debate about world sociology that *International Sociology* and its parent organisation, the International Sociological Association (ISA), were sponsoring. The concept of 'indigenous sociology' was creating a stir, and Akiwowo's contribution seemed to be a perfect example.

Akiwowo was a well-known figure, having been on the ISA executive committee. A few years earlier he had written a detailed survey of 'Sociology in Africa Today' that discussed the different national situations and the difficulties for African sociologists in communicating with each other, and expressed the hope that nevertheless they could: 'reorient the discipline to African reality through an integrated system of conceptual schemes, theories, and methodological techniques drawn up in relation to both African and European thought-ways and social practices' (Akiwowo 1980: 67). The 1986 'Contributions' paper tried to realise this proposal, and it made a radical departure from the structure of knowledge usual in postcolonial countries. Instead of importing concepts from Europe and North America and applying them to local data, Akiwowo proposed to find concepts in Nigeria and export them to the rest of the world. Specifically, he proposed to find them in a resource that metropolitan social theory never used—the ritual oral poetry of the community.

'Contributions' is a short and uncompromising text. Most of its fifteen pages consist of a line-by-line translation of a Yoruba-language ritual poem from Oyo state in western Nigeria, with a running commentary on its meaning and a glossary of its terms. The poem (strictly, a group of poems and a song), to be recited at the foundation of a new settlement, tells a creation story and describes how the different beings of the creation come together in communities. Akiwowo's commentary emphasises the idea of *asuwada*, defined as 'the purposive clumping of diverse *iwa*' (beings), as the principle of creation and the key to the world as we now find it. The poem also briefly relates the violation of the common good by a mythical being who steals some seed from the divine mother; and asserts the importance of social harmony.

In short concluding sections, Akiwowo summarises the ontological principles he finds in the text, and nine sociological propositions he derives from it. Examples of the latter are (p. 353):

1. The unit of social life is the individual's life, being, existence, or character . . .
3. The corporeal individual, essentially, cannot continue-in-being without a community.
4. Since the social life of a group of individual beings is sustained by a spirit of sodality, any form of self-alienation for the purpose of pursuing a purely selfish aim is, morally speaking, an error or sin . . .
6. A genuine social being is one who works daily, and sacrifices willingly, in varying ways, his or her cherished freedom and material acquisitions for self-improvement as well as for the common good. For without one, the other cannot be achieved . . .

As a reader from another cultural background, I did not find this easy to follow. The language and characters of this creation myth, and the world-view it expresses, are entirely unfamiliar. Well and good—that's what indigenous sociology is supposed to be. Akiwowo gives little help by way of background on the text. I learned from other authors (especially Payne 1992) that this poetry is associated with a socially elite tradition of divination and advising, so it is not exactly folk poetry. As I understand it, Akiwowo is trying to extract sociological principles from the accumulated wisdom and observations of society by Yoruba community elders and intellectuals, as condensed in the myths of an oral literature tradition.

This approach did not spring to life in 1986. Akiwowo had been developing it through the 1980s at the University of Ife, in collaboration with a group of younger scholars there. This in turn was part of a wider movement, in Africa and beyond, to revalue oral sources for history and social analysis (Vansina 1985; White, Miescher and Cohen 2001).

In 1988, *International Sociology* published a follow-up paper by one of these former colleagues, Moses Makinde, called 'Asuwada Principle: An analysis of Akiwowo's Contributions to the Sociology of Knowledge from an African Perspective'. Makinde supports the intention of deriving sociological ideas from 'African culture and philosophy'—the addition of 'philosophy' is significant, as I will show later.

Makinde tries to systematise the sociological thought in 'Contributions'. He boils down Akiwowo's list of propositions into three fundamental 'axioms' concerning the principle of *asuwada*, from which the others follow:

1. The unit of social life is the individual's life, being, existence or character.
2. Although each human being is metaphysically a unique emanation—an *emi*—of a Divine Being, each individual's life, as a corporeal self, needs the fellowship of other corporeal selves to feel and be whole and complete.
3. The corporeal individual, essentially, cannot continue-in-being without a community.

The core of Makinde's paper moves on from these presuppositions to more substantive issues, particularly Akiwowo's ideas about the different forms of social connection. The key distinction is between *ajobi*, the connection between blood relatives, and *ajogbe*, the connection between people who live together or beside each other. *Ajobi*, consanguinity or kinship, is seen as the fundamental unit of an African society, and together with *ajogbe* bonds, acts to create social harmony.

But breakdown can occur. Makinde quotes Akiwowo's description of the severe attenuation of *ajobi* kinship bonds following the advent of the Europeans in West Africa, rising individualism, new forms of money, unequal wealth, and rivalry rather than solidarity among siblings. Then, only *ajogbe* co-residence bonds remain. But Makinde argues that these too may fail, and in that case the general principle of *asuwada* has broken down. This crisis of the social, Makinde suggests, has now become common, especially in Third World countries.

Here Makinde introduces Akiwowo's concept of *ifogbontaayese*, 'using wisdom to remake the world'. Technological development alone is insufficient—indeed, it is a source of the difficulty. Makinde suggests that the crisis can be combated by intellectuals coming together across disciplines, especially the social sciences, for the purpose of making the societies of the world better places to live in—thus following the principle of *asuwada* themselves.

Two years later, *International Sociology* published a third paper by scholars from the University of Ife (now Obafemi Awolowo University). It was called 'Towards an African Sociological Tradition: A Rejoinder to Akiwowo and Makinde'. Its tone was very different. Olatunde Bayo Lawuyi, an anthropologist, and Olufemi Taiwo, a philosopher, do not reject the idea of 'doing sociology in African idioms'. But they argue that Akiwowo and Makinde have failed to do it.

In courteous but firm language, Lawuyi and Taiwo show that Akiwowo's and Makinde's readings of the oral poetry tradition yield concepts with shifting meanings. The usage of *asuwada* itself blurs three distinct ideas (a principle of creation, the character of things tending to clump together, and humans coming together for a common end). The concept of *iwa* (beings) is equally blurry, and the idea of *ajobi* is used by Akiwowo in two incompatible senses. *Ajobi* (kinship) and *ajogbe* (co-residence) are sometimes seen as forms of social life that can exist together, sometimes as a sequence with the latter following the breakdown of the former.

Further, Lawuyi and Taiwo show that Akiwowo and Makinde produce different understandings though they are reasoning from the same oral poetry material. Makinde shifts the meaning of *ajogbe* towards the concept of society-as-a-whole, thus making *ajobi* a unit within it. In Akiwowo's account, the two are coordinate forms of social relationship.

The logical critique is devastating, and there is more to come. Lawuyi and Taiwo argue that Akiwowo has not succeeded in doing sociology in Yoruba. Instead, the effort has largely amounted to a search for Yoruba-language equivalents for English-language sociological terms. The project hasn't actually generated an indigenous sociology: 'We do not dispute the claim that Akiwowo's discoveries show that the everyday basis for sociology is there in Yoruba. What we deny is that either of our interlocutors has given us a sociological theory in Yoruba' (Lawuyi and Taiwo 1990: 67).

Lawuyi and Taiwo raise another important problem about Akiwowo's and Makinde's project. The idea of *ifogbontaayese* (using wisdom to remake the world) appeared earlier in Akiwowo's writings published in Nigeria, and speaks to his political intentions. Akiwowo had been concerned about the disintegrating effect of individualism on African societies, arguing that Africans should return to indigenous cultures to discover the criteria for relevant knowledge. Lawuyi and Taiwo argue that this necessarily produces a culture-bound idea of knowledge. Further, Lawuyi and Taiwo suggest, the argument over-simplifies African reality and misses the social forces shaping knowledge itself, since the social evaluation of knowledge 'invariably reflects both the distribution of power and the principles of social control' (1990: 72).

Akiwowo has written two replies to these criticisms, published in 1991 and 1999. The first, 'Responses to Makinde/Lawuyi and Taiwo', was short, rejecting the criticisms with scorn. Lawuyi and Taiwo were accused of failing to read Akiwowo's text correctly, failing to understand the Yoruba universe of discourse, and especially the philosophy behind these poems, and failing to realise that sentences in Yoruba had multiple nuances. Akiwowo specifically denied there was a problem of culture-bound knowledge in his use of mythical material, citing Joseph Campbell's claims about the universality of myth.

The second reply, 'Indigenous Sociologies: Extending the Scope of the Argument', was published after Akiwowo had moved to the United States. It is longer and more measured, though it is clear he is still troubled by the criticisms. He defends the distinctiveness of indigenous thought via the example of a Yoruba psychiatrist who used local myth to understand mental problems.

In this paper, Akiwowo revisits and to some extent revises his conceptual system. He starts with the problem of the breakdown of the *asuwada* principle raised by Makinde. Akiwowo now suggests that this implicates the human spirit, that the spiritual factor in social relations has to be recognised, and that individual differences in spirituality affect the working of the *asuwada* principle. Akiwowo then offers a glossary of Yoruba terms relevant to understanding the *asuwada* principle, expounds some of them, and re-tells another mythological story that illustrates the coming together of beings into a harmony—in this case, the parts of the body.

Akiwowo's choice of a particular body of oral poetry as the source of indigenous concepts was not at issue in this debate, though perhaps it should have been. This sourcing means that his sociological concepts are drawn from the outlook of a narrow group within Nigerian society, relatively privileged and strongly traditionalist.

Given a body of Yoruba-language cultural material to work from, how do we actually get to sociological concepts? The method is never very clear in Akiwowo or Makinde. What is clear from the controversy as a whole is that there is no unambiguous way of doing the job. Akiwowo produces one set of concepts, then a modified set; Makinde produces a somewhat different interpretation of the issues; and Lawuyi and Taiwo have misunderstood the whole exercise, in Akiwowo's view.

This is a familiar problem in other cultural settings. As an Australian, I am familiar with local controversies about Australian identity and the meaning of Australian myths and symbols. But what is at stake here is not just the ethnographic interpretation of a local culture. The question is the grounding of concepts that are intended to circulate beyond Yoruba culture and, as Akiwowo's 1986 paper put it, 'contribute to a general body of explanatory principles' for sociology across the world. If four Yoruba-speaking specialists don't agree on how to get sociological meaning from these texts, then how should I, as a sociologist in another part of the world, relate to them?

The problem is compounded when Akiwowo, defending his system in 1999, produces more mythological material from other oral sources. Let's assume that I am trying to use the *asuwada* principle and the concepts of *ajobi* and *ajogbe* in my sociological research in Australia. I don't have access to the general background of Yoruba language and culture, nor to Ifa divination ritual in particular, let alone the extra texts that Akiwowo knows. The chances are that I would not only go astray in my interpretation of the terms, as Akiwowo thinks his local interlocutors have, but would go very badly astray. I would not so much be using an indigenous sociology from Nigeria as constructing my own syncretic system, which would make little sense to other sociologists either in Australia or Nigeria.

As far as I know, there are no sociologists from other countries who actually have used Akiwowo's concepts in substantive research. In 1992, the US sociologist Mark Payne published a paper praising Akiwowo's ideas, and defending the oral literature tradition and divination practices as useful sources of sociological insight. But he does not actually *do* any sociology with these concepts. On this point, the situation remains exactly as Lawuyi and Taifo described it: the *possibility* of a Yoruba-based sociology has been demonstrated, but *substantively* it hasn't yet been done.

There seems to be, if we can judge from this example, a problem about putting indigenous sociology into play in other cultural contexts, and perhaps even in what Akiwowo calls the 'parent culture' of the indigenous sociology. The high hopes of 20 years ago that indigenous sociologies would challenge the conceptual system of metropolitan sociology seem to have led nowhere.

Yet there is something more to be said. Akiwowo's bold project may have produced few fruits in terms of concepts useful in a global discourse. But he is saying something significant about Africa, which is expressed in his choice of Yoruba terms though it probably isn't dependent on them. His writing implies a *social diagnosis* of the critical problems of contemporary Nigeria, and by extension the problems of other countries in the region. Such a diagnosis does not depend on the terms of an indigenous sociology, though it may certainly draw insight from them. Any international reader can learn something from it.

Specifically, Akiwowo's use of the *ajobi/ajogbe* couple suggests a reading of the process of change from a kinship-based society, under the impact of colonialism and the postcolonial economy. His emphasis on the *asuwada* principle itself suggests his concern about fundamental social integration and the threats to it. Even the moralising tone of the 'propositions' in his 1986 article suggest his concern about these threats, and imply the need for resistance to them.

What appears as a radical epistemological project from the point of view of international sociology is—if I am reading it rightly—also a conservative response to social change in West Africa, from the point of view of a traditionalist older man seeking to restore social integration and balance. The controversy with Lawuyi and Taiwo has a generational element in it. Akiwowo's attempt to construct an African sociology from indigenous cultural materials was not an unusual kind of project for intellectuals of his generation. The main action, however, did not occur in sociology.

From 'African philosophy' to the sociology of post-colonial knowledge

In the 'Contributions' paper of 1986, Akiwowo cites a certain philosophy text, which had no resonance for *International Sociology* (it meant so little that the journal misspelt the author's name) but was highly significant for

African intellectuals. This was *Bantu Philosophy* by the Belgian missionary Placide Tempels (1959), originally published in French in 1945—the starting point of a huge debate about culture and philosophy in Africa. It is worth examining this debate because in it fundamental problems about any indigenous social science have been raised.

The story of the Belgian invasion and exploitation of central Africa is now reasonably well known. It is one of the more horrifying stories in the blood-stained history of colonial conquest. Its brutality gradually leaked out to European and North American audiences via progressive journalists, one of whom was Robert E. Park, later a key figure in the Chicago school of sociology (Lyman 1992).

A number of Catholic missionary orders arrived in the Congo at the end of the nineteenth century and set about converting the natives. Valentine Mudimbe describes the process in his magnificent survey *The Invention of Africa* (1988) and its sequel *The Idea of Africa* (1994). The task was one of cultural change as much as change in faith. The 'colonising structure', as Mudimbe calls the apparatus of rule, undertook the domination of space, the integration of local economies into the capitalist system, and the re-forming of the natives' minds.

A few decades into the twentieth century, much of the population was at least notionally Christian, indigenous men were becoming priests, and the problem changed. It became important to show that local cultures held capabilities on which Christianity could build. This was the task undertaken by Tempels in *Bantu Philosophy*.

To understand its impact, it is important to realise how fierce the European denigration of Africans had been. Colonisers' contempt for the colonised is a common feature of imperialism. North American indigenous people were slandered as treacherous, Bengalis as effeminate, Chinese as decadent, and so on. Africa, the last major region of the world to be colonised completely, got the full barrage of metropolitan contempt. Much as Aboriginal Australia came to stand for the ultra-primitive, Africa came to epitomise the European idea of a zone of savagery, incapable of improvement by its own efforts.

Tempels argued that colonial uplift had failed because, in thinking of black Africans as savage people with primitive minds, Europeans failed to see the well-developed *implicit* philosophy that Africans already possessed. *Bantu Philosophy* sets this philosophy out in detail. Bantu thought rests on an ontology, a theory of being that equates being with 'vital force'. Where Europeans see an object or a person, Africans see a force of life. These forces are in interaction with each other, usually hierarchical. Thus a person lives in a community under the direction of headmen who embody a greater life-force; the living necessarily have relations with the dead (hence ancestor worship); and one life-force can dominate or damage another (hence witchcraft). This ontology leads to a theory of the person, *muntu*, in a kind of philosophical psychology; and to an ethics, strongly communal. All of these beliefs are based on an underlying belief in the strongest vital force of all: God.

Reading Tempels' text 60 years later, I found it difficult to grasp how it could have had such an impact. The method by which he arrives at his philosophical formalisations is so muddy that it is impossible to reconstruct, or to test, his argument. His claims are vastly over-generalised—'In the minds of the Bantu . . .' or 'In African eyes . . .' (1959: 46, 76, 124). Tempels was, at best, an amateur at ethnography. His evidence is anecdotal, and there are large areas of indigenous life that he does not consider at all, such as the economy and social institutions. In this he followed the idealist style of French anthropology in his generation (Copans 1971). Tempels' research is markedly inferior to ethnographic work in other parts of Africa published before World War II, such as Jomo Kenyatta's *Facing Mount Kenya* (1938).

What shines through the book, nevertheless, is Tempels' passionate rejection of the Eurocentric belief that Africans have no worthwhile culture and no ethics. His book is addressed to white 'colonials *of goodwill*' (1959: 184, his italics). Tempels wanted the Belgians to stop destroying indigenous culture and 'help the Bantu to build their own Bantu civilization, a stable and noble one of their own' (1959: 174). Tempels was, in fact, one of a dissident faction among the colonisers, who defended native rights (Hountondji 2002a: 212–16). To persuade his compatriots, Tempels wrote warmly of the coherence and profundity of African thought, speaking of 'a lofty wisdom' from which Europeans too could learn. There is a half-veiled suggestion in *Bantu Philosophy* that the Bantu are closer to God than the Europeans are. Given the record of Europeans in the Congo, who could disagree?

But this praise only applies to certain Africans—those who stick with traditional culture. Full of praise for 'obstinate, conservative and philosophy-filled' groups like the Baluba (1959: 161), Tempels was openly contemptuous of Europeanised Africans, the *évolués* as Belgian and French colonialism called them (literally 'the evolved ones'—a history of colonial attitudes in one word). To Tempels, these people were rootless, money-obsessed, 'empty and unsatisfied souls', 'moral and intellectual tramps', 'a class of pseudo-Europeans, without principles, character, purposes, or sense' (1959: 180, 184).

This part of Tempels' argument resembles the ideas of some other intellectuals not far to the south, who also had a theory about the Bantu. The idea of a fundamental cultural gap between Bantu and European was part of the justification for 'rightful race-separation', in the thought of Afrikaner scholars such as Geoffrey Cronjé, who in the 1940s developed a sociological justification for the emergent Apartheid regime in South Africa (Cronjé 1947; Coetzee 1991). But these beliefs were not universal among white South African intellectuals. A fierce debate ignited between critics and supporters of Apartheid, and about strategies of opposition to the regime—the theme, for instance, of Nadine Gordimer's beautiful novel *Burger's Daughter* (1979).

Tempels' book was, without a doubt, a justification for colonialism—purified colonialism, in which missionaries and educators would combine the best of Christianity with the best of Bantu ontology to lead the Africans upwards. Tempels did not see coming the tidal wave of decolonisation that soon transformed Africa, led precisely by those *évolués* he despised—radicals like Kwame Nkrumah (1957), educated in both the Gold Coast and the United States, who in 1951 won a landslide election in what was to become Ghana. Tempels' paternalist model of change was immediately obsolete. During the two decades of anti-colonial political and cultural struggle that followed World War II, it was the other side of his thought, the praise of African philosophy, that had a remarkable influence.

The publication of *Bantu Philosophy* triggered a whole industry of ethnophilosophy from the 1940s to the 1980s. Tempels' amateur ethnography was soon replaced by much more sophisticated work. Alexis Kagamé from Rwanda wrote in *La philosophie bantu-rwandaise de l'être* (1956), an elaborate account of indigenous ontology based on a close analysis of word forms in the local language, supplemented by proverbs, fables, traditional stories and dynastic poems. Kagamé went on to compile a vast comparative study of 180 Bantu languages and dialects on which he based a survey of *La philosophie bantu comparée* (1976). He defended the concept of a 'Bantu civilisation' and claimed to reveal its formal logic, ontology, doctrine of the person, and idea of a prime cause.

Meanwhile, in East Africa, John Mbiti published his survey of *African Religions and Philosophy* (1969), which offered an even vaster survey of indigenous thought across the continent, covering not only ontology and theology but also ethnicity, the life-course, marriage, intellectuals, witchcraft and ethics. Though he started by recognising diversity, he too drifted into sweeping generalisations about the African view of the world, of which the most famous was his claim that:

> according to traditional concepts, time is a two-dimensional phenomenon, with a long past, a present, and virtually no future. The linear concept of time in western thought, with an indefinite past, present and infinite future, is practically foreign to African thinking (Mbiti 1969: 17).

Research in this tradition was still continuing in the 1980s. A fine example is Kwame Gyekye's *An Essay on African Philosophical Thought: The Akan Conceptual Scheme* (1987). Gyekye interviewed a number of 'wise men . . . the gurus of traditional wisdom' among the Akan communities of Ghana, collected proverbs and legends, and came up with an account of 'the Akan conception' of being, the person, destiny, ethics, logic, the relation between the individual and the community, and so on. Like Kagamé and Mbiti, he moved on from local material to generalisations about the common ground among African cultures, arguing that modern philosophers should concern themselves with, and build on, these 'intellectual foundations of African culture and experience' (1987: 212).

Because the rise of ethnophilosophy was exactly contemporary with decolonisation, the discovery of philosophies based in indigenous cultures became a vehicle for the reassertion of African dignity. Gyekye (1987: 33) cites a fascinating document, a resolution about philosophy from the 1959 Congress of Negro Writers and Artists, which states that African philosophy should be based on 'the traditions, tales, myths and proverbs' of the people, and should draw from them 'the laws of a true African wisdom'. Philosophers doing this should rid themselves of any inferiority feelings *vis-à-vis* the West.

The idea of African philosophy, then, was an intellectual parallel to the better-known reassertion of African creativity in the *négritude* movement of the 1930s and 1940s. Poets such as Léopold Senghor and Aimé Césaire celebrated the experience of those who were negated, defined as 'other', by white European culture. The movement was given enormous publicity in the metropole by Jean-Paul Sartre's essay 'Black Orpheus', which appeared within a few years of Tempels' *Bantu Philosophy* and Alan Paton's famous novel *Cry, the Beloved Country*, marking a high point for white intellectuals in the development of black consciousness. The literary movement became increasingly politicised as the struggles for colonial independence developed—influencing, among others, Frantz Fanon and Steve Biko.

'African philosophy', then, played a part in contesting the culture of imperialism and in legitimating African independence. But was it actually philosophy? The question had been raised by Tempels himself. By the 1960s, more doubts were being expressed. In 1976 they were crystallised in a brilliant, witty and angry book called *African Philosophy: Myth and Reality*, by the young Dahomeyan philosopher Paulin Hountondji.

Hountondji is scathing about the idea of an immanent African philosophy that could be discovered in customs, chants and myths. He points to the lack of a clear textual base for the ethnophilosophers' interpretations, and the contradictory doctrines they produced. This 'philosophy' was not constructed by rigorous and testable methods; it is, in fact, a loose projection of the ethnophilosophers' own ideas:

> . . . that which exists, that which is incontrovertibly given is that [ethnophilosophical] literature. As for the object it claims to restore, it is at most a way of speaking, a verbal invention, a mythos. When I speak of African philosophy I mean that literature, and I try to understand why it has so far made such strenuous efforts to hide behind the screen, all the more opaque for being imaginary, of an implicit 'philosophy' conceived as an unthinking, spontaneous, collective system of thought, common to all Africans or at least to all members severally, past, present and future, of such-and-such an African ethnic group. I try to understand why most African authors, when trying to engage with philosophy, have so far thought it necessary to project the misunderstood reality of their own discourse onto such palpable fiction (Hountondji 1976: 55).

As he later put it, this was an evasion of responsibility:

> [Ethnophilosophers] developed a sort of philosophy in the third person, consisting of sentences like this: 'They think so and so,' 'They say so and so,' etc. They renounced, in a sense, speaking and arguing on their own behalf. They renounced intellectual responsibility (Hountondji 1996: 83).

Further, ethnophilosophy was based on bad social analysis. It made an implausible assumption of consensus within African cultures, 'the myth of primitive unanimity, with its suggestion that in "primitive" societies—that is to say, non-Western societies—everybody always agrees with everybody else' (Hountondji 1976: 60). It made a false assumption that African societies were culturally static, so an unchanging world-view could be discovered in them. Far from putting authentic African philosophical work into wider circulation, ethnophilosophy reproduced the colonisers' gaze on African culture.

In short, Hountondji argues, the whole school of ethnophilosophy from Tempels onward was a 'mad and hopeless enterprise' based on 'a huge misconception' (1976: 52, 75–6)—unscientific, arbitrary and now politically reactionary.

Hountondji understood that ethnophilosophy and the *négritude* movement were responses to the colonialist contempt for primitive thought, a contempt expressed not only by sunburned planters in pith helmets, but also by distinguished intellectuals in Paris. But assertion of the distinctness of African culture, progressive in the time of anticolonial struggle, changed its political colour in the neocolonial era. It now became part of the ideology of dictatorial postindependence states. Hountondji was pungent in his criticism of these regimes and their self-serving cultural orthodoxies. He had personal experience of teaching in Zaire in the time of the Mobutu dictatorship and its dogma of 'authenticity'.

Hountondji was by no means alone in making such criticisms. For instance, the Ghanaian philosopher Kwasi Wiredu, in *Philosophy and an African Culture* (1980), made a clear distinction between 'folk thought' on the one hand, and philosophy as a critical practice, based on reason and argument, on the other. If African philosophy meant only traditional culture, Wiredu argued, philosophers would have to abandon modern logic and epistemology as 'un-African' and 'content ourselves with repeating the proverbs and folk conceptions of our forefathers'.

What remains for African philosophy after this truly devastating critique? In Hountondji's and Wiredu's view, everything remains. They have merely been clearing away a damaging myth, which has become an obstruction to intellectual development. As Wiredu (1980: 36) argued: 'African philosophy, as distinct from African traditional world-views, is the philosophy that is being produced by contemporary African philosophers. It is still in the making.'

These arguments were not received with universal acclaim. Hountondji in particular trod on so many toes that *African Philosophy* became the centre of its own controversy, some of it vicious. Hountondji was accused by the left of being a petit-bourgeois individualist, and by the right of betraying African people and culture. Ethnophilosophers saw him as committed to a Eurocentric view of philosophy. He was charged with being a neocolonialist, an elitist, an idealist, a writing-fetishist, a snob and an intellectual fraud. No wonder, looking back on the controversy, he called it a 'polluted debate' (Gyekye 1987; Serequeberhan 1991; Hountondji 1990, 2002a: 162ff).

Yet, over time, the critique of ethnophilosophy prevailed. The critics were not abandoning issues about Africa, but thinking about them in a different way. Both Wiredu and Hountondji were concerned with the *reconstruction* of African cultures. Hountondji's first book, *Libertés* (1973), had been centrally concerned with the connections among intellectual integrity, freedom and popular participation in political change.

Hountondji did not wish to abandon local cultural knowledge, but he insisted that ethnophilosophy and ethnoscience (the academic discipline that tries to reconstruct non-Western cultures' views of plants, animals, the natural world, mathematics, etc.) represented a European gaze on it. So African intellectuals who pursued these approaches were adopting a European point of view; their work was 'extroverted'. What was needed, rather, was a realistic approach to local knowledges that allowed them to be seen in relation to other knowledges, criticised and reappropriated in forms relevant to the development of African societies. The unfolding of these views steadily moved Hountondji from conventional philosophy towards the sociology of knowledge.

The productiveness of this approach is seen in *Les savoirs endogènes:*

pistes pour une recherche (*Endogenous knowledge: research trails*) published
by the Council for the Development of Social Science Research in Africa,
CODESRIA, in Dakar (Hountondji 1994). This volume collects studies on
endogenous technologies such as ironworking, on conceptual structures
such as number systems, medicine and pharmacology, and on the forms
of transmission of knowledge.

Hountondji's introduction to this book, together with a number of
articles published at about the same time, generalised his observation about
the extroversion of African science. The analysis is based on a materialist
view of knowledge as part of a total social process of production, and
Hountondji explicitly connects his argument with the economic analysis of
Samir Amin in *Accumulation on a World Scale*. Under colonialism, the
integration of subsistence economies into the world capitalist market
produced a distinctive pattern in the production of knowledge:

> With respect to modern science, the heart of the process is neither
> the stage of data collection nor that of the application of theoretical
> findings to practical issues. Rather, it lies between the two, in the
> stages of theory building, interpretation of raw information and the
> theoretical processing of the data collected . . . The one essential
> shortcoming of scientific activity in colonial Africa was the lack of
> these specific theory-building procedures and infrastructures
> (Hountondji 1995: 2).

In the colonies, the *theoretical* stage of science was omitted. Accordingly,
the colonies became a field for the collection of raw material—scientific
data—that was sent to the metropole where theory was produced.
Examples of this process abound in the history of European science.
Witness Sir Joseph Banks, for decades the president of the Royal Society
in London. Banks received a huge volume of specimens and observations
from all over the expanding British empire, as well as holding the original
biological loot from 'Botany Bay' in Australia, collected in 1770 during his
famous voyage with Captain Cook (O'Brian 1987).

Colonial relationships of knowledge became increasingly institutionalised through museums and universities. Hountondji (1995, 2002b)
shows that this structure persists powerfully in the postcolonial period. He
offers thirteen 'indices of extroversion' in a sardonic and all-too-believable

diagnosis of the dilemmas of today's intellectuals in the periphery. One example will suffice: scientists from the periphery trying to publish their work in metropolitan academic journals. Such journals have no expectation that theory will come from the South. Therefore:

> African scholars are often tempted, especially in the social sciences, to lock themselves up into an empirical description of the most peculiar features of their societies, without any consistent effort to interpret, elaborate on, or theorize about these features. In so doing, they implicitly agree to act as informants, though learned informants, for Western science and scientists (Hountondji 1995: 4).

That is exactly the problem that the indigenous sociology movement was trying to address. Hountondji's profound critique of African philosophy is easily applied to this movement. There is the same vagueness of method, the same implausible assumption of homogeneous and static cultures, the same complicity with nationalism, and the same difficulty in connecting with international dialogue except on terms of unequal exchange.

Yet Hountondji's later work opens up a more positive line of thought. Local knowledge is, indeed, important in economic and social development. But to make use of it, Hountonji argues, it is necessary to be concerned with the *truth* of indigenous knowledge, the reasons for its effectiveness, as well as the reasons it is so much bound up with myth and magic.

This is the argument I had in mind when suggesting that Akiwowo's work commands attention particularly for its diagnosis of social change in West Africa. The *knowledge of social situations* embedded in non-metropolitan discourses about local society is knowledge of the same order—as detailed, subtle, grounded in experience, and contestable—as metropolitan discourse about metropolitan society.

On Hountondji's view of science, problems of the same order would appear in both the metropole and the periphery, in converting informal knowledge of social situations into the formal discourse of social science. In both cases, there must be a process of critique to overcome the determinations of social structure. As Diawara (2000) observes, the knowledge of a local group is:

> knowledge that constitutes itself exactly through the clash of local and universal knowledge, their dialogues and their transmission

processes . . . This local knowledge is not distributed evenly over the whole society but varies with social group, status, ethnicity and gender. The possession, passing on and negotiation of this local knowledge are thus inextricably bound up with social differences and power relations . . . Far from a static ensemble, this knowledge is an object of incessant reinterpretation according to varying situations and interests (2000: 368–9).

But though similar in kind, the problems of producing knowledge in the metropole and the periphery are differently structured *in practice*. This follows from the global inequalities that have constituted the metropole as the home of theory, or 'science' as such, and the periphery as either the source of data, or the arena in which metropolitan knowledge is applied.

African Renaissance and African intellectuals

In May 1996, speaking at the national convention that was to adopt a democratic constitution, South African Deputy President Thabo Mbeki opened his address by declaring: 'I am an African!' The following year Mbeki adopted the term 'African Renaissance' for his vision of a new wave of cultural and economic development. Since Mbeki became President in succession to Nelson Mandela, this idea has provided the framing for South Africa's foreign policy. There have been several books about the 'African Renaissance', at least one institute to promote it, and a widening debate about the idea.

The powerful rhetoric of 'African Renaissance' was light on proposals, however, and needed to be filled out. A document of 1997 listed five priority areas for South Africa's engagement with the rest of the continent: cultural exchange; the emancipation of African women; mobilisation of youth; the promotion of democracy; and sustainable economic development. It is clear that the very idea was inspiring to many local people. For instance, Bothlale Tema (2002: 129), a matter-of-fact science educator, speaks of it as a 'wondrous moment'; while Vale and Maseko (2002: 130), sober policy analysts, speak of the 'emancipatory moment that Mbeki has captured'.

When the African National Congress came to power through a series of compromises with the former government, South African business and global capital, it gradually shed its former commitment to socialism and adopted a mild neoliberalism domestically (Jacobs and Calland 2002). The vision of economic development for Africa, the centre of what Vale and Maseko (2002) call the 'globalist' interpretation of the African Renaissance, emphasises free markets, scaling down of the public sector, good governance, attracting private investment, and better infrastructure. Critics see this as little more than a regional version of neoliberal globalisation. Even so, the agenda has not been easy to implement. Taylor and Williams (2001) show how the devastating war in the Congo, reignited in 1998 with participation from several neighbouring states, is inconsistent with the premises of the African Renaissance. Far from being potential allies in African unity, reform and development, political elites in central Africa make huge profits from war and instability, which allow them to run patronage networks to bolster their own rule.

There is, however, a second interpretation of 'African Renaissance', which Vale and Maseko call the 'Africanist' interpretation. In this, Mbeki's ideas fall within the tradition of cultural reassertion that goes back to the *négritude* movement and the pan-Africanism of Nkrumah (Ahluwalia 2002). Some of the strongest supporters of the African Renaissance idea have adopted this interpretation (Makgoba 1999; Ntuli 2002). Pitika Ntuli, for instance, draws a dichotomy between 'the Western Way' and 'the African Way'. In a style strongly reminiscent of ethnophilosophy, Ntuli argues that the African cosmo-vision is holistic, and integrated with society, ceremonial, rebirth and reproduction. But his version is politicised. Ntuli believes the African Way is being betrayed by Westernised intellectuals who, for instance, criticise the 'virginity testing' of girls, which Ntuli believes is a sign of moral renewal. (Mbeki's principle of the emancipation of African women seems to have got lost somewhere.) It is clear that Ntuli thinks the African Renaissance project justifies hauling dissident intellectuals into line.

African Renaissance in a cultural sense is closely connected with the revalidation of indigenous knowledge. As Catherine Odora Hoppers (2002) relates, the South African parliament asked the country's science councils to reconsider the subject of indigenous knowledge, launching a research agenda to correct the 'epistemological disenfranchisement' of local people. Raymond Suttner (2006) too has argued for indigenous knowledge as real knowledge, and argues that South Africa needs an inclusive culture that realises the suppressed creativity of African people.

Ari Sitas (2006) sees in the African Renaissance idea the stimulus to a new sociology, tracing the 'reclamation journeys' that sociologists such as Akiwowo have made into indigenous knowledge, and arguing for an interplay between general and specific knowledges.

Not everyone, however, is uncritically supportive. Sitas acknowledges the complexity within the European tradition, and the danger of basing contemporary knowledge on dubious ideas about unique traditional cultures. The psychologist Livingstone Mqotsi (2002: 170) forthrightly criticises Afrocentric thought and the policy of those in power 'to resuscitate tribalism and primeval institutions . . . Africa is not populated by a special breed of humans endowed with special attributes'.

Pal Ahluwalia (2002) similarly warns against the African Renaissance model drifting towards racial essentialism. Here the argument about forms of knowledge intersects in troublesome ways with identity politics. In a dichotomous discourse that equates 'African' with indigenous ethnic identity, there is no place for significant groups of intellectuals whose African identity has other grounds. They include white writers who shared in the African cultural revival and the struggle against Apartheid (e.g. Davidson, Fugard), members of the black African diaspora (Du Bois, Fanon), intellectuals from Arab Africa (Amin), and the many locally born intellectual workers of European, Indian or interracial backgrounds who have a role in current projects of reform and development (see Connell 2007).

These difficulties will not be solved by more elaborate categories, but by thinking more carefully about the circumstances of intellectual work. In a penetrating discussion of the African Renaissance idea, Mahmood Mamdani (1999) recalled how, under the Apartheid system, segregated universities had functioned 'more as detention centres for black intellectuals than as centres that would nourish intellectual thought'. Mamdani noted that racialised thinking persisted in the post-Apartheid period, and it was now crucial to attempt the 'deracialisation of intellectual production'. This implied deracialised institutions, plus intellectual freedom. But deracialised knowledge about Africa could only be produced by an 'Africa-focused intelligentsia'. This was difficult in South Africa, where the institutions of science and higher education continued to be 'hostile to Africa-focused thought'. More had been achieved in other parts of Africa—for instance, with the Dakar school of cultural research or the Dar es Salaam school of political economy.

Mamdani thus pointed to the same issue that concerned Hountondji: the conditions of existence of intellectual workers in Africa, in the context of a global economy and metropolitan cultural hegemony. This is unquestionably a sore point. In a bitter reflection, Thandika Mkandawire (2000) traced the history of the relationship between intellectuals and post-independence governments across black Africa. Intellectuals had mostly supported nation-building in the 1950s and 1960s, but repressive regimes closed the spaces for debate and often demanded ideological conformity. African social scientists in particular were cut off from policy-making. When neoliberalism and Structural Adjustment Programs arrived in the 1980s and 1990s, the alienation was renewed. Governments turned to foreign advisers, while NGOs wanted only consultancies, not basic research programs, assuming that 'poor research was good enough for the poor'.

The difficulty of finding ground for the development of African social sciences is emphasised by those who have looked at the institutions mentioned by Mamdani. Checking the curricula of universities in Sub-Saharan Africa, Peter Crossman and René Devisch (2002) and Birgit Brock-Utne (2002) find little Africanisation of content, or teaching in indigenous languages, 40 years after political independence. Like NGO funding, aid directly intended for the social sciences tends to support small-scale, practically oriented studies. Witness the projects supported or reported through the Organisation for Social Science Research in Eastern and Southern Africa. They include local studies of youth leadership, AIDS risk, stress among public servants, food security, gender and small enterprises, sexual abuse (*OSSREA Bulletin* 2005). All are worthy topics but, as Hountondji observed, the stage of theory-building is missing.

So far, it seems, the African Renaissance has not given rise to an *intellectual* ferment that would inspire new developments in social thought. Yet such a thing has happened in the past. Mudimbe's (1988) vast survey *The Invention of Africa* traces epistemological ruptures in thought about Africa, especially the one that challenged the reading of Africa as 'other' to the European. Picking up steam in the 1920s and completed in the 1950s, this epistemological break—including the new African historiography, the critique of ethnography, the *négritude* movement and African independence political thought—made possible the very idea of an Africa-focused intelligentsia to which Mamdani much later appealed.

In this spirit, I recall a study from a generation even before that of

Kenyatta and Tempels. In 1916 in London, Solomon Tshekisho Plaatje published *Native Life in South Africa*. This was not a travelogue, nor an ethnography, nor a tale of life on an African farm. It was an account of the impact of the 1913 *Natives' Land Act*, pushed through the all-white South African parliament in the wake of union between the British and Afrikaner colonies. The purpose of the Act was to force black tenant farmers off their land, to create a wage labour force for the benefit of white property owners, and to set up black homelands (as they were later called). It was, in short, an enclosure act along racial lines, and a key move towards Apartheid.

Plaatje was a court translator turned journalist, at the time the general secretary of the recently founded South African Native National Congress (soon to become the ANC). He travelled the country by bicycle to research the impact of the Act on displaced families driven off their land. The book describes cases from his fieldwork, and also documents speeches, parliamentary debates and newpaper reports. Plaatje began writing it on board the ship to England, to appeal to the imperial government to intervene. His case included passionate reporting about the social consequences of the Act, irony about the Christian pretensions of South Africa's rulers, a critique of racial hatred and of the implacability of the Boer politicians, an appeal to imperial citizenship, and a veiled prediction of the bloodshed that might result from the path of racial segregation.

The British felt deep sympathy. But the year the delegation arrived was 1914 and the imperial government had other fish to fry. As Lloyd George later told Plaatje, the British could hardly interfere in the internal affairs of a dominion to which they had just given self-government.

So the delegation, and the book, failed in their political purpose. Yet the book has enduring importance. If we are looking for classics of world sociology, *Native Life in South Africa* is certainly one. It is not only a pioneering piece of fieldwork, done under great difficulty, and a striking dissection of racism, in both respects comparable to the work of W.E.B. du Bois in the same generation. Plaatje's work is also an acute analysis of a political and social conjuncture. It shows how, in the colonial situation, the control of land and the disruption of land tenure are central to the pattern of domination, the play of interests, the consciousness of groups and the process of social change. It is a striking example of social diagnosis, and it highlights an issue that metropolitan sociology almost entirely missed. I will return to this issue in Chapter 9.

6

Islam and Western dominance

The Prophet of Islam was appointed to complete the movement which has existed throughout history in opposition to deception, falsehood, polytheism, discord, hypocrisy, aristocracy, and class differences. This was made a goal of the struggle by the announcement that all humanity is of one race, one source, one nature, and of one God.

—Ali Shariati (1972)

In this chapter, I present my encounters with the writings of three Iranian intellectuals who grappled with the problem of Western dominance in the Muslim world. There is a broader Muslim literature on this subject; Shi'ism, though the majority tradition in Iran, is a minority in Islam as a whole. I focused on this tradition both because I have more background in Iranian than Arab or Indonesian history, and because of the significance of the Iranian revolution of 1979 in reshaping the Muslim world's relations with the metropole. Islam is—contrary to media stereotypes and 'clash of civilisations' ideologues—undergoing vast change and renovation, and these authors form a significant strand in this process.

When I say encounters with their writings, I should say encounters with translations. I have no knowledge of Farsi (Persian) or Arabic. I am not only dependent on translators' renderings of text, but also on their choice of texts to translate. Fortunately, the key books by al-Afghani and Al-e Ahmad have been translated in full, as have a sample of Shariati's lectures on social issues; otherwise this chapter would not be possible at all.

I have tried to fill the gaps by studying biographies, general histories, anthologies and specialist articles. Nevertheless, I emphasise that this chapter is not offered as a technical study of their oeuvre, but specifically as an encounter in social theory. I believe it is an encounter that other Anglophone social theorists should have.

Refutation of the Materialists

During the second half of the nineteenth century CE, the formations that we call the social sciences came into existence in Western Europe and North America. At the same time in the Islamic world, an even more fraught transition was beginning, which also involved knowledge and moral discourse about the social—though it was structured in different ways. A central figure in this transition was Sayyid Jamal ad-Din, known to fame as al-Afghani.[1]

---

1   For those unfamiliar with these naming customs: 'Sayyid' is an honorific signifying that the person's family is descended from the family of the Prophet. 'Al-Afghani' is a common type of alternative to the personal name; it means, more or less, 'of Afghanistan' and was used by Jamal ad-Din after his first important political post, as an adviser to the Emir of Afghanistan. Adopted by someone from Shi'ite Iran, the name also suggests solidarity with Sunnis.

Al-Afghani's best known works were written in the 1880s when he was already middle-aged; he was a younger contemporary of Herbert Spencer and Friedrich Engels, a little older than Ferdinand Tönnies. But his conditions of life were dramatically different from theirs. He spent most of his adult life travelling across the Islamic world, from Kolkata to Cairo, with periods also in Christian countries, living off his wits and his scholarship, rarely able to settle anywhere for more than a few years. He was deeply involved in elite politics, being adviser at various times to monarchs in Afghanistan, Iran and the Ottoman empire. He was also involved in reform politics in several countries, and helped to inspire important social movements in Egypt and Iran. He was expelled from, or had to flee, four countries at different times. He seems to have been a wonderful orator and teacher; he also created one of the first newspapers to be read across the Islamic world. He had a loyal following, and probably inspired the assassination of a Shah. He was regarded by the British as a Russian agent and was equally distrusted by the Russians. At the end, he died in detention, trapped by the regime that was the main beneficiary of his pan-Islamic campaign.

This was not a life made for quiet scholarly reflection. Al-Afghani wrote only one book, *The Truth about the Neicheri Sect and an Explanation of the Neicheris*, better known as *Refutation of the Materialists* (the title of its Arabic translation). Most of his written work comprised essays for newspapers and magazines. Much of his influence was certainly due to face-to-face teaching, not surprising in what was still mainly an oral culture. Though there are some records of his teaching and conversation, there is controversy about his exact views. For all that, it is clear that al-Afghani was an original thinker and had a powerful intellectual impact. Rather than systems in the manner of Spencer or Engels, he created starting points for cultural change. He opened up problems and created models of argument that were developed by later thinkers in many different ways.

We should see al-Afghani as an intellectual of a historically new kind— as we should see the social scientists of Europe—made possible by the upheavals of culture, education and political systems resulting from imperialism. Al-Afghani was a practitioner in two cultures, that of the imperialists and that of the colonised, and worked at the intersection of the two. He was one of the first thinkers anywhere in the world who tried to mobilise the resources of *both* cultures to generate a vigorous answer, at both practical and intellectual levels, to the imperialists.

The problem was acute. Al-Afghani came to maturity in the period that has been aptly called 'the zenith of European power' (Bury 1960). He lived in a region partly occupied by European military forces, with the rest swept by European political pressure and economic penetration. Most remaining Muslim governments were puppets of the imperial powers, or completely intimidated by them. Al-Afghani saw this at first hand, visiting India soon after the great rising of 1857 had been crushed. He saw the feeble Qajar regime in Iran pulled this way and that between the Russians and the British, and tried unsuccessfully to negotiate a peace between the British and the Mahdist movement in Sudan.

To someone concerned with the dignity of Islam, this was intolerable. Al-Afghani became a lifelong opponent of the British empire, the superpower in the Muslim world at the time (much as the United States is now). Most of his political work concerned attempts, which mostly failed in the short term, to strengthen Islamic regimes and create anti-British resistance. But he also inquired into the reasons for the terrible weakness of Islamic society.

There are several strands to al-Afghani's thought on this problem. He saw trends that had sapped the strength of Islam from within, such as tyrannous rulers who had destroyed cultural resources. He saw a Muslim clerical intelligentsia, the *ulama*, who had replaced living religion with a dusty scholasticism. He saw rifts among Muslims—the Shi'ite/Sunni split among them—that opened the path to conquest from outside.

He also developed a more complex cultural analysis, and for this I turn to his longest text, the *Refutation of the Materialists*. On the face of it, the *Refutation* is not about imperialism at all. It is a defence of religion against irreligion, specifically the form of irreligion represented by materialist philosophy.

With much rhetorical exaggeration, al-Afghani presents materialism as a conscious conspiracy against religion. More interesting is the specific charge he brings against the materialists of past and present, that their ideas cause licence, anarchy and communism. That is to say, he focuses on the *social* effects of false doctrine. More interesting still is his defence of religion, which is praised because it makes for virtuous people and social cohesion. Al-Afghani develops this point at length. Religion promotes three key beliefs (that man is the noblest creature; that one's own society is the noblest; and that there is an afterlife), and three qualities in people and nations (a sense of shame; trustworthiness; and truthfulness). Once these beliefs and qualities are established, society will flourish; without them, society declines. Thus religion is the key to progress: 'Since it is known that religion is unquestionably the source of man's welfare, therefore, if it is placed on firm foundations and sound bases, that religion will naturally become the complete source of total happiness and perfect tranquillity. Above all it will be the cause of material and moral progress' (1968: 169).

Other religions can have these effects, but the best religion is Islam. Again, al-Afghani's reasons are interesting. Islam is superior to other religions, he argues, because it is the most *rational*. It has no doctrines that depend on irrational faith or priestly authority:

> The Islamic religion is the only religion that censures belief without proof and the following of conjectures; reproves blind submission; seeks to show proof of things to its followers; everywhere addresses itself to reason; considers all happiness the result of wisdom and clearsightedness; attributes perdition to stupidity and lack of insight; and sets up proofs for each fundamental belief in such a way that it will be useful to all people (1968: 172).

With this ringing declaration, al-Afghani is not abandoning his critique of contemporary Muslim society. He meets the obvious objection thus:

> If someone says: If the Islamic religion is as you say, then why are the Muslims in such a sad condition? I will answer: When they were truly Muslims, they were what they were and the world bears witness to their excellence. As for the present, I will content myself with this holy text: 'God does not change the condition of a people unless they change what is in themselves' (1968: 173).[2]

Two lines of social analysis converge in the *Refutation*. The first is a sociology of social cohesion in which economic and political well-being depend on the cultural foundations of human action—cultural foundations that al-Afghani presented in the language of morality and religion. It was entirely consistent that al-Afghani in other writing emphasised imperialism's threat to Islam, and Islam as the basis for resistance.

---

2   Qur'an 13:11; I have used a more modern translation.

The *Refutation* was written in 1881 when al-Afghani was in India, as a critique of a contrasting Muslim response to conquest, the Aligarh movement. Led by Sayyid Ahmad Khan, this trend emphasised the pursuit of modernity, Western-style education, rationalist reform of Islam and political accomodation with the British (Malik 1980). Ahmad Khan explicitly supported equality for women, which he saw as Islamic principle though denied in Muslim practice. The Aligarh movement was an early statement of a modernising logic later followed in many parts of the colonised world. To al-Afghani, it represented a disastrous concession to imperial power, specifically undermining Islam. Al-Afghani was a moderniser too, but he wanted to modernise from a position of Islamic strength, not weakness.

This was expressed in his later life by commitment to a pan-Islamic movement centred on the Caliphate in Istanbul. He also began to see the *ulama* as potential allies of the movement to strengthen Islamic societies. In 1891, in the struggle against the Iranian Qajar regime's concession of a tobacco monopoly to a British company, al-Afghani made a famous appeal to the leader of the *ulama*, Haj Mirza Hasan Shirazi, to join the opposition. In this conflict, the united resistance of secular modernisers, *ulama* and masses defeated the Shah and the British, and created a vital precedent for future politics.

The other key line of thought concerns rationality. Al-Afghani was the inheritor of a rationalist tradition in Islamic philosophy that had been strong in Iran. (It is much less widely known to Westerners than the mystical tradition of Sufism.) In his essay 'The Benefits of Philosophy', al-Afghani argues for the unity of knowledge, invoking the key Islamic theological concept of *tawhid*, the absolute unity of God. For him there was no separate Islamic science. Muslim intellectuals had drawn freely on Greek, Roman and Persian knowledge in the past, and Islam should be vigorously associated with the progress of universal science in the present.

He therefore called on the *ulama* to get with it: to study electricity, steam power, the phonograph, the camera, 'the entire sphere of new sciences and inventions and fresh creations' (1968: 121–2). Al-Afghani kept abreast of technology and used it himself—for instance, promoting newspapers as a new means for creating a Muslim public sphere. In part of his career he used the most traditional of political techniques, as personal adviser to Muslim monarchs; in another part he pursued a radical technique of distance politics, living in Europe and disseminating his ideas across the Muslim world via print.

To al-Afghani (as, ironically, also to Ahmad Khan at Aligarh), Islamic revival was in large part an educational problem. The disintegrating effects of materialism and imperialism, which in his world were intertwined, had to be countered by good education. This required moving away from the sterile repetition typical of religious schools. Knowledge, he argued in the *Refutation* and other texts, was the key to social wealth and productivity. If the great question of philosophy is now: 'What is the cause of the poverty, indigence, helplessness, and distress of the Muslims, and is there a cure for this important phenomenon and great misfortune or not?' (1968: 120), then it is incumbent on any Muslim with intellectual resources to focus on this problem and do something about it.

Al-Afghani's English-language biographer suggests that the source of his influence was his finding *within Islam* the bases for rationalist and modernising thought (Keddie 1972). His modernising agenda was therefore not automatically seen as an alien introduction. To put it another way, al-Afghani refused the modernity/traditionalism dichotomy so familiar in Western social thought.

That makes his thought significant in a broader perspective again. Al-Afghani had, from long experience, an acute sense of the global power relations of his era. He was not deceived by the ideological construction of imperial power as a reflection of cultural worth, the idea embedded in the nineteenth century concept of 'progress' (see Chapter 1). He saw the British straightforwardly as a band of robbers and tyrants.

But he also saw their power as having major cultural effects, and therefore as requiring a new kind of response, not just an imitation. To defend and purify the culture of the colonised, *and at the same time* acquire science, technology and social techniques from the imperialists—therefore to change the balance of global power by a cultural/political regeneration within the colonised world—was the difficult path al-Afghani thought was now necessary.

Al-Afghani's rhetoric is unfamiliar to me, and some of his attitudes are as unattractive as those of his European contemporaries. But I respect his dedication, his evident courage and above all his creativity. In his life and writings, one finds a vision of the world that has a breadth, a level of insight, a moral force and a practical edge that are rare in any generation.

Westoxication

In 1962 the censored version of a short book by a well-known literary figure was privately printed in Tehran. The government banned it, but copies leaked out to the Iranian diaspora. In 1964 the author, Jalal Al-e Ahmad, prepared a complete uncensored version. The government seized the book during printing and bankrupted the publisher. The complete text was not published until 1978. In the meantime, editions of the censored text had been published outside Iran and the book had become a symbol of Iranian intellectual opposition. When it was freely available in Iran, on the eve of the revolution, it became a best-seller.

The book was titled *Gharbzadegi*, a made-up word that translators have struggled to render in English. 'Westoxication' and 'Plagued by the West' are among the better efforts; 'Westafflictedness' and 'Occidation' are among the worse. Translators John Green and Ahmad Alizadeh, who prefer 'Weststruckness', remark that the Farsi roots have connotations of contagion and of a blow being delivered—and Al-e Ahmad certainly starts his text with the metaphor of a disease, 'I say that Westoxication is like cholera'. But there is also a connotation of infatuation. I will use '*Gharbzadegi*' for the book and 'Westoxication' for the concept.

Gharbzadegi is a tricky book for an outsider to appreciate. It is written in a popular style specifically for Iranian readers. There are allusions, jokes and satire which would have increased the book's local popularity but do not help it to travel.

The text is also hard to follow because it is, to be blunt, disorganised. Al-e Ahmad (1982a) chats to the reader, excuses himself, interrupts himself, thinks of a new topic and darts off after it, then repeats himself. He is opinionated, laying about with scathing comments on the schools, the army, the *ulama* and the intellectuals, but he does not follow through very far on any argument. His jeers at Westernised women come close to misogyny. He is a vivid writer with a sharp eye and a notable sense of humour, but is in no sense a systematic thinker. (In another essay, Al-e Ahmad (1982b: 98) makes this same criticism of his own generation of Iranian writers: 'We're in a hurry. We write too much. We're seldom careful.') Exasperated Iranian critics point to errors of fact and interpretation in *Gharbzadegi*, and even an outsider can see some of them.

And yet, for all its messiness, *Gharbzadegi* contains a powerful argument. In international perspective, it was one of the first attempts to dissect the cultural dimension of neocolonialism and it launched ideas that were later to become very familiar. It was also notable in suggesting a feasible strategy of resistance to cultural domination. *Gharbzadegi* is recognised as an important moment in the history of the Iranian opposition. I think it should be recognised more widely.

The grip of the Qajar monarchy had been broken by the 'Constitutional Revolution' of 1905–11, which installed a shaky parliamentary regime. This was subverted by internal and external forces, especially by the British, who had become dependent on Iran's oil during World War I. A period of turbulence was ended by an army takeover; with covert British support, the general Reza Khan took power and in 1925 installed himself as Shah. Reza Shah pursued a modernising strategy based on that of Kemal's regime in Turkey, creating a secular state and beginning industrialisation. But he wandered too close to the Germans. During World War II, the British and Russians threw him out, giving themselves complete control of the oil and a supply route to the Soviet Union (Keddie 1981).

After the war, there was a democratic opening, leading to the election of the reformist Mossadeq government which tried to pursue neutralism and development, eventually nationalising the oil industry. This triggered a violent reaction from the Western powers, who backed a right-wing coup against Mossadeq in 1953. The United States promptly replaced the British as the main controllers of Iranian oil and politics. By 1955, the government was a personal dictatorship in the hands of Mohammed Reza Shah. This regime became one of the most brutal of the pro-American Cold War dictatorships, though it never quite matched the Suharto regime in Indonesia which waded to power in 1965 through the blood of half a million people.

Mohammed Reza Shah renewed his father's policy of secular modernisation-from-above, using oil revenues and US aid to fund a military build-up, economic and educational expansion, and spectacular development works such as big dams. But little autonomous industrialisation occurred; rather, imports soared. Rising levels of consumption and a Western lifestyle for the wealthy—gently satirised in the tales of upper-class family life by Amirshahi (1995)—did not trickle down to the working class. So there was growing inequality, exacerbated by a mass inflow of unemployed rural workers to the cities. Popular discontent was put down by force, and opposition figures were gaoled, exiled or killed. The Shah's infamous secret police organisation, SAVAK, was set up in 1957 and trained by the Americans and Israelis.

This was the situation addressed by *Gharbzadegi*, written in 1961 as a submission to an official inquiry on the goals of education. It required a good deal of courage to write such critical ideas, let alone show them to the Shah's government.

Al-e Ahmad, who was born about the time Reza Shah seized power, came from a religious family—his father and an older brother were members of the *ulama*. He therefore had a grasp of Shi'ite ideas and practice, yet moved into secular radical politics. As a young man in the 1940s, he trained as a teacher, and became an active member of the left-wing Tudeh party. After leaving Tudeh in one of its splits, he was a supporter of Mossadeq. After the 1953 coup, he left party politics and concentrated on literary work. He was already a prolific writer, and continued for the rest of his life to pour out short stories, novels, essays and commentary on culture, religion and society (Al-e Ahmad 1982b).

Gharbzadegi opens with a sketch of East–West divisions as a conflict between global rich and global poor, and moves on through several chapters on Islamic, mainly Iranian, history. East–West rivalry is a very old story, Al-e Ahmad argues, but in the last 300 years it has changed character, turning into a relation of domination: 'Now the spirit of competition is forgotten. It's now been replaced by a feeling of helplessness and dependence' (1982a: 34).

Al-e Ahmad comments that under the Safavid dynasty, which had made Shi'ite Islam the state religion, Iranians began to want the approval of Western travellers and diplomats. This opens a major theme of *Gharbzadegi*, the critique of Western orientalism. Nearly 20 years before Edward Said's famous book on the subject, Al-e Ahmad saw Western researchers on Islamic societies as key agents of the system of domination. Complicit with corporations and governments, the Orientalists gather intelligence. But they also produce cultural effects, as their interpretations of Iranian culture override the indigenous ones: 'The westoxicated man even describes, understands, and explains himself in the language of orientalists! ... He has placed himself, an imagined thing, under the orientalist's microscope, and he depends on what the orientalist sees, not on what he is, feels, and experiences' (p. 121). This critique is different from Said's, but in a way more frightening: Western intellectual domination sustains the inauthenticity of the subject in neocolonialism.

The empty self in Iranian modernity is another of the central themes of *Gharbzadegi*. The quotation above comes from the key Chapter 7, in which Al-e Ahmad offers a close-up portrait of 'the Westoxicated man'. A man, literally, is meant. Women have little place in the argument, and at this point Al-e Ahmad's account of Westoxication becomes a portrait of an alienated and impotent form of masculinity formed in neocolonial conditions: 'a donkey in a lion's suit'.

This portrait is a satire, but a disturbing one. The new men, Al-e Ahmad indicates, have a veneer of Western education without having its depth; at the same time, they have lost their grounding in local culture and specifically in religion. The result is not an anti-religious attitude, but simply alienation. Indifference marks the whole outlook of the Westoxicated elite:

> The usual practice in this country is to confer power on those who are rootless and without personality, if not on the ruthless and the corrupt . . . If we're to do a good job of following the West, someone must lead the nation who's easily led, who isn't genuine, who's unprincipled, has no roots, and is not of the soil of this land (1982a: 116).

The situation calls for men who are tactful, compliant, flexible, who follow fashion, who have no passion, no commitment to others and no depth of knowledge. What they do have is fear; desire for Western material goods and a consumer lifestyle; and the attitude that the Australian literary critic Phillips, at about the same time, called the 'cultural cringe' towards Europe. As Al-e Ahmad puts it, the Westoxicated man follows Western news, reads Western literature, and even learns about Eastern philosophy from Western books.

Al-e Ahmad reserves special anger for modernising secular Iranian intellectuals. At various points through the book, he criticises them fiercely as agents of Westoxication, much as al-Afghani had criticised the Aligarh movement as 'materialists'. Al-e Ahmad thinks no better of the flocks of foreign advisers who came into Iran under the Shah's regime to promote the modernisation of the economy and institutions, especially those from UN agencies. (His criticism of this group, which must have sounded idiosyncratic in 1962, prefigured the worldwide criticism of advisers from the IMF and World Bank in the 1990s.)

This cultural and psychological situation is certainly a result of Western political control, exerted over Iran because of the oil resources; however, there is also something deeper going on. Among the most powerful images of *Gharbzadegi* is that of the machine. The Westoxicated society is dominated by machinery. It is dominated in the specific sense that the society is dependent on machines—ranging from tractors and cars to television sets, refineries and weapons—but does not know how to design, produce or even maintain them.

The machine is, for Al-e Ahmad, both a fact and a symbol. As fact, it reveals the dependence of the new Iranian economy on imports, the weakness of technical education and the disruption of old production systems. In a vivid image, he describes travelling through villages and towns and seeing hundreds of still, disused windmills. This was not an accidental observation. Al-e Ahmad, known as a writer of social-realist short stories, had spent time travelling into the countryside to make ethnographic observations of village life, and had inspired other urban intellectuals to do the same (Mirsepassi 2000: 104). As symbol, the machine stands for out-of-control change in Iranian society, and for the desire of Iranians for the very things that are disrupting their society.

His awareness of that desire distinguishes Al-e Ahmad from most commentators, then and now, on global cultural domination. The desire to enter the globally dominant culture, to possess its artefacts, to follow its customs and to be esteemed by its emissaries, is both powerful and protean in Iranian society. Al-e Ahmad uses the analogy of an amulet or talisman— 'Machines are talismans for us westoxicated folk' (1982a: 97)—which the owner wears for its magical effectiveness without understanding how it works. Al-e Ahmad never draws on psychoanalytic ideas, but in this account of desire and the fetishism of possessions he is close to the Freudian left in the metropole.

Gharbzadegi also contains more conventional commentary on social change, 'a society in disorder': 'It's a mixture of a pastoral economy and a village economy with the manners of a newly formed urbanity, ruled by big foreign economic interests like a trust or a cartel. We're a living museum of old and new social institutions. We have all of this at once' (1982a: 129). Al-e Ahmad sketches change in the lives of nomadic pastoralists, village farmers, rural–urban migrants, and so on. At one point he also notes change in the lives of women. In a highly ambivalent passage, he appears to attack women's emancipation as part of Westoxication, producing a 'feigned liberation' in the cities; but he also argues that women in the villages have long carried the 'primary burden of life'. This is condescending, but not as hostile as Ayatollah Khomeini, who arrived on the national political scene in the year *Gharbzadegi* was published with a fierce, and successful, attack on women's right to vote.

Given the accumulation of cultural distortions and social problems represented by Westoxication, what can be done in response? Al-e Ahmad is reasonably optimistic. The way to deal with a machine civilisation is not to reject machines. Al-e Ahmad is badly misrepresented by commentators who see him as an anti-technology 'nativist' (e.g. Boroujerdi 1996; for a convincing critique, see Partovi 1998). The point is to get control of them: 'Machines are a natural springboard for us, one that we must use to make the longest possible leap. We must adopt machines, but we must not remain slaves to them' (1982a: 96).

Only a society that *makes* machines, rather than always importing them, can control their power and use them in a labour-intensive, more appropriate agriculture that would reduce imports and support the population. To have a machine-producing economy, however, would require a workforce that did not yet exist in Iran. So Al-e Ahmad argued for massive changes in education, getting rid of an irrelevant academic curriculum and greatly expanding technical education. Specialists were needed—one characteristic of Westoxication was the lack of real specialists—but specialists with character. A cultural and psychological revolution was also required.

To Al-e Ahmad in the 1960s, such cultural and psychological change could only come from religion. Islam appeared, in his survey of history early in the book, as the only social totality that had effectively resisted colonialism and Christianity. Thinking about Iranian resistance in the past, Al-e Ahmad saw that 'a precious jewel lay hidden in the hearts of the people, like a seed for any uprising against a government of oppressors and the corrupt' (1982a: 61). But the *ulama*, with a few notable exceptions, had failed to recognise it.

Gharbzadegi pictures the clerics of Iran as timid, passive, backward-looking, preoccupied with the trivia of religious ritual, stuck in a cocoon, 'a petrified fossil fit only for a museum' (1982a: 69). In other writing, such as his famous short story 'The Sitar', about a poor musician whose new instrument is smashed by a self-satisfied zealot, Al-e Ahmad (1982b: 58–62) had criticised formalistic religion. Here he directly criticises the *ulama*.

This is very like al-Afghani's criticisms 80 years earlier. Hard words are written not because Al-e Ahmad is anti-religious, but because, like al-Afghani, he thinks the *ulama could* act differently. They hold enormous power in their hands, for the mass of the population keep their religious faith. The *ulama* were the only significant force in Iran that had resisted Westoxication. Therefore they are now the key to cultural and political regeneration.

Al-e Ahmad does not carry this argument further in *Gharbzadegi*, but it became the theme of his next book, on intellectuals and politics. This book (not yet translated, so I rely on secondary accounts such as Vahdat 2002) expands the criticism of Westernised intellectuals. It develops the idea that the late nineteenth and twentieth centuries CE had created a chasm between secular modernisers and the defenders of Islamic law, which now had to be bridged. Only when the two groups acted together did real reforms with popular support happen in Iranian history. Al-e Ahmad thus pointed to the kind of alliance that actually materialised a decade later in the run-up to the revolution. But he did not live to see it, dying in his mid-forties in 1969.

To read *Gharbzadegi* as a book with continuing importance for an international audience is to read it against the grain. Al-e Ahmad was obviously writing for his own time and for a local audience who could fill in the gaps for themselves. The whole book is, in a sense, a sketch—a brilliant sketch to be sure.

Its argument is particularly truncated on the question of action. That is hardly surprising for writing produced under censorship. But this does leave obscure a crucial step in Al-e Ahmad's argument: the thesis of a religious basis for resistance to Westoxication. That is exactly the problem addressed by Ali Shariati, who came to prominence as Al-e Ahmad passed from the scene.

In the footsteps of martyrs

Ali Shariati, ten years younger, was several things Al-e Ahmad was not: a systematic thinker, a conscious social scientist, a religious innovator and a preacher. Shariati was a powerful orator and a poet, and at times a humourist. His use of oral teaching gave him a greater freedom from censorship—up to a point, since he was arrested several times by the Shah's police, and finally died in exile. He seemed to many a martyr. His photograph was carried alongside pictures of Ayatollah Khomeini in the mass demonstrations that led to the overthrow of the Shah in 1979, and it is said that his ideas were at that time more widely circulated and more influential than Khomeini's own.

Shariati shared with Al-e Ahmad, and for that matter al-Afghani, a fierce opposition to imperialism, a critique of Western culture and economy, a belief in Islamic renewal, and a conviction that the roots of renewal already existed in Islam. But there was a profound difference in intellectual style as well as political practice. I can read Al-e Ahmad— adjusting for his specific style, audience and context—as a cultural critic of a familiar kind. I cannot read Shariati in that way. His texts require a much greater effort for an outsider to grasp, and I remain less certain of understanding them. I have therefore relied more heavily on Farsi-speaking scholars to test my interpretations and help place his writing in context. (I have particularly relied on the fine work of Abrahamian 1989; Bayat 1990; Behdad 1994; Rahnema 1998; and Ghamari-Tabrizi 2004.)

Reading Shariati demands a particular effort to evaluate the texts. They consist mainly of transcriptions of his lectures, some revised by the author and some not. Some circulated underground in stencilled sheets, others were formally published. A fraction have been translated into English, some by Shariati enthusiasts and some not, and the quality of the translations varies widely. One of the major texts that has been translated, a critique of Marxism, seems to have been doctored by the Shah's secret police to create dissension among the left, and it is unclear how much it represents Shariati's views at all (Bayat 1990). It is certain that Shariati's ideas did evolve over the decades of his political and intellectual activity. I will focus on the period 1968–72, when he developed his most distinctive views.

Ali Shariati's personal story has been often told, and often mythologised; only with the recent biography by Rahnema (1998) did the details become clear. He grew up in the provincial city of Mashhad in northeastern Iran, the son of an activist member of the *ulama* who created a centre for progressive Islamic thought. Ali thus had a substantial background in Shi'ite culture, without being formally trained in the religious schools. As a young man he was involved in the Islamic socialist circles that supported Mossadeq but kept clear of the communist Tudeh party. At one point, the Shariatis, father and son, had the distinction of being arrested together in a sweep by the security police. Ali trained as a teacher, and while working in the local schools also took himself to university, during the rapid expansion of secular higher education that was a key part of the regime's modernisation program. At graduation he won an official scholarship to do a higher degree abroad, and so went to Paris.

Besides getting a secular higher education and practical experience in opposition politics, Ali Shariati also deepened his religious education, in the heterodox Sufi tradition. Over his lifetime, periods of political engagement alternated with periods of mystical religious experience. During these times he withdrew from politics—indeed, from most social life. He also suffered from bouts of depression; he cannot have been easy to live with. But when he did come back to politics, it was with religious convictions grounded in personal experience of the divine—therefore not easily shaken.

In Paris for five years from 1959–1964, Shariati came into contact with the French intellectual left, especially Gurvitch's revision of Marxism and Sartre's activist existentialism, and with the African anticolonial movement, especially Fanon. Recently married, Shariati started a family, and became involved in overseas student politics. Returning to Iran he was arrested at the border, and denied employment as a lecturer. A job at Mashhad University was finally opened to him, and he began to teach Islamic history and sociology. His lectures were increasingly popular; he spoke at campuses around the country, and by 1971 worried the regime so much that SAVAK had him sacked from his university job. But he was already lecturing at a reform Islamic centre in Tehran, the Hosseiniyeh Ershad, which the government did not directly control, and in 1971–72 became their main lecturer. His reinterpretation of Islam became enormously popular with younger intellectuals in the capital, and large crowds came to his lectures. Tapes and transcripts circulated underground, evading censorship. Fierce criticism arose from the orthodox *ulama* at Shariati's politicisation of religion.

At this time, armed resistance had broken out, with both Marxist and Islamic guerrilla groups in action. The regime eventually concluded that

Hosseiniyeh Ershad was a guerrilla-recruiting centre and closed it down. Shariati went underground; some months later he gave himself up in an attempt to save his ageing father, whom the regime had arrested as a hostage. Ali Shariati was imprisoned without trial for sixteen months, and repeatedly interrogated by the security services; he may not have been tortured, but he was held in a notorious prison where many others were. On release he was ill, depressed and jobless. In 1977 he escaped from the country, but part of his family was trapped. The month after leaving Iran, Shariati was dead of a heart attack. Rumours flew that he had been murdered by SAVAK. Probably it was the cumulative effect of prison, fear, heavy smoking and acute stress. Indirectly, perhaps, SAVAK killed him.

I will start to consider Shariati's sociology not with his conceptual statements, but with a text that gives a sense of *why* he was building an intellectual system (Shariati 1986b). One of the major events of the Shi'ite calendar is the anniversary of the death of the Imam Hossein, grandson of the Prophet, killed at Karbala (in what is now Iraq) by the troops of the then Caliph. On this anniversary, Shariati gave a lecture at the Hosseiniyeh Ershad on the subject of 'martyrdom'. Not long before, some members of the resistance, including two of Shariati's students, had been captured and condemned to death by the government.

Shariati's text is a long exposition of the meaning of martyrdom, centring on the story of Hossein. The Third Imam is a central symbolic figure for the Shi'a, and this anniversary is a great occasion for ritual mourning. Shariati gives the familiar story a radical reading. He portrays the first 60 years of Islamic history as the story of a social revolution, set in motion by the Prophet himself on divine principles of social justice—as explained in the epigraph to this chapter.

This revolution was gradually corrupted, as the Muslims became a world power and the Ummayid clan took control and set up a monarchy. In the second generation after the Prophet's death, Hossein was the only remaining representative of the original Islamic movement, but had neither power nor recognition. He openly declared opposition to the ruling regime and faced death, not in resigned submission to God's will but as an activist gesture. The message he sent out to the world did indeed galvanise a tradition of resistance that places a 'mark of cancellation' on all governments. Shariati argues that struggle against oppression and injustice—even to the death, even against overwhelming power—is inherent in Islam.

Even in translation, this is a very moving text, and its impact in the original is not hard to understand. In place of the fossilised official religion that al-Afghani and Al-e Ahmad had denounced in their times, Shariati evokes from the most orthodox sources, Qur'anic texts and familiar traditions, a dynamic Islam committed to justice and social transformation. From a traditional figure of sorrow and defeat, he evokes a model of heroic activism, giving deep religious significance to the sacrifice made by young militants in the present.

Further, Shariati finds in this ancient story certain patterns of social relations that have much wider significance. Shariati does not erect a system of sociology on some axiomatic base of religious 'values'. The relation is much more intimate: he finds sociological principles *in* the religion. While the idea of reading the Qur'an as a sourcebook on social dynamics might disturb conventional Muslim thinkers (and Western social scientists too), it seemed the most natural thing in the world to Shariati. The passage quoted in the epigraph, for instance, evokes a definite theory of class as well as an ethic of social equality and anti-racism.

Shariati's theory of class, though often called Marxist, is only that in the loosest sense; its European analogues would include Bakunin's anarchism and Mosca's elite theory as well. In several texts, including 'Martyrdom', Shariati evokes a structure of slave and master, exploiter and exploited, that has existed throughout history since the transition from hunter-gatherer to agricultural society. In a long chapter of his 1969 book *Islamology* (his most important academic publication, a course of lectures on Islamic studies), he uses the Muslim version of the Cain-and-Abel legend to dramatise the creation of class society:

> Cain is not inherently evil ... What makes Cain evil is an anti-human social system, a class society, a regime of private ownership that cultivates slavery and mastery and turns men into wolves, foxes or sheep. It is a setting where hostility, rivalry, cruelty and venality flourish; humiliation and lordship—the hunger of some and the gluttony of others, greed, opulence and deception: a setting where the philosophy of life is founded on plundering, exploitation, enslavement, consuming and abusing, lying and flattering ... where all things

revolve around egoism and the sacrifice of all things to the ego, a vile, crude and avaricious ego (Shariati 1979: 107).

This was the structure that the Prophet faced, and overcame, in his day; this was the structure that the Ummayids restored, and Hossein challenged. This is also, I think, intended as a description of life in the Shah's Iran.

In the following chapter of *Islamology*, Shariati offers a criticism of Marx's theory of modes of production, suggesting that the underlying structure of class relations remains constant through changes in production relations; and elaborates his own model of the ruling class centred on forms of power. An original single power has evolved through history into a three-part system of domination, with a political, an economic and a religious manifestation—the state, the owners of property and the official clergy. Again he finds a Qur'anic basis for these ideas (1979: 115). The scandalous part of this model is Shariati's identification of the clergy as a full component of the dominant class; this connects with his analysis of religious history, to which I shall return.

Shariati accepts a conventional Marxist view of bourgeois society and industrial capitalism as the contemporary form of class domination in the West, but he adds a critique that is closer to the Western counter-culture of his day. In a lecture given in the oil city of Abadan, he remarks that 'the spirit dominating the new culture and civilization is bourgeois: the spirit of money-making, business, power-seeking, tool-making, consumption and hedonism' (Shariati 1981: 25). He criticises the loss, in modern European history, of religious culture and of fundamental dimensions of human nature: love, idealism, values and existential significance.

Like most Third World radicals of his generation, Shariati sees neocolonialism as an extension of metropolitan capitalism. In none of the texts I have read, or read about, does Shariati discuss the specific mechanisms *producing* imperialism as a system of global power. But he has a lot to say on the mechanisms through which imperialism operates in the colonised world. As with al-Afghani and Al-e Ahmad, the core of his argument concerns cultural domination.

Since the basis of non-capitalist cultures lies in their religion, the colonialists logically attempt to destroy or to neutralise religion. This will destroy the cultural identity or 'selfhood' which provides the alternative to capitalist social relations. Over the top is laid a modernity in which Western styles of thinking, beliefs and even artistic tastes are imposed, and Western-style consumption can be introduced.

In this task the imperialists have important allies within the colonised society. In the long text 'What is to be Done?', based on a Hosseiniyeh Ershad lecture from his most militant period, Shariati (1986a) identifies two groups in particular. The first comprises the Westernising secular intellectuals who, in the name of liberal reform, are playing the colonialists' game of cultural disruption. The second consists of the traditional clerical intellectuals, who have closer touch with the masses but deceive them with a fossilised religion that encourages only passivity. The result is a contradictory situation for youth in particular, which Shariati sketches sympathetically in *Islamology*—brought up in touch with local culture and religion, yet processed through a Western education system reflecting ideas that have no local roots.

An interpretation of Islam is central to this complex of ideas. Al-Afghani's religious views were enigmatic and Al-e Ahmad's only summarily stated, but Shariati's are out in a blaze of sunlight. He did, after all, teach and publish a whole course of study on Islam, wrote a book on his mystical experiences, and lost few opportunities to discuss religious questions. As Ghamari-Tabrizi (2004) puts it, Shariati's is a public religion. I don't claim to understand the full spectrum of his religious thought, but the points closest to social analysis are clear enough.

Of these, the most striking is his view of Islam as a this-worldly, socially engaged religion. To quote one of many such statements, in 'What is to be Done?' Shariati declares:

> Islam is a realistic religion and loves nature, power, beauty, wealth, affluence, progress, and the fulfilment of all human needs . . . Its Prophet is a man of life, politics, power, and even beauty. Its book, more than being concerned with metaphysics and death, speaks about nature, life, world, society and history . . . It invites people to submit themselves to God, and urges revolt against oppression, injustice, ignorance and inequality . . . Its history has been written with rebellion and struggle against distortion of reality, as well as against oppression of the masses (Shariati 1986a: 43–44).

This is a position Shariati may not always have held—in his Sufi-influenced periods of mysticism he seems to have practised a religion of withdrawal—but in the texts of 1968–72 these ideas are put forward powerfully. They are plainly directed against the Islam of ritual and resignation which Shariati saw as the main content of orthodox Shi'ism.

In this critique of backward-looking religion, Shariati was not alone. A similar idea of radical Islam was developed by the early Mojahedin in the years before their armed struggle against the Shah began (Abrahamian 1989). There is even significant overlap with the idea of an activist religion held by Ayatollah Khomeini, though he and the Mojahedin later became bitter enemies (Vahdat 2002: 153ff). Shariati develops the idea in distinctive ways. Shariati insists that Islam is not just socially involved, but is specifically a *revolutionary* religion, committed from the start to social equality, and committed against power structures of all kinds. He finds Qur'anic texts to support this. He deduces it from Islamic theological principles, specifically *tawhid*, the absolute unity of God, which has as its corollary the unity and therefore equality of humankind.

This principle of equality extends to women. Shariati argues, in many places and citing Qur'anic texts, that women and men are created with the same nature, and have the same entitlement to respect. He is sharply critical of the veil, which he regards as a derogatory non-Islamic tradition, and also of the seclusion of women. He defends women's education and political participation—the presence of women at his Hosseiniyeh Ershad lectures was one of the traditionalists' complaints against him. Nevertheless, in a 1971 lecture on the life of Fatima, daughter of the Prophet and mother of Hossein, he holds up an Islamic ideal of womanhood which is still based on women's services to men in the family. He defended women's education because it would make them better mothers; and, like his conservative opponents, he seems to have been afraid of women's independent sexuality (Ferdows 1983). As with so many radical men of his generation around the world, the radicalism became ambiguous in the realm of gender.

In other respects, Shariati sees a tradition of struggle against domination as the core of religious history, at least in the 'Abrahamic' prophetic religions: Islam, Christianity and Judaism. This connects to his model of class: over against the structure of power, there is a mass upon whom power is exercised. It is in the religious doctrine that a positive meaning for this mass is found. In *Islamology*, Shariati (1979: 116ff) discusses the Qur'anic concept of *al-nas*, the people, whom he treats virtually as the presence of God on earth, and the concept of *umma*, the Islamic community, which he describes as a society in motion towards a common goal. I don't think there is complete consistency among his lectures, but there is no doubt of his general intention to valorise the mass of the people as the central concern of both true religion and social reform.

It is the *ulama*'s misuse of their contact with the masses that is the basis of Shariati's anger against them. Like Al-e Ahmad, he sees the creation of official Shi'ism under the Safavid dynasty as a religious disaster; but Shariati further sees the alignment of clergy and state power as a recurrent pattern in religious history, found in early Islam, in mediaeval Christianity and elsewhere. He gives this pattern a sharp theological interpretation: revolutionary religion is monotheistic; orthodox state-aligned religion is polytheistic and pseudo-Islamic.

The struggle against the worship of false gods is a central theme in the Qur'an, as it is in the Bible. Shariati is here defining orthodox Shi'ism as a fraud that substitutes for Islam. No wonder his clerical opponents were upset. Shariati was subject, during his life and after his death, to very hostile attacks from conservative clerics and their supporters. There was also more measured criticism from Islamic scholars, who pointed to Shariati's lack of training in Islamic jurisprudence, his inaccurate use of Islamic history, and theological problems in his positions on reason and prophethood. As his influence spread, some of the Ayatollahs took the serious formal step of issuing advice to the faithful (*fatwas*) not to go to his lectures nor read his books (Rahnema 1998: 206–9, 266–76).

Yet Shariati's argument on polytheism is not so much sectarian as sociological. A class society produces alienation that takes a religious form. In a lecture delivered on the road in Abadan, Shariati argues that a society based on social division generates in the experience of its members a religion with multiple divinities, which in turn provides a justification for the divided social order:

> It is the earth's picture reflected upon the sky, that is, the ruling clergy by justifying the polytheistic-like monotheism justifies the change from racial class monotheism to racial class polytheism . . . When man's intrinsic unity is changed to man's inherent plurality, God's intrinsic unity will also change to inherent plurality which is polytheistic order (Shariati 1981: 21).

In another version of the argument, at the Hosseiniyeh Ershad: 'The people are habituated to a life of infatuation with the idea of the hereafter, while forgetting their own present condition as well as that of their enemies. Islam is turned into a tool by which Muslims are distracted from their fate' (Shariati 1986a: 39–40).

In making such arguments, Shariati is bluntly contesting the *ulama*'s monopoly of religious knowledge. It is not surprising that he sometimes appeals to the model of the protestant reformation in Europe, and to the precedent of Mohammed Abduh, an Egyptian follower of al-Afghani who very influentially promoted a return to popular understanding of the text of the Qur'an itself.

Shariati is also taking a strong position on the question of *ijtihad*, judgment or interpretation. Whether the 'door of *ijtihad*' is now closed—that is, whether the main doctrines of faith and jurisprudence have been settled—is a vexed question among schools of Islamic thought. Shi'ite tradition has generally maintained the door is still open, but the procedure is restricted (Cole 1983). Shariati flings the door open as wide as it can go. In a remarkable document of 1971 that spells out his plan for Hosseineyeh Ershad as an international research centre, Shariati treats *ijtihad* as a principle of freedom of thought and scientific adventurousness, as well as Islamic renewal. On this basis he projects a new intellectual era:

> A new breed of Muslim scientists will take over, who feel Islam in their hearts and minds, who have scientific familiarity with Islamic culture, civilization, and schools of thought, who know scientific research methodology, know the progress of sciences in the contemporary world, and in short, know both cultures (1986a: 114).

Assuming Shariati saw himself as one of the 'new breed', we may infer that to know both cultures means not to know them separately, but to develop analyses that operate organically in both. Shariati sought a unified hermeneutic, and we should read his repeated invocation of Qur'anic texts and Islamic traditions in this light. Here Shariati could draw on a Shi'ite tradition about the infinite richness of the divine message: 'understanding the multi-dimensional language of the Qur'an and discovering the inner meaning of the Qur'an which, like nature, has different aspects when looked upon from different angles' (1986a: 110). He was not just giving religious illustrations of contemporary arguments, but trying to discover common structures in the two domains, and therefore find valid contemporary meanings in ancient texts and stories. Hence, for instance, his celebration of Abu Zarr, a companion of the Prophet, whose biography Shariati had translated as a young man, and whom he continued to find a shining model of Islamic egalitarianism.

We also have to understand Shariati's arguments in terms of the conflicts in which he was engaged. In 1968–72, Shariati was defending Islam against the rising tide of atheistic Marxism among the young; he was defending activist Islam and revolution against the conservatism of the *ulama*; he was defending socialism and equality against capitalist development; he was defending all of these against the Shah's dictatorship; and he was defending the Third World against Western imperialism and cultural control.

Much of his writing, therefore, is embattled, and it is hardly surprising that a good deal of his conceptualisation is sketchy. The urgency in his texts is palpable. He was living in a turbulent society; some of his students were becoming involved in an armed uprising; and he was living on a knife-edge of tolerance from a violent regime—which silenced his voice soon enough. Not only the justification of change, but also the strategy of change, was a central problem in his thought.

Here, according to his biographer, there are two Shariatis—or perhaps one Shariati whose judgment about the historical moment changed dramatically. At the time he wrote *Islamology*, he believed that there was still a vast task of cultural preparation for social change to be done. There had to be a critical appropriation of Western culture while Islam urgently needed renewal from its own resources. This work had to be done in all countries dominated by imperialism. If domination worked by cultural control, then resistance must involve cultural contestation and the rediscovery of local identity or selfhood, contesting the 'futility' that resulted from the imposition of bourgeois culture. It was this dimension he celebrated in the politics of other Third World intellectuals, from Fanon and Kenyatta to Gandhi and Tagore—and in the Islamic world, al-Afghani and Abduh. The ambitious scope of *Islamology*, and the vast agenda of research and popular education that Shariati planned for the Hosseineyeh Ershad, show the scale of this task of recovery and creative development.

But by the time Shariati wrote the latter document, the armed struggle had begun and a political crisis was building. It seems he became persuaded that a revolutionary situation had appeared, and his lectures in 1972 are virtually incitements to insurrection. He was out by only a few years. He began to see the Shi'ite community as a vast social movement heading towards the overthrow of the regime and the creation of a new order, a revolutionary party in its own right.

The task of building a transformative culture was defined by Shariati as the task of creating an 'ideology'. His concept of ideology is very different from the Marxist: it is closer to Mannheim's concept of 'utopia'. It means a dynamic system of ideas capable of changing the world. As Shariati put it in a lecture on ideology: 'Each ideologue, then, is responsible to change the status quo relative to his ideals and convictions' (Shariati 1981: 85). Clearly, a religion can be an ideology, and Shariati saw Islam in this light. He saw his own task as creating an Islamic ideology for the conditions of the present.

This was not his task alone; rather, it was the task of a certain kind of intellectual. One of the most interesting parts of Shariati's thought is his sociology of intellectuals. I have already mentioned how he saw the conservative clergy as an intellectual wing of the ruling class. In the specific conditions of neocolonial Iran, Shariati saw the clerical intellectuals being challenged by an ascendant group of secular, Westernising intellectuals. This group included scientists and technologists, and had a base in the secular education system. Both groups colluded in imperialist domination, as we have seen.

This is not far from Al-e Ahmad's picture in *Gharbzadegi*, but Shariati complicates it with the dimension of ideology. Over against these groups— though drawn in part from both of them—there exist thinkers who perform a function of cultural transformation. These he calls *rushanfekr*, another Farsi term that seems almost impossible to translate: 'enlightened souls' and 'free thinkers' are among the attempts. Shariati describes this group differently in different lectures, but his general intention is clear. He has in mind thinkers who perform a prophetic function, without themselves being prophets. In a 1971 lecture he discusses *rushanfekr* at length, and calls them 'those who have a sense of responsibility with regard to their time and society and wish to do something about it' (1986a: 4).

This is a careful formulation and every phrase matters. First, such people are defined not by their technical knowledge, but by their sense of a large responsibility; they are people who give a lead to others, who think forward and define directions of change for the society. They may come from the intelligentsia but they also come from the masses. Second, they have a responsibility for a specific time and society. Their role is not to produce universal truths, but to understand the concrete situation of their own society, to grasp its inner truth, and to spread that understanding to others. The problems of Europe are not the same as the problems of Asia, and the solutions will therefore differ. (Shariati makes a good joke out of a hypothetical follower of Sartre attempting to spread existentialism among the poor in India.) Third, they wish to do something about it; it is not enough to have the insights. Therefore, enlightened thinkers must have contact with the people, and must be trusted by them, to make the transformation of consciousness possible.

This is not the model of a Leninist vanguard. Shariati is clear about the danger of such people claiming positions of political leadership, and gives dire examples from anti-colonial movements in North Africa. 'Their sole job is to bestow awareness on the masses, that's all . . . to return the alienated society to its real self' (1981: 110). It is specifically a role of cultural leadership, with a strong implication of energy and creativity. How such people are generated, Shariati does not say; at times he almost suggests they are appointed by God—and that may really be what he thought.

The concept of *rushanfekr* thus qualifies Shariati's otherwise very heavy account of cultural domination of the Third World by imperialism, and of Iranian society by imitative bourgeois culture and conservative religion. The term is too free-floating to be given a clear social definition. But it certainly symbolised to Shariati's audiences the vulnerability of systems of domination, the permanent possibility of agency, opposition and change.

With Shariati, more than most intellectuals, the attempt to create a theoretical geometry, a formal deductive system of 'Shariati's social theory', is doomed to failure. (For such an attempt, see Akhavi 1983.) And yet he *was* a systematic thinker in another sense, following a logic grounded in the neocolonial situation, in his reading of Islam, and in the demands of social action.

It seems that his logic had a powerful impact, at least on the younger urban generation in the 1970s. After the revolution, the story was different. In violent struggles over the direction of the revolution, those movements closest to Shariati's radicalism were defeated. An armed confrontation in 1981 was won by the conservative forces around Khomeini. More than ten thousand Mojahedin activists and other dissidents were killed and the opposition leadership fled into exile.

The victorious religious leadership defended private property, closed down gender reform and purged the universities. The long-term result is a highly unequal society in which movements of political reform alternate with the assertion of conservative religious authority. New forms of Westoxication for the affluent filter in, while working-class incomes seem to have fallen (McGeough 2006). Ali Shariati's wife was quoted in the 1980s as saying that if he were alive then, he would be in prison. But if he held to the key ideas of his classic work, he would think that Shi'ite authoritarianism too had its vulnerabilities, its possibilities for popular opposition and change.

7

Dependency, autonomy and culture

An intelligent knowledge of the ideas of others must not be confused with that mental subjection to them from which we are slowly learning to free ourselves.

—Raúl Prebisch (1950)

Latin America was the first large region of the world to be controlled by European invaders. As Aníbal Quijano (2000) observes, 500 years of colonialism and neocolonialism have embedded a powerful orientation to Europe among Latin American intellectuals. The link is emotional as well as conceptual. When the great Chilean poet Gabriela Mistral heard of the outbreak of war in Europe, she wrote movingly of the 'Old Mother' who sheltered us, now burning in war (Mistral 2003: 285).

A great deal of Latin American social science shows the pattern we have seen in Australia and Africa—imported concepts and methods applied to the raw materials of local society. Deference to the theorists of the metropole finds remarkable expression in a recent book called *The Other Mirror: Grand Theory through the Lens of Latin America*. The editors, Miguel Angel Centeno and Fernando López-Alves (2001: 3), anxiously specify that they 'are not proposing a "Latin American" theory to supplant a "European" one'. Rather, they 'offer' Latin America to the English-speaking reader as another case reflecting new variations of mainstream social science themes.

Northern theory written in the South can certainly be impressive. A good example is José Joaquin Brünner's *Globalización cultural y posmodernidad* (1998), a Chilean contribution to the debate on globalisation which can stand with any of the metropolitan texts discussed in Chapter 3. Indeed, it shares most of that literature's assumptions and language, seeing cultural globalisation as composed of postmodernity, postindustrial capitalism, liberal democracy and the communications revolution. Most of the literature that Brünner cites is the modern metropolitan canon—Giddens, Habermas, Baudrillard, Dahrendorf. When he writes about inequalities he does so in the same way that Europeans do, by citing United Nations statistics. Towards the end of the book, he discusses centre–periphery relations and asserts that cultures in the periphery are flourishing. These points would be exceptional in a metropolitan text on globalisation from the 1990s. Yet, overall, Brünner's book is written from the point of view of a generalised Western culture. His main conceptual, political and historical points of reference are European.

But we should remember that Latin America was also the first part of the world to break European colonial control on a continental scale. The search for intellectual independence has led in many directions, from the reconsideration of the local past in Octavio Paz's famous meditation on Mexico, *The Labyrinth of Solitude* (1950), to the dependency school's rethinking of the structure of the world economy.

I cannot map this whole tradition of thought in one chapter. I hope, rather, to follow a significant thread within it—a discussion of autonomy and power which, over a 50-year period, started with economics and ended with culture while continuously questioning political strategies for change.

Centre and periphery

I begin with a document that is little read nowadays, but has a claim to be one of the most important statements in twentieth century social science.

In 1949, a recently created United Nations body, the Economic Commission for Latin America (CEPAL), was working on a general survey of economic affairs in the region. A regional body was exceptional in the UN framework at the time, and CEPAL's creation had been opposed by the United States. To write the introduction to the statistical report, a consultant was brought in, an Argentine economist called Raúl Prebisch.

Prebisch had started as an orthodox economist, working as an academic and simultaneously as a public servant in Buenos Aires. Under the conservative regime of the 1930s, he became general manager of the Central Bank of Argentina, until he was sacked after a coup in 1943. Over the next few years, he developed a critique both of orthodox economics, obsessed with equilibria, and of Keynes, whom he saw as insufficiently realistic. Prebisch was concerned with the dynamism of economic systems, operating through economic cycles, and increasingly with the differences between the economies that were 'cyclical centres' and the economies of the periphery. His awareness of alternative strategies was also shaped by the practical experience of those Latin American countries that had responded to the Depression of the 1930s and the trade crisis in World War II by increasing local manufactures (Love 1986; Dosman 2001; Mallorquín 2006).

With this background, Prebisch wrote a strong text which caused something of a sensation at the CEPAL conference in Havana in 1949. Hoping to damp down any reaction, UN officials separated it from the official survey and published it as an individual essay called *The Economic Development of Latin America and its Principal Problems*. The tactic backfired spectacularly. Prebisch's personal fame rocketed and the essay was hailed as a key statement of strategy for developing countries. By the end of 1950, he had been appointed executive secretary of CEPAL, based in Santiago de Chile. Here he was able to bring together, on a permanent basis, a talented group of economic and social researchers—what we might now call a think-tank for development strategy (Dosman 2001; Toye and Toye 2004).

Prebisch's interest in such a strategy flowed from his conviction that action was becoming urgent, and *laissez-faire* economics could not produce a solution. For the next two decades, CEPAL strongly advocated the strategy of 'import substitution industrialisation', to reduce dependence on imported manufactures and to diversify exports. Whether due to this advocacy or not, the policy was widely adopted in Latin America (and some other parts of the periphery, including Australia) from the 1940s to the 1970s. By and large, the strategy worked, producing higher growth rates and productivity—though it also faced problems of inflation and encountered limits to industrialisation (Kay 1989; Vellinga 2002).

By the early 1960s, the Cold War confrontation between the United States and the Soviet Union had eased a little, and the United Nations became the scene of a new configuration of international politics. Countries of the global South began to see themselves as having common interests which were blocked by the power of the global North—in many cases, their former colonial masters—and began to press for economic concessions. This came to a head at the first UN Conference on Trade and Development (UNCTAD) in 1964, whose agenda was dominated by a group of 77 developing countries, the G77. Raúl Prebisch was appointed secretary-general of the conference, and his opening report, *Towards a New Trade Policy for Development*—written after extensive consultations in Europe, Asia and the Pacific—was a powerful statement of the developing countries' case for trade reform. After reviewing the history of the international economy, it looked at the problems of development, patterns of trade and the role of developed countries. It ended with a plea for mutual aid: 'These pages are therefore an act of faith' (Prebisch 1964: 123)—essentially, faith in international cooperation.

In the aftermath of the conference, with pressure from the G77, UNCTAD was made a permanent agency of the United Nations and

Prebisch was made its secretary-general. He now had a global audience and a means of action, as he tried to make UNCTAD an effective forum for trade negotiations and international development policies that would actually shift resources towards the South.

Not much international cooperation was forthcoming. Prebisch's agenda met heavy resistance from the rich countries led by the United States. The G77 began to break apart, and North–South tensions rose. Prebisch, travelling endlessly, struggled with little success to get international commodity agreements, or an international financial system to support developing countries. He had a major success on one point, getting agreement on tariff preference for the *industrial* exports of developing countries—a key complement to the CEPAL industrial-development strategy (Toye and Toye 2004; Pollock et al. 2006).

In 1968, after seeing UNCTAD through its second general conference, Prebisch retired—he was overloaded and ill, and his marriage was showing the strain—and returned to a Latin American base and to theoretical work. For some years, nevertheless, Prebisch had been the focus of the first coherent, world-level articulation of economic ideas and socioeconomic strategies from the viewpoint of the global South. There are few social scientists who have ever played so pivotal a role.

The Economic Development of Latin America and its Principal Problems is as much an intellectual agenda as a policy prescription. (There is a story that the whole thing was written in three days and three nights.) Industrialisation was already happening in some Latin American countries; Prebisch provided a theoretical justification for it, and showed how the process could be sustained. The crucial point was that 'the raising of the standard of living of the masses'—which remained the ultimate goal in all Prebisch's work—could not be achieved by the growth of agriculture alone. Prebisch gave several reasons for this, the most famous being his thesis that, over the long run, the terms of trade move against exporters of agricultural products in favour of exporters of industrial products. The result is a massive global inequality in the benefits of economic growth: 'In other words, while the centres kept the whole benefit of the technical development of their industries, the peripheral countries transferred to them a share of the fruits of their own technical progress' (Prebisch 1950: 10).

As this passage shows, Prebisch made a fundamental distinction between the economies of the 'centre' and the economies of the 'periphery'. He did not invent these terms, but he certainly popularised them—indeed, made them essential ideas in discussions of world development. Centre and periphery had different economic structures, different economic problems, and therefore needed different economic policies.

This did not mean they could be separated. Prebisch saw the global economy as a necessarily interlinked system. This became a key point that divided 'CEPAL-ism' from the Marxist under-development theorists of the 1960s and 1970s, notably Frank and Amin, who proposed delinking peripheral economies from global capitalism. To Prebisch, the centre was a vital source of trade, capital and technology for the periphery. It was also a source of dire economic problems, including boom and bust cycles (the way the 1930s collapse had been exported to Latin America was much in Prebisch's mind), and of course the terms of trade problem.

One of the most striking features of *Principal Problems* is the attention Prebisch devotes to analysing the centre, especially the US economy and the US dollar, which take up two of the seven chapters. In 1949, Prebisch was writing at the high tide of US economic and military power, before the German *Wirtschaftswunder* or the Japanese boom. He realistically saw the United States—as consumer, producer, innovator, investor and controller of the world's reserve currency—as having enormous importance for Latin American development.

The link could not be broken, but it could be reshaped, if Latin American governments would get down to the job. Prebisch assumed capitalist development, not a Soviet-style economy, but he also assumed a highly interventionist state. The state would work through tariffs, exchange controls, taxes, development planning, anti-cyclical policy, and so on, to prod and cajole the economy towards sustained growth.

For instance, a key problem was the shortage of capital to allow higher technology and rising productivity. The incomes of the Latin American masses were already so low that very little more could be squeezed out of them. The higher income groups, who could be saving, instead spent much of their income on imported consumer goods, trying to sustain the lifestyle that they saw in the developed countries. This irresponsibility of Latin American elites, as Prebisch obviously saw it—he calls their behaviour 'improper' (1950: 37), which given his general style is equivalent to a charge of dancing at midnight with demons—both hindered capital formation and worsened the problem of financing useful imports. A tough-minded developmentalist government could fix that.

At the end of the day, Prebisch's strategies depended on a change of consciousness among intellectuals and policy-makers in the periphery. This led him, in several brief passages of *Principal Problems*, to a striking sociology-of-knowledge view of economics. Classical free-market economics, he argued, reflected the historical experience of the global centre, not the realities of the periphery:

> One of the most conspicuous deficiencies of general economic theory, from the point of view of the periphery, is its false sense of universality. It could hardly be expected that the economists of the great countries, absorbed by serious problems of their own, should devote preferential attention to a study of those of Latin America. The study of Latin America's economic life is primarily the concern of its own economists. Only if this regional economy can be explained rationally and with scientific objectivity, can effective proposals for practical action be achieved (1950: 7).

Not that the economists of the centre could be ignored. With tongue in cheek, Prebisch quotes Keynes in defence of the 'truths of great significance' embedded in classical equilibrium theory (1950: 36). But he also argues forcibly that the assumptions of classical theory do not hold in the periphery—that is the opening argument of the whole text—so new scientific analyses as well as new practical strategies are required. That requires training a new generation of intellectuals, capable of the necessary independence of mind. Within a couple of years of writing, Prebisch had begun to do just that, through CEPAL.

In retrospect, the limits of Prebisch's intellectual world are clear. *Principal Problems* treated economic growth as an absolute good; towards the end of his life, Prebisch (1981a) began to acknowledge environmental problems. The 'economy' that Prebisch theorised was very definitely the men's economy. Women were mentioned just once in *Principal Problems*, as a reserve labour force, and domestic production was not considered part of the economy at all. Of course, these limits were common to almost all economic thought at the time. Within them, the beginning that Prebisch made to an economic theory for the underdeveloped countries proved extraordinarily fruitful—and not just in economics.

Ruling classes and Donald Duck

Prebisch attracted other social sciences besides economics to CEPAL. One of the sociologists who came, in exile from the military dictatorship just established in Brazil, was Fernando Henrique Cardoso. The CEPAL approach was already under challenge from the left, from Marxist or Marxist-inspired analyses which saw the future of Latin America not in capitalist development but in socialism.

During 1965–67, while Prebisch was fighting the good fight at UNCTAD, Cardoso and Enzo Faletto were working on an ambitious historical sociology of development. The resulting book, *Dependency and Development in Latin America*, was first circulated in mimeograph form, then formally published in Buenos Aires in 1971. It is one of the most important statements of the radical alternatives to Prebisch's model, and one of the most remarkable texts of historical sociology in its generation.

Cardoso and Faletto (1979) argued for a more holistic view of development than was found either in CEPAL economics or in Marxist structural dependency theory. In their view, economic change involved a complex interplay between class politics, the formation of the state, and peripheral economies' insertion into a changing global system. From this interplay, multiple outcomes were possible.

Therefore, it was important not just to make a rhetorical acknowledgment of diversity, but to map the actual trajectories of historical change. The core of *Dependency and Development* is a continent-wide narrative of change, starting with the first attempts to create national states after the wars of independence from Spain. The book traces the uncertain emergence of middle classes in the nineteenth century as alternative power centres to the land-owning oligarchies; the process of urbanisation in the twentieth century and the emergence of the 'worker-popular mass' as a political actor; the attempts at import substitution industrialisation; and the 'new dependence' in a restructured world economy run by multinational corporations, making the earlier populist-nationalist politics obsolete.

It is a dramatic story, and it has a dramatic ending. Cardoso and Faletto were among the first to suggest we were entering a new phase of history marked by 'the formation of a supranational market' (1979: 170)—the idea later named 'globalisation'. They diagnosed, accurately enough, the growth of new technocratic elites in Latin America closely associated with the state (military dictatorships being one form of this); and growing social inequality and exclusion.

Within this broad outline, the course of events in different countries could be significantly different. Cardoso and Faletto emphasise the difference between two major patterns of dependence. One is 'enclave' economies, where major industries were capitalised and controlled directly from the global centre—examples being the nitrate and copper industries in Chile, and the banana industry in central America. In such a situation, rule by a landowning oligarchy could survive, and the dynamic of development was limited.

The second is the pattern of dependent development shown by Argentina and Brazil, where export industries developed through a national bourgeoisie. This group achieved control of the state and acquired a certain capacity to finance industrialisation and integrate the popular masses into the political order. But it did not contest the dominance of the metropole. Here Cardoso and Faletto reach one of their most important theoretical conclusions: 'development' is not the opposite of 'dependence'. Development can occur in a way that maintains dependence; new forms of dependence emerge historically and this process is still going on.

In the 1950s and 1960s, social scientists in the metropole responded to the postcolonial situation by producing theories of modernisation and development, which assumed that the poorer parts of the world would progress by following the path trodden by Europe and North America. The best known—though it was little more than a schematic popularisation— was W.W. Rostow's *The Stages of Economic Growth* (1960), which became a kind of Cold War manifesto for the US political elite. Cardoso and Faletto were understandably scornful of 'theoretical schemes' based on the history of the present-day developed countries (1979: 172). Indeed, they saw a participatory socialism as the periphery's real alternative to dependency, though they acknowledged the political difficulty of following 'new paths in society' (1979: 213).

Modernisation theory was pointless because the course of development in centre and periphery had diverged ever since industrial economies began to form in Europe—at much the same time as Latin America achieved political independence. British wealth and power were vital in shaping nineteenth century Latin American development patterns:

> The very existence of an economic 'periphery' cannot be understood without reference to the economic drive of advanced capitalist economies, which were responsible for the formation of a capitalist periphery and for the integration of traditional noncapitalist economies into the world market (Cardoso and Faletto 1979: xvii).

Neither Britain then, nor the United States now, could control the whole periphery directly. External power had to act through local social forces. The core of Cardoso and Faletto's dialectical sociology is the interplay between global structures and local political dynamics—the formation of the local state and the struggles to control and reshape it.

The 'fundamental historical actors' that Cardoso and Faletto see in this political drama are 'classes and groups defined within specific forms of production' (1979: 201). Here their sociology becomes decidedly schematic. Social classes are defined simply as economic categories. The groups so defined mysteriously acquire an awareness of common interests and a capacity for political action. Cardoso and Faletto give no attention to the problem of class formation, do not explore problems of hegemony, and do not consider the intersections of class with other structures. Like others of their generation, they cannot see beyond the men's economy.

Their strength, therefore, is not in a subtle analysis of the structure of Latin American society. It is rather in their analyses of the historically changing relationships between systems of domination within Latin America and the structures of the international economy. In this regard, *Dependency and Development* has implications far beyond Latin America and is still, I think, an intellectually important text. It offers a carefully thought out method for the analysis of transnational social processes that is far more sophisticated than most of the metropolitan literature on 'globalisation' that appeared 25 years later.

In the same year, 1971, another innovative reading of dependence was published across the mountains in Chile. The authors were Ariel Dorfman, a poet, novelist and literary critic, and Armand Mattelart, a media sociologist originally from Belgium. In writing it, as Dorfman recalls in his autobiography *Heading South, Looking North* (1998), they were caught up in the astonishing ferment of Salvador Allende's first year in office. The peaceful Chilean road to socialism, as the Unidad Popular regime saw it, involved not only economic reform but also a huge effort at popular education, including the publication of millions of books and magazines, and the production of new radio programs. Part of this effort was directed at Chile's youth. It was natural for writers involved in this effort to be interested in the popular literature for children that already existed.

I remember that *How to Read Donald Duck*, when it began to circulate in the English-speaking world in the mid-1970s, caused a certain stir. Disney tried to have it seized when copies arrived in the United States. Even on the left there was some angst. These people from Chile were important role models; they had elected a socialist president and they had been so radical that they provoked a military coup. Why were such people playing around with children's comic books? For Heaven's sake, there are some things that proper revolutionaries just don't do!

But they did, and the result is a fascinating document of radical politics as well as a pioneering work in cultural studies (as the field was beginning to be called in the metropole). *How to Read Donald Duck* is at one level an empirical study of mass media content, based on a close reading of about 100 issues of Disney's comic books. Far from innocent childhood fantasy, Dorfman and Mattelart (1975) show that the stories construct a world of a definite social, cultural and political character.

This is a world with a fixed social hierarchy, though a somewhat peculiar one. There are no parents—rather, uncles, aunts, nieces and nephews exist in abundance. So both sexual reproduction and family authority are concealed, except for a stereotyped sexualisation of women, as seen in Daisy Duck's high heels. Wealth is present—indeed, comically exaggerated in the form of Scrooge McDuck's money bins—but is pictured as treasure waiting to be found, not the product of anyone's labour. 'In the world of Disney, no one has to work in order to produce' (1975: 64). Urban working-class people, when present at all, are mainly criminals (the Beagle Boys).

But the Third World is certainly present. By Dorfman and Mattelart's count, as many as half the stories have the heroes setting off from Duckburg to adventures in exotic, primitive locations such as Aztecland, Inca-Blinca or Unsteadystan. The inhabitants turn out to be naive or noble savages, often being ripped off by evil-doers from whom the ducks save them. They are utterly unable to change their circumstances by their own efforts.

So these mass-circulation entertainments construct for children images of a hierarchical, unchanging local and global order. Dorfman and Mattelart acknowledge that the Disney stories allow many minor inversions. For instance, when the duck nephews are in conflict with Donald, it is usually the children who are wise, careful and far-sighted, and the adult who is stupid. In this respect, the Disney comics are more sophisticated than, say, Superman comics. At the end of each story, however, the world returns to its usual order. Gyro Gearloose never gets rich, Scrooge never gets poor, and if the noble savages do well, it is because some developer has installed a tourist hotel that allows them to preserve their exotic ways.

Dorfman and Mattelart theorise the effect by saying that the Disney comics invert the real relation between material base and cultural superstructure. They create a bourgeois fantasy world—not propaganda for the American Way of Life so much as propaganda for an American Dream of Life:

> It is the manner in which the U.S. dreams and redeems itself, and then imposes that dream upon others for its own salvation, which poses the danger for the dependent countries. It forces us Latin Americans to see ourselves as they see us . . . Reading Disney is like having one's own exploited condition rammed with honey down one's throat (1975: 95–96).

Donald Duck thus contributes to under-development, by helping block the formation of a consciousness of the realities of exploitation, and a consciousness of the possibility of change—'the notion that time *produces* something is naturally eliminated' (1975: 86).

There is more to Dorfman and Mattelart's analysis, as they comment on other themes and on all the leading characters in Disney's cast list. But this is their main argument. It shows how, even with the unpromising tools provided by conventional Marxism, Latin American radicals began to construct an account of the internal mechanisms of metropolitan cultural domination. The problem had many similarities to the 'Westoxication' that Al-e Ahmad had addressed a few years before (see Chapter 6).

Unlike Al-e Ahmad, Dorfman and Mattelart dodged the issue of what to do about it. In a defensive passage at the end of their book, they write that no one is able to propose an individual solution to these problems, and what happens after Disney 'will be decided by the social practice of the peoples seeking emancipation' (1975: 99). And probably they thought that was really happening in the Unidad Popular movement. But when *How to Read Donald Duck* was published, Unidad Popular had just two years to live.

The Day after the Death of a Revolution

In September 1973 the generals struck, the Moneda palace was bombed, Allende died, and both government and movement were destroyed. Ariel Dorfman was on the military's death list, and only just escaped from the country. Dorfman later published a moving book of poems about terror and exile. In one of them (Dorfman 1988: 61) he recalls how the movement in Chile had failed to see what was coming towards it. Unfortunately for copyright reasons I cannot quote the poem here. But I can reflect on the author's point that progressives had simply failed to recognise the consequences of military culture, and their own vulnerability to violence. Chile had, after all, an established constitutional regime, and electoral support for Unidad Popular seemed to be growing. But opposition was hardening too, and finding outside support.

The Chilean military regime was not the first—not even the most violent—of the Latin American authoritarian regimes, but it was brutal enough. In its first few years, which the historian Tomás Moulian (2002) calls 'the phase of the terrorist dictatorship', left-wing militants and intellectuals were hunted down. Many of them were tortured—a specialised prison was set up for the purpose at Villa Grimaldi on Santiago's eastern fringe (later bulldozed to hide the evidence, now a memorial park)—and hundreds were killed.

The situation was worse in the Argentine dictatorship, where in the dirty war against the regime's opponents the 'disappeared' (presumably murdered) numbered above ten thousand. The dictatorship in Brazil held power for more than two decades and deported, imprisoned, tortured or murdered thousands. The dictatorship in Uruguay held democracy at bay for more than a decade. Even in Mexico, under the civilian regime of the Institutional Revolutionary Party, about 300 of the younger intelligentsia were shot dead in 1968, at Tlatelolco Square.

I recall these details not to be morbid, but to emphasise the high stakes in Latin American debates about autonomy and dependence; and also to begin to explain the intellectual change that followed. The state terrorism that decapitated Unidad Popular and dispersed its supporters also destroyed its model of economic and cultural autonomy. The Brazilian dictatorship managed to achieve high growth rates without redistribution, without democracy and without de-linking from the metropole, violating the predictions of both CEPAL and the dependency school. As Cristóbal Kay (1989) observes in his history of under-development and dependency theories, all of these schools of thought were losing political credibility in the 1970s—ironically, just before a vast debt crisis engulfed the continent and proved the need for an analysis of Latin America's vulnerability.

The ground was thus cleared for a new model of development, which Chile under General Pinochet was the first country in the world to adopt. Neoliberalism, the political and social agenda built around free-market economics that came to dominate Latin America in the 1980s and 1990s, is in no sense Southern theory. It is, on the contrary, a classic product of the 'false sense of universality' in economics that Prebisch had criticised in *Principal Problems*. The neoliberals who took control of Chile's economy under Pinochet made this point themselves, by inviting to the 1975 conference that shaped national policy two luminaries of the University of Chicago Economics School—Arnold Harberger and Milton Friedman—who obliged them by arguing for shock treatment, not gradual change (Silva 1996). The Chilean people made the point too, by nicknaming the group of economists, bureaucrats and new-rich entrepreneurs (often the same people) who implemented this policy 'the Chicago Boys'.

The impact of neoliberalism in Latin America is now very well documented (for excellent English-language accounts, see Silva 1996; Nochteff and Abeles 2000; Huber and Solt 2004), and I will not recite the story here. What I would emphasise is that neoliberalism arrived in an atmosphere of crisis, partly internal—as represented by the violence of the dictatorships themselves—and partly external, the debt crisis of the 1980s. An international liquidity squeeze, new far-right governments in the United States and Britain led by Reagan and Thatcher who choked off the North–South dialogue in global forums, and the capture of the International Monetary Fund by neoliberals supported by these governments, forced neoliberal policies on to economies across the continent.

Neoliberalism not only meant selling off the public enterprises that had been built up by the labour of previous generations, dismantling the welfare state and redistributing income towards the rich. It also represented a crisis of impotence for popular politics. The effect of the economic shock treatment, as Nochteff and Abeles (2000: 131–2) describe it for Argentina, was to disrupt institutions, erode popular trust, weaken checks and balances, and create a 'private state' in which the only effective powers were big corporations and the political elite.

The advent of neoliberalism thus had much wider effects than merely economic. As a number of thoughtful commentators have observed, this whole course of events also represented a crisis for social science in Latin America. The old object of knowledge, national society and economy, is no longer a viable unit, and the former connection between social-scientific knowledge and projects of social change has been broken (Garretón 2000). Latin American critical thought came to a standstill as neoliberalism introduced new problems and discussed them in a new language, and connection between critical thought and social movements was lost (Sader 2002).

That is the situation addressed by the Chilean sociologist Martín Hopenhayn in a series of essays collected in *No Apocalypse, No Integration*. His opening chapter, 'The Day After the Death of a Revolution', evokes the mood of loss and doubt:

> What the societies of Latin America most share today are social deterioration, formal democracy, privatizing euphoria and shock politics . . . The following pages might seem skeptical. They don't indicate new avenues for change nor do they revitalize old impulses for radical transformation. Rather, they trace the crisis and the consequences following the shattered dream of integration (Hopenhayn 2001: 1–2).

The central concern of *No Apocalypse* is the end of the grand socialist and planned-development projects that had given a focus to both politics and social science over the previous half-century. The end of these projects requires a search for new ways of thinking and new forms of knowledge. This involves, before anything else, a great scaling-down of ambition. 'At present, the field of the social sciences has slipped into greater academic and political humility' (2001: 121)—so much so that the previous heroic figure of the social scientist as reformer might well appear to be a mistake of history.

Hopenhayn's essay 'Is the Social Thinkable Without Metanarratives?' (2001: 119–41) brings together the implications for Southern theory. The social sciences in Latin America are now suffering both a crisis of intelligibility and a crisis of organicity. The three leading paradigms of the previous generation were CEPAL-style development theory, dependency theory and Marxism (represented in this chapter by the three main texts discussed above). Social change itself has produced complexities that these frameworks cannot comprehend. At the same time, the assumption of an organic connection between the production of knowledge and intervention in social reality via popular reform movements has been smashed. The planning state, the social mechanism on which all three paradigms in fact depended, has lost its credibility.

Hopenhayn sees external events—the economic crisis at the beginning of the 1980s and the collapse of Soviet communism at the end—as contributing to this disillusion, but also thinks the social sciences had made themselves vulnerable. The form they took in Latin America repre-sented an extreme expression of European Enlightenment optimism about the power of reason, and the capacity of intellectuals to put themselves on the side of history and progress. He reviews the familiar critiques of such doctrines of rationality—postmodern, Frankfurt School and neoliberal—to suggest there is no way back to the once-dominant models of knowledge and intellectual practice.

At this point in his argument, Hopenhayn is using pure metropolitan theory to hammer intellectuals of the periphery—an all too familiar pattern in the controversies about development economics! In another essay, Hopenhayn directly addresses the local relevance of European postmodern thought, especially Lyotard and Baudrillard. He suggests their ideas have important parallels with the new condition of Latin America. So the postmodern themes of complexity, indeterminacy and the local are helpful in understanding contemporary society, and in justifying social science's new interest in everyday life rather than large structures.

Yet Hopenhayn wants to borrow only selectively from Northern theorists. In particular, he emphasises that moving towards a postmodern sensibility should not mean falling into a cool or cynical acceptance of poverty, social exclusion or alienation. He is very clear about the growth of social inequality in Latin America under neoliberalism, producing 'a status quo where the (internationally) integrated are starkly juxtaposed with the (nationally) excluded' (2001: 4).

While criticising instrumental reason, Hopenhayn defends utopian reason. He ends the book with a nice essay in praise of utopian thought, emphasising the need for open rather than millennialist utopias. In earlier research, Hopenhayn and his colleagues had explored small-scale development projects. In *No Apocalypse*, he praises the 'alternative development' movement, which emphasises grassroots action, diversity and social involvement rather than party politics or the sovereign market. This, Hopenhayn seems to think, is the most promising venue for a new relationship between practice and theory.

But there is also another argument in the book, curious and suggestive. The planning state may have lost all legitimacy, and the social science paradigms associated with it have gone into the dustbin of history. But the reasons why those approaches were created have not gone away. At the end of his chapter on postmodernism and neoliberalism, Hopenhayn recalls Prebisch. Many of Prebisch's analyses and predictions have proved correct in the new neoliberal world. Moreover, 'we do not possess another interpretive focus capable of giving a specific sense of totality and coherence to the heterogeneity characteristic of the processes of modernization in Latin America' (2001: 90).

Others too have suggested that, since neoliberal ideas have flourished for years with little debate, it is time for a new structuralism (Kay 1998). In fact, Prebisch had been one of the first to attempt this, as unstoppable in age as he had been in youth. After his return to Latin America and to CEPAL, now in his seventies, Prebisch wrote a series of papers, synthesised in *Capitalismo periférico* (1981b), reflecting on the lessons of the 30 years since *Principal Problems*. In this book he reinforced the arguments about structural difference between centre and periphery, and added a political sociology of dependent economies to account for the limited success of industrialisation strategies, and the turn to violence under the dictatorships. He made a sharp critique of the 'fake liberalism' that offered prosperity to the rich while consolidating social injustice; and expressed his continued belief that economic autonomy for the periphery is possible, whatever new strategies might be required to achieve it.

New dimensions of struggle

One reason for the sense of greater social complexity noted by Garretón and Hopenhayn is the multiplication of identities and the arrival of new social actors. Perhaps the most important—certainly the most difficult to fit into any of the familiar social science paradigms—is the Latin American women's movement.

All the theorists so far mentioned in this chapter have been men, and not one of them seems to have thought that men's power in society, or dominance of discourses about society, was a problem. Of course, Latin America is not unique in this. Men dominate most of the metropolitan and peripheral discourses discussed in the earlier chapters of this book.

As Sonia Montecino (2001) argues in an essay on social diversity in Chile, in a society accustomed to thinking in terms of unity it is a difficult task to bring out difference. The feminine, the indigenous, the local can be asserted in acts of resistance and reappropriation. But to do so runs against dominant modes of thought. This applies on the left as well as on the right. Women in Latin America, as in other parts of the world, have often faced strong resistance from the men running trade unions, socialist parties and anti-globalisation campaigns (for Central America, see Mendez 2002; for Australia and Canada, see Franzway 1999).

It takes a struggle to get men to recognise injustice in their own habitual practices, or in gender arrangements from which they benefit: wife-beating, sexual harassment in the workplace, unequal pay and the double shift. It takes another struggle for significant numbers of men to recognise women—whom they have long seen as a domestic support system for a masculine public world—as legitimate leaders, representatives and organisational power-holders. In 2006 a breakthrough occurred, and the first woman from a progressive coalition, Michelle Bachelet of Chile, was elected head of government.

Montecino analyses the shift in feminine identities by assuming that historical changes occur both in the structure of gender relations and in subjectivities. Chilean culture was traditionally marked by an identification of womanhood with motherhood. Hence the cult of the suffering Mother in religion, and the construction of images of masculinity in relation to a maternal figure—the absent father, or the mother's son. This is a deeply entrenched cultural pattern, and Montecino cites recent survey evidence showing that Chilean women are still mostly identified with their role as mothers and Chilean men with their role as workers. She observes that an identification with the maternal role can lead to real difficulties about sexuality as women age.

Yet economic change, specifically the incorporation of women into the paid workforce, has been disrupting this identity. As women emerged into the public realm, issues about their subordination to men also emerged. Paid work became a new basis for women's identity, and a permanent tension with the ideology of maternity was set up. Given the pattern of economic change, this shift occurred earlier for working-class women than for middle-class women. Montecino finds survey evidence showing that there is now widespread acceptance of women working outside the home. Support is strongest among women themselves, among young people, in the cities, on the left, and in the working class. In relation to gender politics, as well as class, the state and economic development, Chile seems to be 'un país dividido', a divided land (Huneeus 2003).

Montecino is clear that changes in identity need not simplify identity. We now see 'identities under tension'. She cites a study of middle-class women's orientation to paid work that distinguishes three strategies: maintenance of the commitment to maternalism; a complementary relation between paid work and maternity; and work as the primary life focus. Ironically, it is middle- and upper-class women's economic power that allows them to pass a good deal of housework and child care over to women domestic employees.

Even more interesting is Montecino's suggestion that a dynamic familiar in Latin American history, the formation of identities in social struggle, clearly applies to women. Collective identities for women are constructed in women's movements, and Latin American women's movements are very diverse—some associated with unions or parties and some autonomous, some indigenous, and so on. Feminist movements, from the early struggles for the vote, have emphasised equality between women and men, as well as gender difference. Survival movements have assumed rather than attacked the traditional gender division of labour. Mothers' movements, such as the famous demonstrations for the 'disappeared' in Argentina, have blended maternalist ideology with calls for human rights. Thus feminist movements have struggled for major change in women's identity, and the power to move into masculine spheres, while mothers' movements have not.

Women's activism was a prominent part of the resistance to dictatorship, and this achievement placed feminist demands on the agendas of progressive political parties. But women's activism also created new grounds on which right-wing parties could campaign against immorality and social breakdown, their usual interpretation of change in women's lives (in Latin America as in Iran).

The complex dialectic of gender involves men as well as women. Latin American feminism has been exceptionally active in promoting research and debate about men, as Matthew Gutmann and Mara Viveros Vigoya (2005) note in a recent survey of this field. Indeed, a research group in Chile led by José Olavarría has, since the mid-1990s, conducted the most sustained program of research and research dialogue on men, male youth and masculinities anywhere in the world (e.g. Olavarría and Moletto 2002). This research abundantly shows the diversity of men's situations and the changing consciousness of younger men—for instance, the growth of interest in engaged fatherhood—as well as the continued presence of conservative models of dominant masculinity.

Mapping multiple identities raises a difficult problem for movements for social change, since difference seems to imply difficulty in mobilising for action. Latin American feminism has been inventive in finding new ways to put pressure on the state. For instance, a women's research group developed a benchmarking technique that took existing government gender-equity commitments, both local and international, as its point of departure and set up systematic measures of progress towards these actually existing goals (Valdés 2001). Montecino (2001) notes that, though street politics has declined, feminism has spread into many other social spaces and engaged in new forms of politics, especially cultural and symbolic politics.

The emergence of new arenas, new social movements and new cultural politics is an important theme in recent Latin American social science (e.g. Garretón 2000; Sader 2002; Gómez 2004). It is also a central theme in the work of an Argentinian/Mexican anthropologist who is currently one of the best-known social scientists in Latin America. Néstor García Canclini has conducted, over three decades, extensive research on social processes ranging from village ceremonies and craft production to urban mass media, museums, art marketing and political imagery. The scope of his research is matched by the quality of his writing, which combines clear exposition of concepts, vivid descriptive detail, imagination, humour, anger and irony. In writing *Hybrid Cultures*, he experimented with the form of the academic treatise and the essay. For pithiness, I cannot recall any comment on the Twin Towers attack of 9/11 that compares with his observation that this represented the clash of '*desperados contra instalados*' [the desperate vs the established] (García Canclini 2002: 16).

García Canclini practises anthropology, but he also questions it. His 1982 book, *Popular Cultures in Capitalism*,[3] a masterpiece of transitional ethnography, began with the crisis of ethnographic and political ideas of culture. In Mexico, the celebration of popular culture has been a theme of nationalist rhetoric since the revolution in the early twentieth century. But, as García Canclini argued, there is no such thing as traditional culture any more.

He demonstrated this by a painstaking investigation of two major sites of 'traditional' activity in rural communities in Michoacán: craft production such as pottery and doll-making, and local fiestas. Both of these practices, he showed, have been profoundly changed by Michoacán's insertion into the national and international capitalist economy. Craft production, for instance, is no longer an activity producing objects needed in a local agricultural way of life. It is mainly a matter of production for markets that have a niche for handmade goods. Crafts have a definite role in Mexican capitalism: absorbing rural unemployment, supplying the tourist industry, and supporting political interpretations of national identity. Similarly, fiestas have been reorganised as tourist events, or as venues combining village products with urban goods and services.

García Canclini shows that these changes produce new forms of subordinate inclusion of villagers into the capitalist system. This argument recalls Cardoso and Faletto's point about the constant generation of new forms of dependence. More specifically, García Canclini (1982: 70) argues that capitalism relates to indigenous cultures by a constant process of 'decontextualisation and restructuring of meaning'. Indigenous culture is

---

3   The very straightforward title, *Culturas populares en el capitalismo*, is weirdly changed in the University of Texas Press translation into *Transforming Modernity*—or perhaps that's not so weird, as it avoids naming 'capitalism'.

not obliterated but fragmented, its elements taken out of their native space and recombined in new contexts—markets, tourist shops, buyers' homes, museums.

In setting up this argument, García Canclini gives a bravura display of Northern theory from Kroeber to Bourdieu. One sentence alone need be quoted: 'From Freud to Deleuze, from Nietzsche to Foucault, we have been told that oppression cannot exist in the anonymity of collective structures alone . . .' (2002: 16). The early part of *Popular Cultures* falls into that familiar genre of metropolitan theory illustrated by data from the periphery. But, as the argument unfolds, it moves beyond that terrain. It stays in touch with the history of colonisation. It sees the fracturing of local agricultural society not as an abstract stage of modernisation but as a product of domination and incorporation. It treats contemporary capitalism as a dynamic imperial system, with a powerful homogenising logic but also with places for the subordinate and different. And it also suggests—though it does not develop—a politics of resistance for indigenous culture.

In *Hybrid Cultures*, and in his best-known book *Consumers and Citizens* (1995), García Canclini moves from the village to the city and to issues about postmodernity, under-development and globalisation. The premise of the argument now is the collapse, across Latin America, of the previous generations' nationalist, populist, state-centred development project and the cultural agendas that went with it. Written towards the end of the 'lost decade' of the 1980s, *Hybrid Cultures* dissects the false assumptions that had been built into that tremendous project.

Conventional ideas of modernity, nationhood, art and traditional culture were all constructed through gestures and institutions that set up oppositions—for instance, fine art versus popular crafts, modern versus pre-modern, nation versus locality and one nation versus another. But social reality itself subverts these oppositions—through migration across borders, the creation of complex border realms, mass media reorganisations of culture, and so on. Much of this complexity García Canclini sums up in the notion of 'hybridity', which he sees as deeply rooted in Latin America's history. Hybridity has always complicated the homogenising drive of development and the fears about peripheral backwardness.

In *Consumers and Citizens*, García Canclini builds more extensively on his research in Mexico City. The stupendous expansion of this city, which grew ten times over between 1940 and 1990, has produced a social entity that is not a social unit, that has little coherence or intelligibility, and which the conventional social sciences struggle to grasp. So do its citizens. Different classes, communities and generations within the city conduct their lives with little integration, passing through the urban space on different trajectories. García Canclini jokes that the best way to understand the 'city without a map' might be to use the epistemological model of a video clip: 'an effervescent montage of discontinuous images' (2001: 84). Events intended to unify, such as the Festival of Mexico City, have little effect. In this setting, the postmodern question about who speaks in anthropological studies is answered: 'What speaks, more than a social agent, is a difference, a fissure . . .' (García Canclini 2001: 63).

There is no shared culture, but there are shared experiences—including mass poverty and barely controlled urban violence. European models of urbanism, coming from a more orderly and prosperous background, are largely irrelevant to the bitter realities of Latin America's mega-cities. Deep fissures appear, between elites oriented to the international economy and culture, and local communities of survival. The nearest thing to a common culture is provided by commercial television, a medium for entertainment and marketing which has a very wide reach among the urban poor.

Recognising the huge contemporary importance of television, film and the new electronic media does not lead García Canclini back to Dorfman and Mattelart's model of imperialist domination. For one thing, he is aware of the media research that shows the active role of the audience and the selective uptake of media content. Yet García Canclini is quite aware of the enormous market power of US media corporations. One of the nicest things in *Consumers and Citizens* is its discussion of how Hollywood creates a kind of world folklore. In the essay on 'Latin America and Europe as Suburbs of Hollywood', García Canclini shows how neoliberal economic policies of global market integration impinge on cultural autonomy and diversity on a world scale, while the privatisation agenda destroys cultural agencies at the national level.

In a short book written at the start of the new decade, *Latinoamericanos buscando lugar en este siglo* (Latin Americans Seeking a Place in This Century), García Canclini returns to this point in a more optimistic vein. National identities are certainly under heavy pressure from neoliberal globalisation. An important case is the takeover of the Latin American publishing industry by international capital, especially from Spain. Some authors, even when published, are not distributed in their home countries because profits are not guaranteed there. 'The authoritarianism of the market' therefore has damaging effects (García Canclini 2002: 53).

But there are important possibilities for *regional* action to defend cultural independence and diversity. In an argument reminiscent of CEPAL 50 years earlier, García Canclini observes that regional markets (e.g. for popular music) are larger than national ones. He proposes that cultural production should be treated as an important industry worthy of government planning and support. A democratic use of new media is possible, allowing cultural production and distribution by the social groups who are currently marginalised or excluded.

García Canclini persistently refuses the dichotomy of elite and subaltern which he sees as the weakness of Latin American marxist analyses of culture: 'A broader and more detailed consideration of the daily interactions of subaltern majorities reveals that Latin American countries are hybrid societies where different forms of disputing and negotiating the meaning of modernity are in constant contention' (García Canclini 2001: 140). The problem is that, during the 1980s and 1990s, the space for political negotiation was closed down. Neoliberal politics operates as a spectacle, with the major decisions taken in forums hidden away from popular participation. Old models of hierarchical domination no longer apply, but the system is very far from democratic.

Since the system urgently does need change, this pushes García Canclini to think about new forms of political action that make sense in the new conditions. At the start of *Consumers and Citizens*, he suggests that 'consumption is good for thinking'. In the final chapter, 'How Civil Society Speaks Today', he argues for a reconstituted public sphere, in which citizenship is based on people's activity as consumers:

> Civil societies appear less and less as national communities, understood on the basis of territorial, linguistic and political unity. They behave, rather, as *interpretive communities of consumers*, that is, ensembles of people who share tastes and interpretive pacts in relation to certain commodities (e.g., gastronomy, sports, music) that provide the basis for shared identities (García Canclini 2001: 159).

The kind of political practice to which this might lead remains unclear, but García Canclini certainly sees multiculturalism as a key to contemporary democracy.

García Canclini's work is increasingly known in the metropole. There he tends to be seen as a regional cultural studies specialist or an idiosyncratic postmodernist. (*Vide* the bizarre and condescending Introduction to *Consumers and Citizens* by its North American translator.) García Canclini has certainly made use of metropolitan postmodern thought, as well as metropolitan Marxism, anthropology, media research and other literatures. (One could wish he had learnt more from feminism.) He was, like Hountondji and Shariati, a graduate student in Paris. And he too has developed a nuanced use of metropolitan theory. Especially in his later work, García Canclini refuses to take any metropolitan theory as a framework, but takes many of them as fruitful sources of ideas.

This does not result in gross eclecticism, because there are two strong organising principles at work in his writing: the social-scientific encounter with Latin American realities; and the search for forms of progressive politics relevant to the situation Latin Americans are actually in. He remarks at the end of *Consumers and Citizens*: 'Postmodern thought provoked us during the 1970s and 1980s to free ourselves from the illusions of metanarratives that augured totalizing or totalitarian emancipations. Perhaps it is time to emancipate ourselves from this disenchantment' (García Canclini 2001: 161). There is a place, he too suggests, for utopias.

8

Power, violence and the pain of colonialism

The aim is not to adjust, alter or refurbish Indian experiences to fit the existing psychological or social theories . . . The aim is to make sense of some of the relevant categories of contemporary knowledge in Indian terms and put them in a competing theory of universalism.

—Ashis Nandy (1983)

India was the 'jewel in the crown', the core of the second British empire. India's independence movement was the inspiration for anti-colonial movements around the world, and its victory changed the shape of world politics. But 1947 also split India, and not just between Hindu and Muslim. Post-independence generations have faced a hard reckoning with the legacy of colonialism, with new forms of dependence, and with new patterns of division, power and conflict. This reckoning occurs across the social sciences—which themselves have complex relations with India's long intellectual traditions and with metropolitan hegemony. In this chapter, I consider this field of forces at work in texts of historiography, gender analysis, anthropology and cultural psychology. These texts not only document a vivid and sometimes tragic mass experience, but also imply new ways of thinking about social science and its future.

Ranajit Guha's insurgency

In 1982, at a time when the new right was consolidating power in Britain and the United States, the clerical regime in Iran had almost destroyed the opposition, neoliberals were taking over the IMF and the gigantic debt crisis of Latin America was beginning, a group of radical historians from India launched a new book series, which evolved into a periodical. Called *Subaltern Studies*, with acknowledgment to Gramsci, it was subtitled *Writings on South Asian History and Society*.

The preface to the first issue, signed by the founding editor Ranajit Guha, declared an aim 'to promote a systematic and informed discussion of subaltern themes in the field of South Asian studies', with contributions from scholars across the humanities and social sciences. A broad field was to be surveyed, but not blandly. This was an intellectual insurgency, 'to rectify the elitist bias characteristic of much research and academic work in this particular area'.

In the brief following essay, 'On some Aspects of the Historiography of Colonial India', Guha (1982) tears apart the main traditions of writing about Indian history, from the British colonisers to the post-independence nationalists. He argues that the traditional focus on the colonial state and the struggles around it crucially leaves out *the politics of the people* (his italics). Alongside the elite actors, the Jinnahs and Nehrus, there is another domain, an *autonomous* domain, of popular life, consciousness and politics. This has its own idioms and values, expressed in events such as peasant uprisings. To document this autonomous domain, to bring to light the logic, limits and impact of this popular politics, is the task of *Subaltern Studies*.

Two decades later, *Subaltern Studies* was famous—not among Indian peasants, but in North American universities. Praised by Edward Said and Gayatri Chakravorty Spivak (Guha and Spivak 1988), *Subaltern Studies* came to be seen as exemplary of postcolonial studies. The series, and the network around it, became a vehicle for postmodern discussions of identity, fragmentation and difference. Something happened that went beyond the normal case of 'academic tourism', as Hountondji called it (see Chapter 5), where Southern intellectuals travel to the metropole and humbly learn its concepts and techniques. *Subaltern Studies* and its contributors were drawn into metropolitan circuits as a kind of collective celebrity.

Along the way, *Subaltern Studies* attracted an extraordinary outpouring of criticism. Its second issue, for instance, was the subject of a 40-page multi-author critical review in another Indian journal. At various times, members of the *Subaltern Studies* group were charged with bad historiography, insufficient revolutionary zeal, not enough Marxism, too much Marxism, too much modernism and too much postmodernism. They were criticised for being too Westernised, for romanticising peasants, and for ignoring the middle classes. They were criticised in the name of Lenin, in the name of Lacan, in the name of Derrida, in the name of Gandhi, in the name of Wallerstein and, ironically, in the name of Gramsci. Two weighty books have been published that consist of nothing but articles about *Subaltern Studies* (Chaturvedi 2000; Ludden 2002; see also Lal 2003).

What more can there be to say? The critical commentary includes some very fine pieces. One is an essay by the historian and former contributor Sumit Sarkar, 'The Decline of the Subaltern in *Subaltern Studies*' (Sarkar 1997). This traces the impact of the periodical's postmodern turn, which Sarkar sees as a kind of Faustian bargain. The connection that brought fame came at a price: a drift away from the project of documenting the poor and the dispossessed, and a narrowing of political horizons within India.

Sarkar's argument helps in understanding the cultural phenomenon that *Subaltern Studies* became. Yet there is something more to be said, for the purposes of this book. The early issues of the series, as well as containing vivid social histories, also expressed a theoretical point of view that has considerable interest.

The project of documenting 'the politics of the people', while it required the fine-grained empirical history that made up the bulk of the early issues, was never an innocent empiricism. Guha's phrase already contained an important theoretical point—that peasant and working-class movements *were political*. They were not, as assumed by both nationalist and Marxist historiography (in Guha's view), spontaneous and undirected outbursts that required either the nationalist elite or the one true revolutionary party to give them political form. In the context of British rule, these movements embodied specifically an anticolonial politics.

This politics was not an offshoot of elite politics. That was the principle of the 'autonomous domain' defined by Guha. Subaltern politics grew out of local ways of life and thus expressed specific forms of consciousness, often in the language of local religion. Some of the most fascinating papers in early *Subaltern Studies* show the local roots of politics very clearly.

A gripping example is 'Four Rebels of Eighteen-Fifty-Seven', in which Gautam Bhadra (1985) excavates, from records of the huge upheavals of that year, tales such as the story of the village rebel Devi Singh. This was 'entirely the affair of a peasant community of a small area', involving attacks on moneylenders as well as British authority, and an attempt to set up an independent government. This small-scale rising was soon put down by force and the leaders were hanged.

Another example is Gyanendra Pandey's (1982) 'Peasant Revolt and Indian Nationalism: The Peasant Movement in Awadh, 1919–22'. Pandey shows that, even in the context of the national non-cooperation movement in those years, local peasant politics was an autonomous movement. It had its own organising mechanisms—*Kisan Sabhas*, or peasants' associations— its own leaders and its own modes of action against landlords and the authorities. Huge demonstrations attracted the attention of the Indian National Congress leaders. When Gandhi came to the area and intervened in the struggle, it was mainly to *restrain* peasant militancy. Pandey argues that this reflects the strategic decision of the Congress leadership for an alliance with Indian elites, which required holding back the social radicalism of the rank and file. The Awadh peasant movement was, in its turn, crushed by police action.

The obvious difficulty with tracing subaltern consciousness is that few of the subaltern groups left written records, and leaders like Devi Singh were killed before they could create oral traditions. *Subaltern Studies*, in one of its most brilliant moves, developed a sociology-of-knowledge approach to the historical record, and set about reading subaltern history *through* the documents created by the colonial elites.

Thus, in the paper on 1857 already mentioned, Bhadra read the memoirs of the British victors, but read them from the point of view of the defeated local communities. Dipesh Chakrabarty (1983), in 'Conditions for Knowledge of Working-Class Conditions', studied the jute workers of Kolkata in the early twentieth century. He showed that the *absence* of documentation about the workforce (even when officially required) is a clue to the real pattern of labour recruitment and control in the jute factories. In 'The Prose of Counter-Insurgency', taking as his main case the Santal rising of 1855, Guha (1983) shows how primary written accounts of peasant risings are constructed to justify the continuity of the British Raj. Later historians tended to reproduce the viewpoint implicit in these documents, or assimilate them to an over-arching narrative of national or revolutionary struggle. Yet, as Guha also shows, by a detailed critical reading of the archive 'the specificity of rebel consciousness' can be reconstructed and the local logic of the movement, including its strong religious component, can be understood.

Being trained in the same profession, and having tried to understand class and change in another kind of colony (Connell and Irving 1980), I have read these papers with admiration and pleasure. They are very skilful historiography. Not only do the authors have an eye for significant detail and a flair for weaving analysis and narrative together. As with Hountondji in Africa and Shariati in Iran, their argument is given urgency by a sharp awareness of power.

In one of the early critiques of *Subaltern Studies*, Rosalind O'Hanlon (1988) argues that the dichotomy of 'subaltern' and 'elite', for which Guha and his colleagues were heavily criticised, was not so much intended to name social categories as to dramatise the pervasiveness of power and domination. It was a way of creating an agenda of investigation, always to look for resistance to power—whether spectacular or unheroic.

I think that O'Hanlon was right, and that the *Subaltern Studies* group's sensitivity to issues of power accounts for the vividness of its members' writing, across a very wide range of topics and historical situations. This is a key way in which *Subaltern Studies* differed from the more conventional Marxism that had been the main force on the Indian intellectual left. Marxist research was very much concerned with getting socioeconomic categories, especially classes, exactly defined and mapped.

Yet the *Subaltern Studies* researchers came out of Marxism, without a doubt. Ranajit Guha, like Al-e Ahmad (Chapter 6), had been a labour movement activist in the 1940s and 1950s. He was specifically a militant of the Communist Party of India, from which he also broke, somewhat later than Al-e Ahmad's departure from Tudeh (Amin and Bhadra 1994). The younger group which Guha gathered to create *Subaltern Studies* were influenced by developments in Marxist thought in the 1960s and 1970s, including the new working-class history coming out of Britain and the structuralist Marxism coming out of Paris. There are, however, few signs of any influence from Third World revolutionary thought in the tradition of Fanon.

The Marxist background was the starting point for Guha's ambitious paper 'Dominance Without Hegemony and its Historiography' (1989), in which he argues that British imperialism never achieved hegemony in the Indian colony. Rather, the Raj was based on coercion behind a thin facade of legality. Guha suggests that the universalising tendencies of bourgeois culture, based on the expansive tendencies of capital, find their historic limit in colonialism. It is an argument that converges with Prebisch's (1981) late critique of liberalism in the periphery.

Marxist thought is also the starting point for early *Subaltern Studies'* most explicit attempt to theorise power, a paper by Partha Chatterjee (1983) called 'More on Modes of Power and the Peasantry'. In a previous paper, a study of the fluctuations of communal conflict in Bengal, Chatterjee had suggested that the explanation lay in the intermingling of contradictory power systems that existed during a transition to capitalism. In 'Modes of Power', Chatterjee sets out to systematise this idea, which he thought applied broadly to large agrarian societies.

The argument starts with the transitions between 'modes of production', understood in classical Marxist terms. Associated with these economic structures, but not reducible to them, are patterns of political struggle, centred on property and on definitions of rights or entitlements. These Chatterjee calls 'modes of power'. He defines three basic forms: communal, where entitlements are allocated on the authority of a whole social collectivity; feudal, where entitlements derive basically from physical force (i.e. a situation of direct domination); and bourgeois, where property rights are guaranteed by generalised law, and indirect domination is achieved through the institutions of representative government.

The most interesting part of Chatterjee's argument concerns the interplay between these modes. Feudal society was not established as a homogenous system; rather, it involved the intrusion of the feudal mode of power into a communal realm. The result was constant resistance to feudal lords, with unstable outcomes. Sudden risings, and sudden reconfigurations, were possible—especially when a feudal monarchy became a third player. The communal mode of power was capable of generating local leadership when needed, but not of institutionalising it. Chatterjee treats the transition to the bourgeois mode of power only briefly, but makes the key point that expanding capitalism does simply obliterate feudalism. Indeed, it can incorporate feudal structures of domination. What capitalism does tend towards is the extinction of the *communal* mode of power. Chatterjee gives a pithy summary of a couple of hundred years of colonialism:

> The usual features here are the intrusion of new extractive mechanisms into the agrarian economy, often with the active legal and armed support of a colonial political authority, leading to a systematic commercialization of agriculture and the incorporation in varying degrees of the agrarian economy into a larger capitalist world-market; the growth of a new industrial sector, usually of a limited nature in comparison with the absolute size of the economy and with varying combinations of foreign, 'comprador' and 'national' capital; the growth of new political institutions and processes based on bourgeois conceptions of law, bureaucracy and representation (Chatterjee 1983: 347).

The impact on pre-existing social structures was extremely uneven in practice, creating 'many unexpected possibilities' through the interplay of different modes of power—hence, we might infer, the variegated picture of subaltern politics documented by *Subaltern Studies*. Chatterjee explicitly contrasts this with the picture of 'capillary' power in Europe presented by Foucault. Chatterjee suggests that, in the 'so-called backward countries', such forms of power have limited reach. It is the complex combinations of modes of power around postcolonial states that are characteristic, opening up 'an entirely new range of possibilities for the ruling classes to exercise their domination'.

This grim conclusion was not *Subaltern Studies*' last word on the subject of power. In later issues, not only did the topics of research shift away from subaltern groups but, as Sarkar (1997) shows, the conceptual framework also shifted. The key dichotomy was no longer between ruling class and subaltern, but between colonial power/knowledge, institutionalised in the modern state, and the non-modern. This is clear in Partha Chatterjee's book *The Nation and its Fragments*, published ten years after the paper on power. The focus is no longer on systems of class power and the changing forms of contestation, but on the discourse of nationalism and modernity, with the state taken to be the axis of power. In short, *Subaltern Studies* and the group of scholars around it moved towards a more conventional postmodernism. I think that is a pity, because Guha's structuralism, and Chatterjee's original conceptualisation of power, were highly illuminating theorisations.

Gender, violence and feminist theory

Among the criticisms of *Subaltern Studies* was that it had little to say about caste, and little to say (despite the involvement of a well-known feminist, Gayatri Spivak) about gender relations. These criticisms are broadly correct, for the early issues. The narratives of peasant risings talk a lot about local leaderships, but hardly notice that the leaders are exclusively men. However, gender issues do creep in. In the fifth volume, Guha (1987) himself wrote a superb paper, 'Chandra's Death', about a peasant family in mid-nineteenth century Bengal. In this he worked from tiny fragments of evidence to build a picture of the gender order in rural society and the responses rural women made to patriarchal power.

Of course, Guha was not the first man to concern himself with the oppression of women. As Chatterjee (1993: Chs 6–7) notes, gender justice had been a major issue in mid-nineteenth century Bengal. Claims about the barbarous Indian treatment of women were part of the British justification of colonial rule; but the issue was also addressed by indigenous intellectuals. Iswarchandra Vidyasagar, an educational reformer and a central figure in the 'Calcutta renaissance' of the mid-nineteenth century, sharply criticised the patriarchal kinship system of his day, including polygamy, child marriage and the ban on widows remarrying. He wrote the scathing lines:

> Let not the unfortunate weaker sex be born in a country where the men have no pity, no dharma, no sense of right and wrong, no ability to discriminate between beneficial and harmful, where preservation of what has been customary is considered the only duty, the only *dharma* . . . By what sin do women come to be born in Bharatvarsha at all? (Quoted in Sarkar 1997: 267)

In the next generation, Bankimchandra Chatterjee [Chattopadhyay], the best-known Indian novelist before Tagore, and famous as the author of the hymn *Bande Mataram* (Hail to the Mother), which became a national song, took an even more radical position. In an essay on 'Equality', he denounced the fact that 'in all countries women are the slaves of men'. He argued not only for widow remarriage and women's property rights, but also for women's right to move in public space, and the need for *men* to share child-care and housework, a position still radical a hundred years later (Chatterjee 1986). Chatterjee later retreated from this view, but other men in the Indian intelligentsia also took up the cause of women's rights, including Sayyid Ahmad Khan, as mentioned in Chapter 6.

The development of a *women's* politics around gender justice was a slow and complex process. Women were present in the nationalist movement in considerable numbers, and not just elite women. Gandhi's mass action campaigns depended on women's support. But mainstream nationalism, as Partha Chatterjee (1993) argues, did not articulate a gender politics in the public realm. A diverse group of women's organisations set up an umbrella organisation, the All India Women's Conference, in the 1920s. This body did articulate an equal-rights perspective, but lost influence after independence. Those women's organisations which had a mass reach were mainly the affiliated groups set up by male-controlled political parties.

Their effect is illuminated by Raka Ray's (1999) study of feminist politics in Kolkata and Mumbai, which looks closely at Paschim Banga Ganatantrik Mahila Samiti, the women's wing of West Bengal's governing Communist Party of India (Marxist). The Samiti functioned mainly to implement the official line coming down from the male leadership, and that line insisted on solidarity between working-class women and men.

The women of the Samiti, while working for women's economic and educational advancement, therefore shied away from any direct challenge to the interests of men—for instance, from making a public issue of domestic violence.

Violence against women was, however, the galvanising issue in other parts of India. Some feminist groups formed in the early 1970s. In the years immediately after Indira Gandhi's temporary dictatorship, the 'Emergency' of 1975–77, feminist organising spread rapidly. A wide range of autonomous women's groups came into existence, periodicals were launched—the best-known, *Manushi*, began publication in 1979—research and teaching began, and public campaigns were undertaken (Kumar 1999).

A few years later, Nandita Gandhi and Nandita Shah (1992) conducted an interview survey of women's groups across the country, and were impressed by the range and diversity of activism. There were campaigns around domestic violence, dowry murders, rape, women's health, women in the workplace, legal reform, and more. But for all this diversity, it was the continuing fact of men's violence—the sense of threat under which women lived—that was central to the movement. As the editorial in the first issue of *Manushi* put it:

> To live as a woman is to live in fear—of molestation, rape, of social stigma in almost every action of ours. We have to be afraid to do so many things—to be outside after dark, to travel alone, to step outside the home, to be alone in the home, to be with others, to acknowledge even to ourselves our own desires—to love, to laugh, to live (Kishwar and Vanita 1984: 243).

We might therefore expect Indian feminism to generate distinctive theories about violence and the nature of a gender system that produced such pervasive fear. But Gandhi and Shah, who subtitled their book *Theory and Practice in the Contemporary Women's Movement in India*, found little theoretical work going on. Women's movement conferences, on their account, focused on empirical documentation of the position of women and on debating problems of activism. And of one occasion when there was a conscious attempt to promote theory, they report ruefully: 'A study circle formed by Shakti, a Bombay based resource centre, to discuss analytical concepts such as patriarchy, feminism and its various streams, had to close down for want of people' (Gandhi and Shah 1992: 288).

Can an energetic, diverse and creative movement, which is grappling with issues about state power, caste inequalities and cultural definitions of women's bodies, function without theory? Perhaps not, because several kinds of theory were soon imported. One was a body of ideas long familiar on the Indian left, Marxist political economy. Indian feminists became involved in the debates, also familiar in the metropole, about productive and unproductive labour, wages for housework, women as a reserve army of labour, Engels on the family, and so on. For instance, Gabriele Dietrich (1992), a participant for fourteen years, devoted a heavyweight chapter of her *Reflections on the Women's Movement in India* to these ideas. She concludes, unsurprisingly, that the women's question cannot be solved within capitalism, but also that an autonomous women's movement is necessary.

Other Indian feminists read the literature of radical feminism produced, mainly in the United States, in the 1970s. The concept of 'patriarchy' as a system of domination was articulated by Women's Liberation at the start of that decade. Not long afterwards, Mary Daly, Susan Griffin, Carolyn Merchant and others reworked this idea into a dichotomous vision of gender in which females are peaceful, cooperative and close to nature while males are aggressive, competitive and hostile to nature. This model was picked up by the woman who, after Spivak, became India's best-known feminist outside India, Vandana Shiva.

In *Staying Alive: Women, Ecology and Development*, Shiva (1989) applies this model, her immediate sources being Merchant and Griffin, to environmental struggles in India. The strengths of the book include a narrative of the Chipko forest protection movement in North India since 1972, in which Shiva emphasises, in a way *Subaltern Studies* never did, the importance of women in local leadership. The book sharply criticises 'Green Revolution' agriculture, on the basis of village-level research on sorghum, and development programs that harvest water. Both are criticised for disrupting village women's labour and the reproduction of local communities and environments.

These analyses, however, are embedded in a righteous rhetoric in which women are always good, ecologically knowledgeable, embedded in nature, caring, quiet and committed to the production of life. Men are mostly bad and noisy, and white Western men are extremely bad and exceptionally noisy, being hell-bent on markets, profits and development. Development is always destructive, always against women's interests, and always resisted by 'women, peasants and tribals'. These good folk, according to Shiva, are involved in the traditional worship of nature as Mother, and support the creative 'feminine principle' known in Indian tradition as 'Prakriti'.

Well. A quarter of the peasants on the Indian subcontinent are Muslim and extremely unlikely to be into nature worship. (It is specifically rejected in the *Qur'an*, see e.g. Sura 13.) The other peasants are divided among hundreds of dialects, castes and religious communities. As Bina Agarwal (1992) observes in a judicious critique, Shiva ignores social, religious, regional and national diversity in constructing an idealised picture of women; she ignores processes of gender change; and she misses the importance of local class power in economic processes.

The arbitrary character of Shiva's text is curiously revealed, for an Australian reader, by her discussion of eucalyptus trees. Here Shiva (1989: 78–82) converts a perfectly valid argument against monoculture of exotics in India into a denunciation of eucalyptus trees themselves, which seem to epitomise the grasping, masculine, anti-life forces that Shiva hates. She does not seem to know that eucalyptus is not a 'single species', but a very large genus with more than 500 varied species, beautifully adapted to the different environments across Australia, and much loved in their native places. (For their career as exotics under British and French colonialism, see Zacharin 1976.)

Yet a third style of metropolitan feminism is invoked in a later issue of *Subaltern Studies*. Susie Tharu and Tejaswini Niranjana (1996) are concerned about the rise of women's activism in right-wing Hindu nationalist agitations, and about how the empowerment of women can be misused by marketers of contraceptive chemicals and misrepresented in discussions of the anti-alcohol movement among village women. What is the theoretical problem here? To Tharu and Niranjana, it is feminism's supposed complicity with humanism and failure to break with the 'humanist subject'. The diagnosis is taken straight from the manual of North American feminist postmodernism.

These texts bring to a head a major problem about theory in the global South. No intellectuals working outside the metropole can ignore the intellectual production of the metropole. For many purposes, it is feasible and labour-saving to import metropolitan theory and simply give it a local gloss. That is understandable where an activist movement faces huge practical problems, which is true for the Indian women's movement. It is also understandable—though the dynamics are different—where a large part of the audience is located in the metropole, which is true for the later *Subaltern Studies* and for Shiva's environmentalism.

The question of Southern theory has, of course, been considered by Indian intellectuals. Chatterjee (1993), for instance, argues for 'an Indian history of peasant struggle' rather than an application of European models. He offers some interesting ideas about how European thought about modernity became a universal model and led to misreadings of colonial society. A more detailed and profound treatment of the problem is found in Veena Das's (1995) *Critical Events: An Anthropological Perspective on Contemporary India*—a book that demonstrates, among other things, that powerful theorising about gender violence is generated from the Indian experience.

Suffering, death and the limits of social science

Veena Das is an experienced anthropologist, and *Critical Events* starts with a reflection on her own profession and its relationship to her own society. India, like Australia (Chapter 4), has long been a data mine for metropolitan social theorists, from Maitland and Maine in the nineteenth century to Dumont's *Homo Hierarchicus* in the 1960s. Their monopoly of intellectual framing has been challenged. Das describes a debate a generation ago in which A.K. Saran asserted, while Dumont denied, the possibility of a social science constructed from an Indian perspective.

To Das, the key question is how to *practise* anthropology in India. Ethnographic research is possible in one's own society, given adjustments of perspective, as recent work on sexuality shows (Bhaskaran 2004). But classic ethnographic technique presupposes the existence of a functioning community, a small, tradition-bound social universe that is to be the object of knowledge. Das strongly questions this presupposition. One of the central themes of her book is that community is *not* a pre-given social entity. Communities have become political actors who claim the right to define history, to regulate the body, to enact violence. Now, 'the community also colonizes the life-world of the individual in the same way as the state colonizes the life-world of the community'. In the conditions of Indian modernity, 'new formations of community and culture have emerged, and indeed have become the sites of major conflicts in contemporary Indian society and polity' (Das 1995: 12).

The anthropologist now proceeds, not by immersion in a warm bath of traditions, but by the painful route of studying those 'major conflicts'. The main text of *Critical Events* discusses a series of conflicts within Indian society in the last two generations: violence against women in the Partition of 1947; the scandalous case of a Muslim woman's claim for maintenance from her divorced husband; the consequences of the death by *sati* of a very young Rajput woman; the emergence of Sikh separatist militancy; and the horrifying chemical disaster at Bhopal in 1984, where two and a half thousand people were killed, and three hundred thousand others affected, in the worst industrial accident in history.

Das's account of Bhopal therefore does not attempt an ethnography of the communities that were devastated by the poison gas leak. Rather, she focuses on the legal battles that followed, and particularly on the medical and judicial arguments and the control of knowledge. There was powerful state intervention. The Government of India took over the proceedings against the Union Carbide company; the Madhya Pradesh regional government took control of clinical information about the impact; and the Supreme Court imposed a settlement (which many thought radically inadequate) on the company and the victims. The medical profession, too, was deeply involved, setting terms for the discussion of impact and responsibility that made it impossible for many of the victims to establish their case. Thus 'the suffering of survivors became an occasion for the exercise of power by the medical profession' (1995: 156).

Yet this pales beside the legal process that Das traces, in which the voices of the victims were silenced over a period of years, and their agency replaced by government and judicial manoeuvering. The details are too complex to recite here, but I will quote in full Das's incandescent summary of the rhetorical role that the suffering of the people came to play:

> The judges were concerned to signal their own humanity and protect the legitimacy of the judicial institution of which they were a part. The 'suffering' of the victims was a useful narrative device which could be evoked to explain why victims had not been consulted; why their protests over the settlement could be redefined as the actions of irresponsible and ignorant people; to explain away the fact that the

judges had not felt obliged to ask the government and its medical establishment to place for public scrutiny what it had accomplished by way of relief and help; to ignore the knowledge that had been generated on the impact of the deadly isocyanate on the health of people; and finally, to obfuscate the fact that they had completely failed to fix responsibility for the accident and had thus converted the issue of multinational liability into that of multinational charity (Das 1995: 163).

Das's anger is obvious—and who could doubt it is justified? But as well as expressing her dismay at the dire course of events, this passage also illustrates her sharp social analysis, focused on the interplay between discourse and institutional power. In the exercise of legal and administrative power, the pain of the mass poisoning victims is translated into the self-justifying discourse of the institutions. The state, in effect, redefines reality—and not in the interest of the people it claims to represent.

The state's capacity to define the situation is also at issue in Das's account of gender violence in the Partition. The last act of British colonial rule was to cut India into parts, and the inauguration of the independent states of Pakistan and India was accompanied by bitter communal conflicts in which hundreds of thousands died, and many millions became refugees across the new borders.

A particular feature of these events was violence by men against women: mass rape, abduction and (reputedly) mutilation of the women of the 'enemy' community, and honour killings of the women of one's own community. Das traces these events, especially among the Sikh and Hindu populations of the Punjab in India's northwest. She reads them as moving beyond the familiar Lévi-Straussian case of women being signs in matrimonial exchanges among men. In situations of crisis, women become signs in a monstrous exchange of pollution and hatred between groups of men, and women's bodies become the men's battleground: 'Hence, each sought to punish the other not only by inflicting pain but also, and more specially, on the women of the other group so that the memory of indignities would never cease to haunt the future' (Das 1995: 186).

Mahatma Gandhi's long campaign for Hindu–Muslim unity failed, and his last campaign was to try to stop this violence. For this he was silenced forever by a Hindu militant (Chadha 1997). The postcolonial Government of India took a stance close to Gandhi's, and indeed the mass violence did stop in early 1948. Government then faced the question of what to do about the thousands of women who had been abducted.

Das's investigation of the improvisations that followed provides a brilliant account of the complexities of gender relations and state power. The governments of India and Pakistan both set up repatriation programs, in effect taking into the realm of the state considerations of purity and honour that had previously been affairs of the family or the village.

On the Indian side, the focus of Das's research, the government called in social workers to solve the interpersonal problems and help with resettlement. The social workers, like the doctors and judges in the Bhopal events, became the authoritative voices defining what was good for the women concerned. To make the machinery work, the state in this case too redefined reality, categorising the women as either Muslim or Hindu/Sikh, overriding all complexities of mixed affiliation or changing relationships and identities.

The result in some cases—it is impossible to know how many—was a fresh human tragedy in which new relationships and blended families were torn apart. Some women evaded the machinery and refused to go back. Das notes that the public symbolism of restoring women and children to their community ignored the resilience of gender relations and family practices, which in many cases had already achieved a reconciliation. It also ignored the ambiguity of events, in which mixed marriages might be an emergency local arrangement protecting women of a minority group from the violence all around, or in which women (contrary to the ideology of purity) might actually prefer life in another community to honour killing at the hands of their male relatives. Even in such desperate circumstances, Das argues, women had a degree of agency to which the official interpretation of events was blind.

In the final chapters of *Critical Events*, Das reflects on the anthropology of pain and on the nature of social science. She considers, but does not accept, the social science tradition going back as far as Durkheim that treats pain (for instance, in initiation) as a means of social integration, that sees social relations inscribed on the body. In events such as the Partition violence, Das suggests, social processes and social science find a limit. The silencing of speech, of the capacity to represent one's suffering, is part of the terror itself. The sexual and reproductive violence of the Partition:

cannot be understood by taking social relations as the model for understanding either relations between persons (even if they had known each other prior to the occurrence of these events), or by taking the relations between different aspects of social structure (such as politics and kinship) as the model (Das 1995: 200).

These events were outside the reproduction of social relations; people had to invent scripts. And in these moments of terror, the fate of the people involved, the good or bad outcomes, were determined by processes beyond human understanding: 'It is in this context that I have gone against the time-honoured tradition in sociology to look for meaning in the face of suffering, and instead suggested that a theory of chaos may be far closer to the victim's understanding of the world as accidental and contingent in nature' (Das 1995: 22).

But that does not mean we should abandon sociology or anthropology. In one of the most original and impressive steps in her argument, Das suggests a different function for social science. Social science should resist complicity with all attempts at establishing monopolies of truth, whether those of the modern state, or those of the 'communities' claiming space in politics, or those of professional communities.

It is a matter of urgency to challenge these meta-narratives, to allow other narratives to come forth, and to relate different narratives to each other. This is a positive, not purely negative, process. It allows alliance (even more, 'consubstantiation') with the truth of the victim, the truth *incarnate* in the victim. This allows new possibilities for pursuing justice, 'and an anthropology which can be seen as forming one body with the victim' (1995: 23, 209).

That is a difficult proposition, though perhaps one that is latent in the tradition of social science that concerns itself with oppression and injustice. It is not difficult to see how it might apply to social science far beyond India, such as Mamdani's (2001) profound analysis of the 1994 genocide in Rwanda. There are complications, however. In the events Das studies, there is little doubt about who the victim is. Mamdani's title, *When Victims Become Killers*, suggests this *can* be in doubt. The 1994 deaths were the worst round in a cycle of oppression, killing, fear and revenge in which both Hutu and Tutsi were agents; a cycle that started much earlier and may not be ended yet.

Yet Mamdani's research strikingly confirms another of Das's arguments. Like Hindu and Muslim in India, Hutu and Tutsi in Rwanda and Burundi, now opposed 'communities', were not primordial social units. They are relatively modern identities, *politically* constructed, and specifically enhanced and shaped by the colonial state.

This is connected to Das's view of the position of social scientists in the periphery. Das is very well read in the European and North American literature, and she is aware that the discipline of anthropology still has a Eurocentric discourse. Yet she emphasises that the 'modes of being in the world' of anthropologists in peripheral countries such as Brazil and India do not mimic those in metropolitan countries (1995: 197).

Different modes of being may lead to different paths towards understanding. Hence Das's own study of critical events, as a way of transcending the old focus on local community, leading to a concern with the limits of social relations models. Right at the end of the book, Das considers the relation between global processes and the search for local understandings, which is often pursued in circumstances where the local is being overwhelmed. It is in that context that a deconstructive and empathic role for social science comes into focus.

Intimate oppositions

Veena Das's research on Partition violence was conducted in collaboration with Ashis Nandy, to whom I now turn. One of the leading public intellectuals in India, Nandy opposes both Hindu and secular nationalism. He is a prolific writer, producing lively essays on literary history, contemporary film, scientific biography, religious conflict, technocracy, and more. I will focus mainly on one text, in which he discusses colonial culture and Gandhian politics, but I also note that this led on to sophisticated diagnoses of contemporary South Asia.

Nandy has a background in clinical psychology, and his debt to Freudian thought is clear. The emotional side of culture and politics is his central concern. Nandy makes free use of Freudian and post-Freudian categories, which sometimes brings him close to the US 'culture and personality' school of psychoanalytic anthropology in the 1940s. But where those theorists had a static view of culture, Nandy works with a model of culture that is plural, constantly changing and deeply implicated in the politics of modernity.

Though Nandy makes free use of metropolitan psychology—and also metropolitan philosophy, history, sociology and cultural analysis—he is far from doing Northern theory in the South. At one point he confesses jokingly to 'the deliberate misuse' of concepts from psychology and sociology, signalling a willingness to borrow but also a determination to argue in Indian terms, as we see in the epigraph to this chapter.

This presupposes a confidence in the 'Indian terms', and Nandy is well justified in his confidence. He has a detailed knowledge of rich Indian traditions of religious, philosophical and political thought, literature and art, and makes free use of these resources in his work. He has written, for instance, a magnificent essay on Rabindranath Tagore's novels as a discourse on the changing character of nationalism and national identity and the political construction of the self (Nandy 2004: 153–233). Nandy has brought to light such marginal characters as the forgotten environmentalist Kapil Bhattacharjee, a critic of dam-building in the 1950s, and—in a different register—Gandhi's Brahmanic murderer Nathuram Godse.

Nandy's (1980) early research addressed the dilemmas of doing Western-style science in colonial India, raising concerns complementary to those of Hountondji in West Africa (see Chapter 5). Nandy's interest in science has continued, but has not moved towards a sociology of knowledge, rather towards a diagnosis of technocratic culture. This, in turn, has been shaped by the analysis of colonialism in his most influential book, *The Intimate Enemy* (1983).

Subtitled 'Loss and Recovery of Self under Colonialism', *The Intimate Enemy* consists of a pithy preface and two long, partly overlapping essays, 'The Psychology of Colonialism' and 'The Uncolonized Mind'. Nandy starts by insisting that colonialism was not just an economic and political structure, but was also a cultural and psychological one, 'a state of mind in the colonizers and the colonized' (1983: 1). This did not begin at the time of first conquest. The bandit-kings of the East India Company were out to rob the locals' purses and had no interest in tampering with their minds. Indeed, the early conquerors had much respect for Indian civilisation. But this changed in the 'second colonisation' of the nineteenth century, when the British did set out to control and change what they now regarded as a primitive culture.

Nandy's key move is to turn the spotlight on the colonisers. The nineteenth century Raj produced profound changes in British culture.

Nandy stresses two: an exaggeration and simplification of masculinity, now constructed in total opposition to femininity; and a valorisation of adulthood as against childhood, which became the dominant metaphor of cultural development. The imperial British, in short, imagined themselves as virile adults governing childlike and/or effeminate races who needed to be nudged, led and coerced towards civilisation and progress.

Some of this has been said in other scholars' histories of imperialism. Nandy's argument is unique in stressing the psychological damage that this system did to the British. It led to a glorification of violence, a contempt for weakness and the feminine, a fear of cultural complexity, a need to wall oneself off from the Oriental other, and a cult of masculine valour. This is seen in exaggerated form among the occupying forces, but also played back into British culture in the homeland. There it fostered the illusion of homogeneity ('the British race') that is one of the most striking features of imperialist ideology. It was duly exported to colonies of settlement such as Australia and Canada, and helped to motivate the slaughter on the Western Front in World War I.

Nandy develops these themes in a subtle analysis of Rudyard Kipling, the most prominent intellectual of the British Empire at high tide. Kipling's childhood identification with native India had always to be denied and overcome in adulthood—though as a hidden current it motivated wonderful writing about India. Kipling, in effect, internalised the necessary violence of colonialism: 'If he did not have any compassion for the victims of the world, he did not have any compassion for a part of himself either' (Nandy, 1983: 69). And Kipling's equilibrium was destroyed when his son was killed on the Western Front in 1915.

But psychological damage was also widespread among the 'exposed sections of Indian society' (1983: 76), forced to come to terms not only with conquest but also with the racial contempt embedded in the developed system of British rule. Some of Nandy's most powerful writing traces the diverging reactions of Indian intellectuals in the nineteenth and early twentieth centuries to this situation. Here his psychological categories—such as identification with the aggressor—come into play, and Nandy is able to analyse the problem that Al-e Ahmad called 'Westoxication' (Chapter 6) in much greater depth.

One response was to copy the exaggerated masculinity of British colonial culture. That was not hard to do, given the ancient social category of *kshatriya*, the warrior class of the Hindu classics, and also given the British tendency to admire 'martial races' among their subjects. This produced attempts at armed revolt:

> They sought to redeem the Indians' masculinity by defeating the British, often fighting against hopeless odds, to free the former once and for all from the historical memory of their own humiliating defeat in violent power-play and 'tough politics'. This gave a second-order legitimacy to what in the dominant culture of the colony had already become the final differentiae of manliness: aggression, achievement, control, competition and power (Nandy 1983: 9).

Such challenges were put down with no great trouble by the British, who had bigger guns and knew what to do with that kind of opposition.

Another response was to exaggerate what the British seemed most to reject: Indian religion. This led into another trap, as revivalists began to reconstruct the fluid and open-ended Hindu spirituality on the model of Christian religion. Yet another response was to adopt the British point of view on the backwardness of Indian culture and leap wholeheartedly into a modernisation program. This might involve Western-style schooling, use of the English language in the home, adopting Western dress, conversion to Christianity or working for the colonial regime.

There were many combinations of these responses. Nandy traces them through short case studies of intellectuals, such as the novelist Bankimchandra Chatterjee, mentioned above, who worked his way through a left-wing positivism in the style of John Stuart Mill to a cult of Krishna structured on European lines (Chatterjee 1986). Nandy's most sustained analysis is of Sri Aurobindo, the first modern Indian guru in the sense of being leader of an authoritarian cult.

Aurobindo's childhood in the late nineteenth century was a mirror-image of Kipling's, starting in a household ruled by a father completely committed to British culture. Taken to England by his parents at seven and left with an English family, sent to school and then university in England, Aurobindo as a lonely young adult worked his way towards a violent rejection of British imperialism. He returned to India, became fluent in four local languages, became a revolutionary nationalist leader, picked up

Chatterjee's imagery of India as a mother needing to be rescued, and by 1908 was in gaol for sedition.

Luckily acquitted, Aurobindo dramatically changed direction and withdrew to contemplative life in an ashram, now seeking yogic rather than martial power. Over the next 30 years, under the influence of a French follower whom Aurobindo assimilated to the figure of The Mother, his group was transformed into a hierarchical, disciplined and conservative cult with Aurobindo as supreme authority. He withdrew into attempts to achieve world peace by increasingly unbelievable yogic practices.

As Nandy observes: 'It is impossible to read the life of Aurobindo without sensing the "inner" pain which went with imperialism in India'—pain experienced in the family, in education, and allowing only a resolution in mysticism, at first political and then cult-like. Nandy takes this as a pointer to a wider cultural reponse, in which Indian society responded to the impossibilities of colonial domination with absurdities and contradictions. In a very characteristic passage, he writes:

> It is the world of a bank-clerk who secretly writes poetry and either hides it from a prosaic world or comically affirms it from the housetop . . . To some, poetry is only poetry and clowns are only clowns . . . To others, poetry—and fooling—could also be a secret defiance, a reaffirmation of the right state of mind in a hard, masculine, anti-poetic world. Defiance need not always be self-conscious. It need not be always backed by the ardent, murderous, moral passions in which the monotheistic faiths, and increasingly the more modern and nationalist versions of Hinduism, specialize (1983: 98).

Which brings us, as it brought Nandy, to Mohandas Karamchand Gandhi: 'one of the few who successfully articulated in politics the consciousness which had remained untamed by British rule in India' (1983: 100).

Gandhi is the central figure in *The Intimate Enemy*, and in Nandy's work as a whole. He is present not as the exemplar of any cultural or psychological pattern, but as the person who cracked the code of colonialism, who discovered the way out of the dead-ends that had defeated all other Hindu reformers. He was the person who found 'the right state of mind' and made it not a secret defiance but a public ethic and a political program.

Gandhi's originality is not easily appreciated from outside India. He is popularly seen as the archetypal mild-mannered pacifist, or as someone who rejected modern technology in favour of the simple life. Neither image is wholly true, and neither captures Gandhi's highly sophisticated response to colonialism. To Nandy, Gandhi's originality lay in his realisation that to fight colonialism on the terms colonialism had created was to be defeated from the start. One had to step outside the logic of being a player or counter-player in the system.

The resource for this was present not in the elite cultures to which earlier reformers had appealed, but in the folk Hinduism they often despised. Gandhi and his supporters created a mass politics of a kind the Indian National Congress before him had never imagined, and which the British regime could neither understand nor control. The methods of *satyagraha*, in India as previously in South Africa, were certainly peaceful but at the same time coercive. They forced the system to reveal its violence, and reveal its failure. Refusing the norms of colonial culture, refusing hegemonic masculinity, modernisation and scientific rationality as well as wealth and office, Gandhi permanently delegitimised the imperial system. India became, to use a more recent term, ungovernable by the British.

But Gandhi did more than invent *satyagraha* and make India ungovernable. His politics were based on an ethic that, like folk Hindu culture, was genuinely inclusive. Gandhi's famous joke against the West—asked by a journalist what he thought of European civilisation, he replied: 'I think it would be a good idea'—was a little uncharacteristic. As Nandy put it in another essay: 'The basic assumption here is that the dehumanized tyrant is as much a victim of his system as those tyrannized; he has to be liberated, too' (Nandy 1987: 35). Far from rejecting the colonising people, religion and culture, Gandhi searched in them for supportive themes and indeed found some. They included the principle of non-violence itself, which he claimed to have found not in the Hindu scriptures but in Jesus's Sermon on the Mount.

It is ethical and cultural inclusiveness that, for Nandy, distinguishes Gandhi's project from that of all other major players in Indian politics, including the modernisers who came to power in 1947. A modernising project was first articulated as a legitimate opposition within British India, discrediting existing culture even at 'the deepest levels of Hindu religious ideas' (1983: 26) and calling for a shift towards rationality, science and linear ideas of historical time. This project was carried forward in the post-independence state, as the ideology of a middle class whose pathology Nandy went on to analyse in many other texts.

He concludes *The Intimate Enemy* by invoking an Indian culture marked by its fluidity, its capacity to live with ambiguities, its trick of surviving by incorporating pressures and thus 'domesticating the West' (1983: 108). Survival of the culture under colonialism required a certain splitting of personality, a certain capacity for ducking and weaving. More positively it involved 'a peculiar robust realism' and 'a certain talent for and faith in life' (1983: 109–10), which are found in abundance in Indian popular culture. It was just this unheroic strength and capacity for survival on which Gandhi built the *satyagrahi* model of resistance. Here, Nandy takes a much rosier view of the power and autonomy of local popular culture than García Canclini does in Mexico (see Chapter 7).

In this book and other essays written about the same time, Nandy defends a view of colonialism and a model of anticolonial politics that are a long way from the insurrectionist politics of Fanon, Guevara or Shariati. In his 1978 essay 'Towards a Third World Utopia', he criticises Fanon's idea of cleansing violence as being insensitive to the cultural resistance of the oppressed (Nandy 1987: 33). He considers this strategy of opposition to be contained within the logic of colonialism, reproducing its hyper-masculinity, cult of violence, loss of emotional connection and dehumanisation of enemies.

Nandy's critique of the postcolonial state is closely connected with his analysis of science. In a key essay, 'Science, Authoritarianism and Culture', written in 1980, he develops a critique of the culture of science as based on the psychological mechanism of 'isolation'—that is, the separation of cognition from affect (Nandy 1987: 95–126). Psychological detachment from the object of study was crucial in allowing Western science to develop. But science is now entwined with powerful technologies and aligned with the state and its ruling elites. Science has become a key to the dominant ideology of the postcolonial state, legitimating the violence that is constantly done in the name of economic development.

Nandy evidently sees the isolation of knowledge from emotion, abstracted perceptions of the world, and commitment to programs rather than people, as a very general pathology of modernised cultures. In 'Towards a Third World Utopia' he remarks on how the modern West:

> has also popularized a devastatingly sterile concept of autonomy and individualism which has increasingly atomized the Western individual. Many non-Western observers of the culture of the modern West . . . have been struck by the way contractual, competitive individualism—and the utter loneliness which flows from it—dominates the Western mass society (Nandy 1987: 50).

In a later essay, 'Culture, Voice and Development', Nandy suggests that the ideology of modernisation is entrenched in the postcolonial middle classes and in the postcolonial state, which is now—at least in the case of India and Sri Lanka—*more* developmentalist than it was at independence. And this ideology is profoundly destructive of pre-existing cultures. Not that it obliterates them; rather, development ideology selects from existing cultures those aspects that underwrite 'the psychological demands of modernity'. It reduces indigenous knowledge to 'transient counter-systems' that survive in corners, no more than minor irritants to the positive sciences linked with the developmentalist state. So victims of the development process have difficulty in finding a voice that can actually be heard (Nandy 2003: 151–70).

Nandy does not reject dealing with the West, nor even adopting large parts of Western culture. Like Al-e Ahmad, he thinks that is unavoidable. As he wrote in his essay on Tagore, colonialism fractured the selves of those Indians who were exposed to the colonial system, and set up the West as 'a crucial vector within the Indian self' (Nandy 2004: 233).

The question is on what terms that 'vector' is incorporated, and what counter-forces keep its pathologies within bounds. Gandhi and Tagore, in their day, found an answer in forms of patriotism that were not nationalist, and in universalist ethics superior to the claims of colonial ideology. Can such a solution be found now?

Nandy's distinctiveness as a theorist flows from his constant weaving together of psychological argument with analysis of culture and politics. In 'Toward a Third World Utopia' he remarks that: 'No vision of the future can ignore that institutional suffering touches the deepest core of human beings, and that societies must work through the culture and psychology of such suffering, in addition to its politics and economics' (Nandy 1987: 26). Nandy's position is not so much a dogmatic psychologism as a very consistent humanism, a respect for ordinary lives and everyday experience.

Contrary to what sociologists might expect, Nandy's psychologism does not lead to an over-emphasis on the individual. Nandy always assumes the personal is political, that larger structures are implicated in personal experience. Indeed, one of his most startling and powerful arguments is about the psychological ties that bind colonial or global systems together— for instance, 'the indissoluble bond between the future of the peripheries of the world and that of the apparently autonomous, powerful, prosperous, imperial centres' (Nandy 1987: 52). Clearly derived from Gandhi's ethical concern for the British, Nandy's arguments repeatedly emphasise the psychological interplay between coloniser and colonised, between developers and developed, between global rich and global poor.

What method are these conclusions based on? Nandy develops some of his ideas in close analyses of literary works or films, political movements or biographies of intellectuals. Some of his argument is based on empirical work—for instance, on the Partition killings. But he is also very free with sweeping generalisations, hypotheses and guesses. He cites approvingly Gandhi's disdain for history as a mode of knowledge, and his preference for myth. It is often unclear how we can know whether or not Nandy is right. His arguments do not face—as, say, the Third World insurrectionists did—a hard test of practice.

There are some troubling limits to Nandy's thought. In *The Intimate Enemy*, the cast list was almost entirely male; the only woman to play a significant role was the sneaky Frenchwoman in Sri Aurobindo's tale. Nandy developed an original and important argument about masculinity, and was also interested in femininity and androgyny, but among men not women. Even in the recent collection *The Romance of the State* (Nandy 2003), half the population of India seems to be missing.

The Australian theorist Phillip Darby (2005) has noted that Nandy wishes to speak beyond the Indian situation, that he is 'attentive to the possibilities of creative change within dominant collectivities'. But how can this be done? In *The Intimate Enemy*, Nandy emphasises the local roots of Gandhi's strategy, its connection with popular Hinduism as well as its tailoring to British culture. Yet he later uses this strategy as a basis for criticising Fanon—indeed, revolutionists and developmentalists on a global scale. This line of thought has recently been pushed about as far as it will go by Vinay Lal in *Empire of Knowledge* (2002).

Conquered cultures *may* be in similar situations in relation to states and global capitalism. But that is not always so, as Cardoso and Faletto showed by mapping different patterns of dependency (Chapter 7). Conquered cultures certainly do not all have the same history and capacities for mobilisation. Gandhi, astonishingly, brought *satyagrahi* movements to a degree of success in two countries: South Africa and India. Could even Gandhi do it again?

Nandy perhaps over-emphasises one strategy of opposition because he tends to homogenise power. The downside of his psychological sophistication is a rather stereotyped view of the state, and a blankness about modern corporate capitalism. The downside of his enthusiasm for popular religion is, as Sarkar (1997: 98) observes, an exaggerated hostility to secularism. In Nandy's critique of developmentalism, it is difficult to see why large numbers of people, not just the middle class, do support development projects and the governments that pursue them. And it is difficult to see in Nandy's arguments the grounds on which—a point Das and Sarkar clearly note—subaltern groups might use state legal procedures or modernist 'rights' ideas to challenge the oppression they experience. In this era of transnational capitalism, I suggest, we need to combine Nandy's wonderful understanding of psycho-cultural processes with a more robust and nuanced analysis of institutions.

PART IV
Antipodean reflections

9

The silence of the land

Everything about Aboriginal society is inextricably interwoven with, and connected to, the land. Culture is the land, the land and spirituality of Aboriginal people, our cultural beliefs or reason for existence is the land. You take that away and you take away our reason for existence. We have grown the land up. We are dancing, singing and painting for the land. We are celebrating the land. Removed from our lands, we are literally removed from ourselves.

—Mick Dodson (1997)

In Chapter 2, I described the cleared space that was a hidden assumption in James Coleman's rational-choice theory of society. The manoeuvres and bargains pursued by his market-style agents occur in an open space miraculously free of previous inhabitants. I suggested further that this cleared space did have a location on the earth's surface. It could be found near Sydney or Chicago, or the other cities of settler colonialism.

Coleman provides an extreme case of a general feature of modern social theory: its lack of interest in place, material context, and specifically the land. Social science usually prefers context-free generalisation. Special prestige accrues to theory which is so abstracted that its statements seem universally true—the indifference curves of consumption economics, the structural models of Lévi-Strauss, the practice models of Bourdieu and Giddens—or which seems applicable everywhere, such as Foucault's models of power and subjecthood.

This was not always so. At the outset, political economy took considerable interest in place and land. *The Wealth of Nations* (1776) has a long chapter called 'Of the Rent of Land', in which Adam Smith discusses the landscape and agricultural systems of various parts of Western and Northern Europe, with an excursus on mines and the value of silver. He does the same for America in a long chapter, 'Of Colonies'. Smith took the trouble to collect a lot of information about rural life, as well as about pin factories, and was concerned with the way rural production differed from place to place.

In *The Wealth of Nations*, Smith assumes that where there is land there is also a landlord—a specific owner of each specific piece of land. Other early economists made the same assumption. David Ricardo actually begins his *Principles of Political Economy and Taxation* by explaining this point:

> The produce of the earth—all that is derived from its surface by the united application of labor, machinery, and capital, is divided among three classes of the community, namely, the proprietor of the land, the owner of the stock or capital necessary for its cultivation, and the laborers by whose industry it is cultivated (Ricardo 1817: 13).

This is a clue to why the land was prominent in their theorising. A landlord group—an aristocracy or gentry—was in fact the ruling class in most of the societies Smith knew. The landed interest dominated politics in eighteenth century Britain, and 'landed society' (Mingay 1963) was a social formation impossible to miss. In the days before corporate agribusiness, each gentry family was connected to specific lands.

No doubt, as Thompson (1965) argues, they treated their lands increasingly in capitalist style, since in most parts of Europe agricultural capitalism preceded industrial capitalism. And this gradually had its reflection in theory. In the 40 years between *The Wealth of Nations* and *Principles of Political Economy and Taxation*, a process of abstraction set in. Ricardo had none of Smith's keen interest in factual detail about industries and places. Much of the time, Ricardo was content to expound his principles by analysing imaginary examples. Thus economics moved on to the path towards placeless abstraction that produced the marginalist revolution in the late nineteenth century and mathematical modelling in the twentieth.

In the late eighteenth and early nineteenth century, however, the idea of a landed interest was still so strong that the British in India construed local elites as the 'natural proprietors' of land, and tried to base their regime on a land-ownership deal (Guha 1989). In the Australian colonies of settlement, there were attempts to create a landowning gentry, sardonically known as the 'squatters', out of the violence and chaos of a pastoral frontier (Connell and Irving 1980). In many of the American colonies, this actually happened. For instance, the landowners were for generations the dominant power in Chile, while in the English-speaking colonies the gentry led a war of independence and, through members such as George Washington and Thomas Jefferson, founded the new state.

In the colonies, however, there was already a population who had their own relationship with the land. This relationship could be very different from the idea of ownership that European colonisers brought with them, the model that Smith and Ricardo presupposed. As noted in Chapter 5, the vital importance of indigenous connections with the land was argued by Sol Plaatje (1916) in *Native Life in South Africa*, in the face of a new wave of expropriation by the neocolonial regime there.

With the revival of indigenous movements in the late twentieth century in Canada, Australia, the Pacific, Mexico and other regions, land rights has become a major political issue. It has not only created new forms of politics involving aboriginal mobilisations, local and national governments, courts, transnational corporations, populist racism, human rights agencies and mass media. Land rights politics has also drawn in, and begun to transform, areas of social-scientific knowledge including law, anthropology and history (Paul and Gray 2002).

The basis of this movement is the fact that many indigenous communities' relationships with the land showed astonishing tenacity in the face of pressures from pastoralists, missionaries, farmers, miners, the state, the tourist industry—indeed, the whole of what Mudimbe (1988) calls 'the colonizing structure'. The social sciences are beginning to learn from this.

I have tried to learn from it by reflecting on the story told in an important Australian study by Nancy Williams (1986), *The Yolngu and their Land*. This book is in part a conventional ethnography, an account by a social scientist of a hunter-gatherer community's kinship system, religion, economy, and so on. But it departs from anthropological orthodoxy in the same direction as Veena Das's *Critical Events* (see Chapter 8), by focusing on a particular conflict, involving the modern state, in which a pattern of relations was remade. This was the pathbreaking *Yirrkala* land case, in the Northern Territory's Supreme Court. Williams sees her role not as that of a neutral observer, but as an informed person with professional skills putting knowledge into circulation on behalf of, and with the permission of, the community.

The people whom Williams calls 'Yolngu' live in the eastern part of Arnhem Land, at the top end of the Northern Territory. (For overseas readers, this is tropical country, in the same region as the famous Kakadu National Park.) Their land includes both coastal areas and grassy inland, so there has been a diversity of food sources. This land was of little interest to white settlers, apart from a Methodist mission established at a place called Yirrkala, until the Australian mining boom of the 1960s. It turned out that there were rich bauxite deposits in the neighbourhood. The church and the right-wing national government, which between them had control of the Aboriginal reserve, allowed Nabalco, a big mining company, to develop a mine. Some of the Yolngu protested against the lack of consultation, sending a famous 'bark petition' to federal parliament (for the text, see Yunupingu 1997: 210–11). Eventually, a group of Yolngu elders took the unprecedented step of launching a court case to stop the development, claiming that their community owned the land.

At the time there was no land rights legislation in Australia. It was generally assumed that the first British colonists had occupied *terra nullius*, land that belonged to nobody, so the only rights in land were those of the British Crown, and the many grants and leases the Crown had made. The weird crux of the *Yirrkala* land case, therefore, was that the Yolngu needed to prove that they had a pre-existing relationship with the land which corresponded to the Adam Smith-style 'proprietary interest' in land that could be recognised in British law.

Not that the Yolngu elders saw it that way. They treated the courtroom as a consultative meeting, intended to produce mutual understanding and consensus, and spent their time carefully explaining to the judge and the lawyers the complex detail of their community's relations with the land. Meanwhile, the lawyers for the defendants (i.e. the mining interests and the government) treated the courtroom as an antagonistic forum, discrediting the Yolngu account as it unfolded, trying to confuse witnesses and trap them into contradictions. The defendants portrayed the Yolngu people as primitives, wandering freely across the land without fixed rights, possessions or boundaries.

The court's judgment, delivered in 1971, went against the Yolngu. The judge (who, to do him justice, made a substantial effort to understand an unprecedented case) concluded that the community did have a definable relationship with the land, expressed in terms of custom and religion, but it was not a proprietary economic interest. It could therefore not be recognised as ownership in British law. The mine went ahead. So did a growing Aboriginal movement for land rights, which in 1976 resulted in legislation that drew substantially on the claims and arguments in the *Yirrkala* case.

Nancy Williams goes to some lengths to prove that the judicial decision in the *Yirrkala* case was wrong in fact. There was indeed a clear structure of economic and political rights in Yolngu land, as well as spiritual—for instance, a 'mosaic' pattern of rights that ensured each group had access to both coastal and inland ecosystems. There was a consistent, though complex, continuity of ownership over time, working through the matrilineal side of the kinship system. Though patrilineal groups appeared as the owners of land, matrilineal relatives had a veto over how it was used. Ownership was publicly recognised in the sense that non-owning groups had to get permission to use the resources of a given site. There was active land management and conservation of resources, a point now familiar about hunter-gatherer economies.

The difficulty was that the ensemble of these rights and relationships was so different from ownership in European or colonial capitalism that there was no easy translation into language familiar to a state instrumentality such as the Supreme Court. For instance, metropolitan law assumes in discussions of ownership a permanent, clearly bounded group—for example, the Xerox Corporation or the Rockefeller family. But in Yolngu usage, and more widely among Australian Aboriginal people, the names applied to groups, and the demarcations drawn between groups, vary greatly according to the topic under discussion and the purpose for which a distinction is being made at the time. Williams criticises classical anthropology, as well as law, for its tendency to reify such mobile distinctions into hard-edged groups—the bands, hordes, clans, moieties, totemic descent groups and so forth that have been the stock-in-trade of Australian ethnography for a hundred years.

The tenure that is recognised in Yolngu relations with the land derives ultimately from the spirit beings who formed the landscape, in the time of the founding dramas of the world that in English is called the Dreaming. The spirit beings created and named the groups on whom the land was bestowed. Their travels across the landscape created links among the groups who are connected with the specific sites along the way. A certain hillside, a river bend, a rock formation, a place where the vegetation changes may be a centre or a boundary. The process of naming is central, and all names have connection with specific sites.

In accounting for the differences between settler and Indigenous land tenure, it has become common to say that in the European system people own the land, while in the Aboriginal system the land owns the people. Williams argues that this formula does not go far enough. The stories about the spirit beings' journeys do not just reflect, they *constitute*, social relations and the groups that practise them. Therefore it is impossible to understand Yolngu social structure without locating it in its particular landscape. The land is *part of* the social order. It is not just infrastructure, and is not something that a Lévi-Strauss can legitimately abstract away from.

The land is therefore capable of entering into organised social knowledge and playing a central role in representations of society. Let me give another example. Fifteen hundred kilometres south of Arnhem Land is the dry country of central Australia—the home of, among others, the

Arrernte people whose religious practices so enthralled Durkheim (see Chapter 4). The 'dot paintings' of Central Desert Aboriginal communities, now made with acrylic paints, circulate as artworks for an international market. This is the most famous contemporary school of Australian visual art (Sutton et al. 1988; Johnson 1994).

In their original form as ground, rock and body painting, and still in their commercial form as acrylic artworks, these paintings express knowledge about Indigenous society. Each traditional design is associated with narratives of spirit beings, in turn associated with particular groups in the community, and the narratives reveal or prescribe relations between groups. Events signified in the design (such as a birth, a meeting, an act of creation) may describe social problems, such as conflicts between kin groups and tensions between generations, and may also suggest solutions.

The crucial point here is that the designs constantly refer to the land. Elements of the design represent places such as waterholes and campsites, and the patterns show relations between elements of the landscape—for instance, by showing spirit beings' routes across the landscape. A particular design should only be drawn by particular people, who have the appropriate relation to the land and the relevant dreaming. Not all of this is obvious in the design. The paintings have layers of meanings, some of which can be revealed to all and sundry, while other meanings are known only to those people with specific responsibilities to the land, the dreamings and the designs.

Here is a well-developed mode of representing social relations, social boundaries, even social conflicts, in relation to the land. Its symbolic language is remote from what we conventionally understand as social science. (I will return to the implications in Chapter 10.)

The issue of relations with the land has been kept alive by the evolving land rights struggles since the *Yirrkala* one, especially by the *Mabo* case decided in 1992. In this astonishing event, the High Court of Australia by a large majority rejected the doctrine of *terra nullius* and asserted that Australian common law did recognise native title, though it did not recognise Aboriginal sovereignty (Goot and Rowse 1994; Reynolds 1996). For a while, there was a new burst of optimism about land rights and reconciliation in Australia, though that has been systematically closed down by the neoliberal national government since 1996.

To readers steeped in metropolitan ideas of the social, and familiar with concepts such as class, culture or alienation, 'land rights' may seem either an exotic or a marginal concept. But it is central to understanding contemporary Aboriginal life, even though a large proportion of Aboriginal people live in cities. This is argued by Mick Dodson, a former director of the Northern Land Council, in the essay 'Land Rights and Social Justice', from which I quoted at the beginning of this chapter.

Dodson starts with exactly those issues of poverty and social exclusion that are familiar in metropolitan social science. He argues that the poverty and lack of infrastructure in contemporary Aboriginal communities in Australia constitute a massive violation of human rights. But human rights for Aboriginal people centre on the relationship with the land: 'Land rights is a social justice issue because the result of not having access to your land is the destruction of culture, language and spirituality' (Dodson 1997: 42). Even the remnant rights, all that are left from 200 years of colonialism, matter. And all too often these are still denied—with gates on the roads to traditional lands literally being locked.

Is this experience completely alien to white settler culture? I don't think so, and I base that on my own experience of an intense relationship with a certain part of the land. This is the country southward from Broken Bay, from the Pacific Ocean in the east to the Hawkesbury River valley in the west, including Port Jackson—better known as Sydney Harbour. Geologically, this country is dominated by the Hawkesbury sandstone, named after a dull English aristocrat. A good part is now obscured by the sprawl of the city of Sydney, but I can feel the creekbeds and watersheds underneath the suburbs. Some of the original open forest survives; its most beautiful trees are angophoras, relatives of the eucalypts (discussed in Chapter 8). Its sunken valleys are lined with mangroves underneath grey and yellow cliffs, where wind erosion carves wonderful shapes from the soft rock. The sea headlands have intricate tidal platforms below, wiry heath on top. In valleys a little way inland, there are patches of temperate rainforest, fed by the storms that blow up from the south. Once there were wetlands, all of them now gone under industrial sites, parks or housing developments.

I was born in this country, though as a war baby I was soon carted away. But four times I have come back to live in the Hawkesbury sandstone country, so I guess this really is where I belong. My connection with this country is a significant part of what grounds me, gives me a sense of continuity and a capacity for resistance, and it has played a part in my intellectual life. Being one of the Hawkesbury sandstone people is not an identity I can readily use in social life, yet I know my connection is not unique. An intense feeling about the same land can be found in Christina Stead's (1934) wonderful novel *Seven Poor Men of Sydney*—indeed, in a whole series of novels, including Patrick White's *The Tree of Man* (1956), David Malouf's *The Great World* (1990) and most recently Kate Grenville's *The Secret River* (2005).

Plainly, this is a very different relationship with country than the relationship at Yirrkala. With the arrival of the British in 1788, the area around Port Jackson became Australia's first colonial frontier. Darug-speaking people, perhaps 5000 strong, lived here. Their destruction began in 1789 with a devastating smallpox epidemic, followed by the British seizing the fertile land and fisheries, provoking the first stage of Aboriginal resistance and frontier violence. The records are fragmentary, and it is difficult to be sure what clans existed and in exactly what areas. It is probable that my house, built a hundred years ago, is built on land for which the Wangal people were responsible a hundred years before that. (The evidence about Sydney's Aboriginal past is scrupulously reviewed by Attenbrow (2002).)

My connection with the land, therefore, is based on dispossession—which is true for the whole of settler society. We cannot wave this history away. We can, however, move towards a sharing of experience and mutual respect, as the reconciliation movement of the 1990s believed. Indeed, it is possible that one of the influences of Aboriginal culture on settler culture—an influence increasingly recognised by historians—was the transmission of a sense of place. My connection with the Hawkesbury sandstone country, at the very least, gives me a sense of what it would be to *lose* connection with the land I love.

The whole history of imperialism, migration and colonial settlement involves dispossession and loss of connection. By 1970 the Yolngu people were fortunate in the strength of their connection with the land. Most of the groups who had spoken Indigenous Australia's 250 languages (Arthur and Morphy 2005) had by then been wiped out, dispersed, relocated to missions and reserves, or obliged to work for the new owners of their land. As the *Yorta Yorta* land rights case of 1998 shows, it is difficult for Aboriginal groups in southeastern Australia, where white settlement was most intensive, to convince a court of their continuing connection with the land (Paul and Gray 2002). Across the colonised world, from Kolkata to California, these processes of disruption and delegitimation are familiar. We can add the whole grim experience of Atlantic slavery to the history of dispossession (Thomas 1997).

Yet dispossession in every case was a local story. I take as an example an excellent, very detailed historical reconstruction of 'how the land was lost' in another part of the Pacific, the Kahana valley on the spectacular northeast coast of O'ahu (Stauffer 2004). The Polynesian people of the Hawai'ian islands had been impacted strongly by white missionaries and traders through the first half of the nineteenth century, but had lost little of their land immediately. There was not a direct colonial conquest as in Australia, or in other parts of Polynesia such as New Zealand and Tahiti.

In 1846–55, the North American-dominated Hawai'ian royal government set up a Western-style land ownership system, recording customary use-rights to land, village by village, and converting them to individual property. It was called the 'Great *Mahele*', or division. (The process has an eerie resemblance to the privatisation of public assets and mutuals by neoliberals since the 1980s.) Despite women's strong position in Hawai'ian culture, the property went to men, since the white officials mostly refused to recognise property rights for women. There was at first much reluctance to register land in this process. Resistance crumbled when the Polynesian aristocracy, the *ali'i*, realised they could get a lot of cash through the process, and applied their prestige and influence to push it through. The *ali'i* soon lost their share of the distribution to American and Chinese businessmen as a result of unsophisticated borrowing or outright sale. The common people proved a tougher nut to crack.

In Kahana, a taro-farming and fishing village, the village people—with impressive determination—held on to their land for another generation. They even set up a successful cooperative in 1874–75, the Kahana Hui, to own and manage the communal lands—part of a wider Hawai'ian cooperative movement at the time. But cooperatives were undermined by a capitalist legal system that made shares into commodities, and the locals-only rule was undermined by the sale of some shares in the Kahana Hui to the King. The stability of family possession was undermined by the commodification of farm and residential land, made worse by the 1874

Mortgage Act passed by the still American-controlled government (led at the time by the country's leading banker), which allowed easy foreclosures.

Stauffer remarks of the Great *Mahele*: 'So it is correct to say that technically the *mahele* did not lose a single acre to aliens. Rather, it produced a set of circumstances that predisposed the almost complete taking of indigenous land' (Stauffer 2004: 76). In the last few decades of the nineteenth century, this 'set of circumstances' worked with ferocious efficiency to dispossess the villagers of Kahana. Population decline, including migration to the city and the effects of leprosy, meant that some families ran out of local heirs. Relatives elsewhere might inherit, or lots were sold to outsiders. The precedent of shares being sold to the King, and to another outsider who was a fellow Mormon (the dominant religious group in the valley), led to the gradual control of the Hui by rich outsiders, especially the Foster family. Under the *Mortgage Act*, local people would borrow money to buy manufactured goods, and then go under. Their land passed to the lenders.

A Chinese-controlled rice farming business was set up in the valley, which gave rental income to the Hui but continued the commodification of the land. Rich people desired the land and pursued parcels over time— for cattle grazing (which destroyed the forest), for a railway and for a beach house (which destroyed the village itself). East coast water was diverted to the west, for the commercial plantation economy that was being set up in O'ahu using Chinese and Japanese labour. This scheme captured most of the Kahana valley's water flow and destroyed irrigation in the valley. By the early twentieth century, local ownership and the village economy in which it had functioned were gone.

Force of arms, then, was not the only way dispossession could occur. Certainly we cannot forget the complete naval domination of the Pacific by Western powers, the backdrop to the decline of the Hawai'ian monarchy. When the United States formally seized the Hawai'ian islands as a colony in 1893, the stunning defeat of a Western navy by Japan at Tsushima was still a decade in the future. By then, 90 per cent of the land of Hawai'i had already been lost. As Stauffer's impressively detailed narrative makes clear, it was social dynamics within the semi-colony that levered the land out of the hands of its indigenous people.

The role of a corrupt and irresponsible aristocracy has already been mentioned. *Ali'i* land in the Kahana valley was sold off as early as 1857.

People with links to the monarchy had a specific role in the Kahana debacle: the King himself, with shares in the Hui; and the Foster family, close supporters of the royals, who wound up with complete control of the valley by 1920. An equally important role was played by Protestant missionary families, who first set out to disrupt the Hawai'ian social order in order to destroy paganism. They succeeded. Then they moved in on the debris, to win commercial and landowning wealth for themselves. Particularly important in Kahana were the Mormons, who first energised the Hui, and then undermined it in the interests of their own international religious and commercial empire.

I have told this story not to suggest a general model of dispossession, but to suggest the opposite: that the general idea of dispossession—one of the most important and under-theorised concepts in social science—needs to sink roots into the mud of particular landscapes.

Taking the land seriously has implications for social science knowledge. A famous English historian, R.H. Tawney, once remarked that for a student of history, the most useful equipment is a stout pair of boots. I apply this advice to the social sciences generally, not restricted—*pace* the Gulbenkian commission (1996)—to the 'idiographic' as against the 'nomothetic' sciences. All of them need to wear out shoe leather. Good researchers in all the social sciences do.

This applies to theorists as well as to fact-grubbing empirical researchers. I want to suggest a new meaning for the term 'grounded theory': linking theory to the ground on which the theorist's boots are planted. To think in this way is to reject the deeply entrenched habit of mind, mentioned at the start of this chapter, by which theory in the social sciences is admired exactly in the degree to which it escapes specific settings and speaks in abstract universals.

There is a counter-position, familiar in Anglophone historiography and reinforced by some currents in postmodernism, that is suspicious of generalisation *per se*. To this way of thinking, the local is the only site of knowledge or the only legitimate site of politics. An entirely understandable concern with false representation can lead in the same direction. For instance, feminist generalisations about patriarchy have been successively subdivided by class, race, sexuality, culture and nationality (Bulbeck 1998). Indeed, a new area of studies of 'intersectionality' has grown up around this problem.

This line of thought is damaging if it leads to a rejection of generalisation—the lifeblood of social science as a cultural formation. Generalisation is involved in communication, in the testing of claims, in scientific imagination and the search for new data, in the application and use of knowledge, in the capacity of knowledge to grow. To reject generalisation in social science would immobilise us.

But that does not mean that we are committed to generalise in abstract universals. The intersectionality literature is helpful here, saying that we always need to think about the specific social contexts from which generalisations grow, and the contexts to which they are being made. Theorising grounded in specific landscapes is not trapped in those landscapes. But it certainly needs another criterion of significance from the criterion that abstract-universal theorising has used, where the more cases that are covered the stronger the argument is supposed to be.

I would see this criterion in the riskiness of social science (discussed further in Chapter 10), and specifically in theory's active relationship with locally generated data. Not only do data criticise theory, theory also criticises data. In this continuous argument, one tries to arrive at a configuration of knowledge that reveals the dynamics of a given moment of human history. All such attempts produce generalisations, but only the weak ones are universals. The power of social science generalisations is multiplied if they can be linked to the characteristics of the context *within* which they apply.

This suggests an argument against pure general theory, in favour of what we might call dirty theory—that is, theorising that is mixed up with specific situations. The goal of dirty theory is not to subsume, but to clarify; not to classify from outside, but to illuminate a situation in its concreteness. And for that purpose—to change the metaphor—all is grist to the mill. Our interest as researchers is to maximise the wealth of materials that are drawn into the analysis and explanation. It is also our interest to multiply, rather than slim down, the theoretical ideas that we have to work with. That includes multiplying the local sources of our thinking, as this book attempts to do.

But might reality itself bypass this argument? The neoliberal takeover bid for the world has epistemic consequences as well as economic and political. A market society built on universal commodification involves universal abstraction as a fundamental part of its reality. It seems to invite representation by the placeless abstractions of neoclassical economics. Disregarding the land is not just one theoretical choice among others; it emerges as a feature of the ideology of neoliberal society.

It is not surprising, then, that neoliberal governments are persistently hostile to indigenous land rights. The current Australian government, when its attention wanders from the pleasant task of privatising the telecommunications system, wants to break down collectively controlled Aboriginal institutions, replace them with individual entrepreneurship, and thus let market forces rule. As market forces did in Hawai'i.

Capital itself has been growing more obviously placeless, as the globalisation literature observes. Since the emergence of the Eurodollar market in the 1960s, an increasing proportion of capital has not been tied to a local currency; nor, therefore, it is tied to a national regulatory and taxation regime. Hot money that surfs the currency markets is one form of the placelessness of capital. The linking of national stock markets is another, a project still underway. This will replace the current pattern of international portfolio investment with a placeless universal market in tokens of ownership. The transnational corporation itself is a third— perhaps the most important of all, since this delocalises the determinations of the employer–employee relation.

Yet the placelessness has limits. Consider a transnational accountant and management consultant such as Ernst & Young, PriceWaterhouseCoopers, or any of their competitors. Such a firm is an extended but quite material reality, with an array of local workplaces in all the countries where the firm operates. The local sites are regularly linked by senior executives who spend a lot of time in long-distance air travel. More importantly, they are linked by a complex electronic communication system. This system centres on a huge corporate database into which the firm's professionals and managers constantly tap, and by which their work is guided. This is not open, limitless cyberspace. It is a carefully guarded and highly specific site, whose specificity is essential to the firm's claim to expertise and hence its capacity to accumulate profits.

So the transnational spaces of globalised corporations have a place-ness about them; and they also have to touch down in ordinary space. This is the argument of Saskia Sassen (1991) in *The Global City*. In a few central places— London, New York and Tokyo—there is a rapid growth of producer services, including legal, accounting, advertising, financial and broking firms, around the vast flow of funds in transnational corporations. Their high-salaried workforces in turn are serviced by real estate, retail, human service and domestic workers, leading to low-wage immigration and changes in local social structure. Sassen (2002) has since repainted this picture, suggesting the recent growth of a world network of about 40 'linked cities' that perform the same control and service functions in a more decentralised way.

Sassen's models, schematic as they are, call attention to the materiality of globalisation processes. The abstraction involved in commodification and international finance does not eliminate space; rather, it reconfigures it. The wealth acquired by the neoliberal economy does not float off into a shimmering transnational ether; it comes to rest in the pockets of particular suits, covering bodies that stand, sit or lie on particular square metres of the land. The power that attaches to contemporary wealth is thus a located power, though not a local one.

That is why so much effort goes into protecting the places of the rich. In all human history, the economic gap between rich and poor has never been as great as it is now. And, to a degree unusual in the history of class relations, the contemporary transnational ruling class has walled itself off from subalterns, in security-guarded apartments, corporate skyscrapers, corporate jets, Maybach cars, and the clusters of mansions carefully documented in Mike Donaldson and Scott Poynting's (2007) *Ruling Class Men*. Mike Davis's (1990) classic *City of Quartz* traced the social history of Los Angeles in the United States, and showed how in recent years, as transnational capital has come to dominate former elites, class and ethnic segregation has literally been built into the fabric of the city. Buildings— indeed, whole precincts—have been designed to keep the poor out; and a private 'security' industry has swollen to provide the means of enforcing exclusion.

The land, therefore, is not irrelevant, even in the citadels of global- isation. We have to understand its social significance in a complex dialectic of place and power, of which the history of colonisation and the consequent land rights struggles of indigenous people are key parts. These struggles, the experiences that underlie them and the arguments advanced in them are now strategic matters of social justice globally. Taking them seriously, and learning from them, is necessary for regenerating social science on a world scale.

10

Social science on a world scale

I went on towards the bamboo house. It was not only from Europe that so much could be learned! This modern age had provided many breasts to suckle me—from among the Natives themselves, from Japan, China, America, India, Arabia, from all the peoples on the face of this earth. They were the mother wolves that gave me life to become a builder of Rome! Is it true you will build a Rome? Yes, I answered myself. How? I don't know. In humility I realised I am a child of all nations, of all ages, past and present.

Pramoedya Ananta Toer (1979)

Studying the social in the world arena

Through this book, I have made free use of different ways of naming global divisions. They include the 'North/South' terminology from UN debates; Raúl Prebisch's language of 'centre/periphery'; the 'West/East' language of Orientalism and its critics; the 'developed/underdeveloped' language of development and dependency theory; the French imperialist 'metropole/colony'. I have rarely used 'First World/Third World', or world-systems theory's 'core/semi-periphery/periphery', though some still find those terms useful too.

Though each of these concepts has its own points of reference, there is obviously a good deal of overlap. The poststructuralist geographer David Slater (2004), reviewing the language of 'North/South' and 'East/West', rightly argues that, through all the ambiguities of terminology, the realities of global division show through. All these expressions refer to the long-lasting pattern of inequality in power, wealth and cultural influence that grew historically out of European and North American imperialism. For that general pattern, I use the hybrid 'metropole/periphery'.

To recognise this pattern, to be able to name the metropole and register the different situations of metropole and periphery, is an absolute requirement for social science to work on a world scale. Theories that do not recognise this pattern (they range from market fundamentalism to global cultural hybridisation) fail at the first test of realism. Theories that embody the 'false sense of universality' Prebisch diagnosed are always based on the same error. They build a model on the experience of the most privileged 600 million people, then assume it accounts for the whole 6000 million who are actually in the world.

No one who thinks for a moment would assume the other 5400 million are all in the same situation. To use concepts like 'periphery' is just the beginning of analysis, not the end. The periphery includes desperately poor countries like Benin and astonishingly rich countries like Australia. As Cardoso and Faletto showed (Chapter 7), even within one region the patterns of dependence and paths of development differ strongly.

As Çardoso and Faletto do, we must bring into the wide picture the local inequalities of wealth and power. The language of 'elite/subaltern' in Chapter 8 refers to the different politics that arose from these differences in colonial India. In Chapter 9, I mentioned Mick Dodson's essay on the situation of Aboriginal people in contemporary Australia, and it is worth quoting some of his statistics:

> The social indicators are grim . . . We are still the ones who are 18 times more likely to be in prisons; they still inadequately house 60 percent of us; we are still the ones dying 18 to 20 years younger than other Australians; still the ones only one-third as likely to complete secondary school, three times as likely to be unemployed . . . 38 percent of Aboriginal communities have a water supply that does not meet World Health Organization standards (Dodson 1997: 40).

As Dodson is well aware, the same problems face indigenous people in other countries, though not many other countries have such abundant economic means for solving them. It is not lack of resources, but the stony indifference of the local ruling class, that prevents such problems being solved in Australia.

The configuration of social forces in the periphery is not fixed. New social actors appear, as shown in both Latin America and India by the mobilisation of women (Chapters 7 and 8); in Australia and other countries by the indigenous land rights movement (Chapter 9); in Iran by the emergence of political Islam (Chapter 6); and in Africa by the independence movements themselves (Chapter 5). A second test of realism for social science, then, is its capacity to recognise the dynamism of the periphery.

This diversity and dynamism have immediate consequences for the making of social science. The production of knowledge is a very different enterprise in an affluent peripheral country such as Australia and a poor peripheral country such as Indonesia. The social theory of a writer like Ashis Nandy in India (Chapter 8), drawing on a rich indigenous intellectual history, reads very differently from the social thought of Afrikaner intellectuals in South Africa, who were cut off by the dynamics of settler colonialism from the resources of indigenous thought (Gilomee 1994). One of the fundamental problems that social science now faces is to connect different formations of knowledge in the periphery with each other. Later in this chapter, I will come to some practical issues in doing this.

In Chapters 2 and 3, I argued that one of the mechanisms constituting Northern theory was the erasure of experience from the periphery.

To undo this erasure is a primary task in reworking the relations between periphery and metropole, to make a shared learning process possible. In the first place, this requires the kind of research undertaken by *Subaltern Studies*, documenting the experience of the oppressed—especially of the people left out of the hegemonic narratives of history and modernity. That was also the task of Sol Plaatje in *Native Life in South Africa*. There are classics of metropolitan social science, too, which have done just that: Eugene Genovese's *Roll, Jordan, Roll: The World the Slaves Made* (1976) comes to mind.

This is different from the task undertaken by mainstream ethnography, building up a library of descriptions of non-Western societies. When Jomo Kenyatta published *Facing Mount Kenya* in 1938, it was not just to add to the Malinowski school's collection of peoples captive on their shelves. It was to contest the real captivity of the Gikuyu people by contesting British colonialism's story about them.

The same point applies now. We cannot arrive at a new formation of knowledge by heaping description on description, however subtle and comprehensive they might be. We should recall Ranajit Guha's emphasis that *Subaltern Studies* was to be concerned with the *politics* of the people, not just with the description of their experience. We should also recall what Mick Dodson was doing with the statistics just quoted: shaping them into an argument for land rights.

What matters, then, is not just the subject-matter of experience but also its vector or intentionality, its relation to the structures around which a politics of change may form. In Plaatje's and Dodson's writing—and indeed in Genovese's—a central fact is the experience of *loss*. There is impressive psychoanalytic work on this theme (e.g. Bowlby 1980), with which social theory has hardly begun to reckon. Yet collective loss, as a social process on a very large scale, is central to the history of colonialism. Chapter 9 gave a well-documented example, the loss of land—and with it the loss of a social order—by one Polynesian coastal settlement. We could multiply cases.

There are other experiences of loss besides land. The missionary incomers in Hawai'i intended that the indigenous people lose their religion. Al-Afghani was by no means naive in seeing the threat to Islam as a key feature of nineteenth century imperialism. Nor was Al-e Ahmad wrong in seeing religious indifference (the loss of faith, not the adoption of another one) as a mark of the Westoxicated man. In Hopenhayn's account of contemporary Latin America, a central theme is the loss of the faith, hope and energy that had been associated with the project of social integration and justice.

There are other aspects of the experience of the colonised that are difficult to represent in social science as now constituted. Chapter 2 noted that the way time is treated in sociological theory is incompatible with the rupture of time and intelligibility represented by colonial conquest. Nor is conquest a once-and-for-all break. The great discontinuity is carried forward into colonial society by the presence of what Valentine Mudimbe (1988) calls 'the colonising structure'—the domination of space, the reshaping of native minds, and the integration of local economies into international capitalism. It is carried forward in postcolonial society too, if we follow Ashis Nandy's (2003) diagnosis, by the developmentalist state as well as by the pressure of the corporate economy.

Néstor García Canclini's (1995) diagnosis of Mexico City points to another kind of unintelligibility, that of the mega-cities of peripheral countries. The integration of national elites into metropolitan culture and global capitalism provides no means of integration (indeed, helps to shred earlier national strategies of integration) for the vast, mostly poor, immigrant population of these cities. Ranajit Guha's formula of 'dominance without hegemony' may be relevant far beyond the case of the British Raj.

Metropolitan social theory comfortably talks about the constitution of society, about the building blocks of social processes, and about the reproduction of social structures. It has been much less keen—and perhaps lacks the concepts—to talk about the destruction of social relations, about discontinuity and dispossession, about the bloodshed and suffering involved in creating the world in which we currently live. There is a deep defensiveness here. When I first published part of the argument of this book, a well-known metropolitan theorist declared, in the same journal, that this was a 'sociological guilt trip' (Collins 1997).

There is, nevertheless, a danger in a tight focus on the periphery. Such experiences as dispossession and discontinuous time may appear a kind of natural catastrophe that simply happened to colonised people. To recall Ariel Dorfman on the 1973 coup in Chile, violence is the act of specific people, who intend its consequences. The targeted group may not see it coming, but the intention—and the possibility of acting otherwise—can in principle be seen. It is vital to recognise the *agency* involved in colonial dispossession, military dictatorship and neoliberal restructuring alike.

Raúl Prebisch devotes more than a quarter of *The Economic Development of Latin America and its Principal Problems* to writing about the United States. It is not enough to name the metropole; the job of social science is to analyse it. This is a question of understanding the social processes—the institutions, interests and strategies—that generate the catastrophes. In the 1960s, new left sociology called this 'studying up', in contrast to the familiar practice where middle-class academics study down on the poor, the marginal and the troubled. Power structure research set out to study the rich instead, and duly produced important findings on the concentration of wealth and the shape of corporate elites, especially in the United States (Domhoff 1975). The strategy is still fruitful (Donaldson and Poynting 2007).

The same logic applies on a world scale, and is seen in the more creative globalisation research, especially linkage studies (Chapter 3). For instance, Leslie Sklair's *The Transnational Capitalist Class* (2001) brings together the results of a long program of research on transnational corporations and their political operations.

Corporations are not the only institutions that allow the rich countries to exercise control and accumulate resources. There is also the metropolitan state, changing from its days of plump imperial pride to its scarecrow neoliberal present, thinning its commitment to citizens' well-being while growing its capacity for external destruction. There are the museums and research institutes that have been key players in the centralisation of data from the colonial world. There are the new sciences and technologies that, as Al-e Ahmad (1962) observed, lie behind the machine civilisation that is the vehicle of Westoxication. Since his day, computer technology has made the point even more forcibly. And there is the problem of tracing the changing locus of power in a system where now, as García Canclini (1999: 13) puts it, the main decisions that shape everyday life 'are taken in places that are inaccessible and difficult to identify'.

No more than with the periphery do we want just a heaping up of descriptions of the metropole. There is already vast documentation of the social life of the United States and Western Europe. That is, after all, the main content of the social sciences today.

From the point of view of understanding society on a world scale, what matters most about metropolitan society is, again, the vector—its ability to function as metropole, and the institutions and processes that support that ability. At this point we can refine the metropole/periphery language a little, though I am afraid my language is still clumsy. The object of knowledge here is the metropole-capacity—or, if we think in more institutional terms, the metropole-apparatus—of the countries that occupy the dominant position in the world economy, international relations and culture.

This apparatus lies behind the colonising structures and the global reach, and understanding it will need the full range of social sciences. For instance, there is a significant gender dimension. Ashis Nandy in *The Intimate Enemy* was one of the first to point to the gender dynamics of the imperial state. Feminist and feminist-influenced research is giving us a much fuller picture of imperial masculinities (Connell 2005). On the other hand, world-systems research has emphasised the political economy of core–periphery relations. One can hardly doubt that the changing forms of capital in metropolitan centres, notably the virtualisation of capital and the development of new instruments of ownership and finance, are important for their current capacity to dominate the international economy.

Production and circulation of knowledge

Social science as a whole is embodied practice. It is something done by particular groups of people in particular settings. This has been clear since feminists raised the issue of what it was to have women rather than men doing the research, as well as being the objects of research (Roberts 1981).

There is always a workforce involved in the production of social-scientific knowledge. If we ask where this workforce is located on the earth's surface, there are no surprises. Social scientists, like other researchers and like the technically trained workforce in general, are concentrated in rich countries. They mostly work for universities, corporations and the state. Their research is funded by the same institutions, plus the indirect corporate funding that comes through foundations in the United States.

Social scientists working in the periphery have a strong orientation to the world centres of their disciplines in the metropole. This is not unique to social science. Natural scientists in Australia also have strong international connections, but they are focused on the United States and Britain, a pattern of quasi-globalisation (Connell and Wood 2002; Connell Crawford and Wood 2005). Much the same was observed by Paulin Hountondji (1995) in the poor peripheral countries of West Africa; there, of course, the metropolitan centre is usually France.

The practices of connection include academic travel (going for training, going to conferences, taking sabbatical leave in the metropole), patronage and sponsorship, publication, and the formation of research networks—which commonly centre on prominent figures in the metropole. Centres can form in the periphery that attract a workforce and develop prestige—CEPAL in Santiago is the most famous in the social sciences; CODESRIA in Dakar a more recent example. But they are few in comparison with the metropole, and may (as CODESRIA does) depend on metropolitan grants. Hosseiniyah Ershad, which Ali Shariati intended to become a world centre of Islamic social research, was crushed by the Iranian government. The institutional base of social science in the periphery is relatively fragile.

The institutional base of the social-scientific workforce is relevant to the kind of knowledge that is produced. Chapter 5 referred to Thandika Mkandawire's (2000) observations on post-independence intellectuals in Africa. In the era of neoliberal restructuring, with governments wanting experts supplied by the IMF and World Bank, local intellectuals looked to NGOs for support and hearing. But aid NGOs wanted only consultancies, not sustained research programs, so basic research was squeezed out from both sides. In Latin America, as in Africa, social scientists were involved in the nation-building projects of the 1950s and 1960s. On Martín Hopenhayn's (2001) argument, their relation with progressive movements and the developmentalist state became the main axis of social science in this period. When the dictatorships and neoliberalism destroyed this context, the project of social science was deeply disrupted, and a very fundamental rethinking had to begin.

It is not surprising that ideas, terminology and research technologies get exported from the metropole to the periphery. I have mentioned the importation of intellectual packages such as US cultural feminism to India and European post-structuralism to Australia and Latin America.

Neoclassical economics is perhaps the package with the biggest impact of all.

Such importation is an extremely common process, involving a trade in texts, which in this respect are not at all disembodied. Texts are also material objects produced by publishers and governed by copyright laws. It has always been difficult for works published in the periphery to circulate in the metropole, and to other parts of the periphery. A fine example is provided by Hountondji's own writing. His first book, *Libertés*, published in Cotonou in 1973, remains almost unknown. His second book, *Sur la philosophie africaine*, published in Paris three years later with some of the same content, became famous.

What circulates, then, is partly dependent on a publishing industry, and this is not static. Publishers have become more dependent on a relatively small number of best-selling authors, and not only in popular fiction. Celebrity intellectuals also exist in the social sciences, and the circulation of their books is both profitable and influential; almost all come from the metropole. Publishing itself has become more centralised, with the rise of firms like Bertelsmann AG. García Canclini (2002) discusses the growth of international corporate control over literary publishing in Latin America, a process familiar in other parts of the world. In Australia, most—though not quite all—independent publishers are now gone.

Global publishing uses globally dominant languages, which these days mainly means English. The Yolngu (Chapter 9) may have a resilient social order but they don't have the numbers to form a market for publishers. *Our Land is Our Life*, the important collection of Aboriginal writing and oral history edited by Galarrwuy Yunupingu from which I have been quoting, is entirely in English. That was a condition for its circulation. The costs of translation will see to it that not a great many writers in other languages will be circulated in English.

Thus the ways in which the production and circulation of knowledge are organised generally produce metropolitan dominance and peripheral marginality in social science. This is a persistent tendency, but not a closed system—otherwise this book would not be possible. There is contestation, and peripheral intellectuals too have agency. This agency is the basis of Ali Shariati's model of *rushanfekr*, the 'enlightened souls' who take responsibility for giving direction to their society. As I argued in Chapter 6, this concept stands not so much for a social category as for the permanent possibility of transformative thought and action. It signals the vulnerability of systems of domination and marginalisation. This too must be factored into any understanding of how social science might work on a world scale.

Relations between knowledges

Imperial expansion forcibly brought together groups of people who had formerly been independent of each other, or who had communicated only remotely. That is the starting point of a problem that has been discussed with particular emphasis in Africa, the articulation of knowledge systems (Odora Hoppers 2002). This problem occurs worldwide, and bears on what we mean by social science in a world context. By a UNESCO count in the early 1990s, there are still at least 10 000 distinct cultures in the world. The report of the relevant UNESCO commission was entitled *Our Creative Diversity* (Eide 2006).

In all cultures, there are ways of representing the social. The 'dot paintings' from Central Desert communities in Australia, discussed in Chapter 9, are a good example. It would be possible for a professional social scientist to learn this symbolic language—or at least the public part of it—and to construct an Indigenous sociology, as Akinsola Akiwowo set about constructing a sociology from Yoruba ritual poetry (Chapter 5). Something like that does happen when Australian anthropologists, as well as community elders, testify in land rights cases. They do not use paintings specifically, but they use the spirit narratives, the local kin terminology and other materials from local culture to picture local society and establish its relationship with specific areas of land. They attempt to translate the local symbolism into a language acceptable in a court hearing.

Apart from court cases over land rights, what would be the point of constructing such an Indigenous sociology? The symbolic systems in designs and narratives are beautiful in themselves. They circulate to a wider audience, transformed as commodities produced for a market, and this has become a successful industry. There is, as far as I know, no missionary impulse in the Central Desert that desires its social concepts to be applied to other societies.

This example might caution us against any general impulse to integrate different systems of knowledge about society. What Central Desert communities need from the dominant culture is not integration, but respect. Respect includes support at the practical level, since the society that produced this body of knowledge is now under severe stress.

Noel Pearson (1997), one of the Aboriginal negotiating team for the 1993 *Native Title Act* that followed the *Mabo* land rights case, makes a similar point about Aboriginal law. 'Native title' is not actually a concept in Aboriginal law. Pearson argues that it is a 'recognition concept', by which settler society's common law recognises a certain form of rights: 'Native title is therefore the space between the two systems, where there is recognition' (Pearson 1997: 154).

Lack of recognition was a keynote of colonial era social science. Theorists like Émile Durkheim were indeed interested in the beliefs of non-Western peoples. But they were not interested in learning the truth or insight contained in those beliefs; they treated them rather as exhibits in a museum of primitiveness. Metropolitan social science has moved beyond nineteenth century notions of the primitive, but as Chapters 2 and 3 showed, the lack of recognition persists.

Metropolitan social science established very early a conceptual style in which theory is monological, declaring one truth in one voice. This can be found as early as Ricardo, Comte and Spencer. It has remained characteristic of the social sciences in the last half-century, though exceptions can be found. (An exhilarating exception is the psychologist Liam Hudson's discussion of unicorns in *The Cult of the Fact*, 1972.) The theorist's monologue encourages—even requires—the discrediting or subsumption of other points of view.

Postmodernism, on the face of it, challenges this way of theorising. Lyotard's *The Postmodern Condition* (1979) is a notably imaginative and insightful text that questioned the grand narratives around which European knowledge systems had been organised. Such a view does encourage the questioning of orthodoxies, and can thus open 'new possibilities for knowledge and social practice' (Seidman 1994: 278). Yet as a movement in the social sciences, postmodernism has not been notably pluralist. Regrettably, it has often adopted the monological style of its predecessors—cultivating its own canon, and trying to discredit other points of view as modernist or essentialist.

A different challenge to dominant frames of thought is the view-from-below in an unequal society. This has a long and rich history, going back to the working-class criticisms of political economy from which Marx and Engels drew. Gyorgy Lukács' formulation of 'the point of view of the proletariat', in the long-suppressed *History and Class Consciousness* (1923), is the classic statement, virtually the origin of the modern sociology of knowledge. Dorothy Smith's formulation of 'a sociology for women' challenges not just the propositions, but the whole cognitive style, of mainstream social science. Raúl Prebisch's idea of an economics for the developing countries has been discussed already, as has Ranajit Guha's agenda for history exploring subaltern points of view.

Two different conceptions of the structure of knowledge can follow. With Lukács, the logic is counter-hegemonic. He thought Marxism represented a better science, a greater truth, than bourgeois thought. This led to a new monological theory in which the previously dominant system of knowledge would be subsumed. With Smith (1987), the logic is disjunctive. She thinks the knowledge produced by a sociology for women (in her later work, a sociology for people) is of another order than the abstractions of conventional social science. It is more concrete, embodied and local. Smith makes no attempt to subsume the dominant system of thought—though she makes a vigorous criticism of it, establishing distance and difference.

These positions have clear, bold outlines. The work discussed in previous chapters under the rubric of 'Southern theory', though certainly embodying a view-from-below on a world scale, has a more complex relationship with dominant systems of knowledge. Existing Southern theory points to a more engaged relationship between knowledge systems, and foreshadows a mutual learning process on a planetary scale.

Consider, for instance, Ali Shariati, whose Shi'ite theology provided a radical alternative to European secularism as a ground for social theory (Chapter 6). Shariati still drew freely on the European sociology of class and concepts of revolution; he drew examples from European history, particularly the protestant reformation; he used the concept of ideology, and drew on Western debates about intellectuals. Or consider the position of Martín Hopenhayn (Chapter 7). The political catastrophes that destroyed integrationist social science in Latin America were locally generated (making all due allowance for the CIA and the IMF!).

Hopenhayn found, in postmodern theoretical developments in the metropole, the best ways of representing the consequences of these events in the periphery.

These two examples are typical. One could add Nandy's use of psychoanalysis, Prebisch's use of economic statistics, Cardoso and Faletto's use of class analysis, Valdés's use of gender difference statistics, Hountondji's adaptation of political economy. Every significant development in the social sciences in the periphery makes *some* use of concepts or techniques from the metropole.

It is therefore not realistic to imagine the future of world social science as a mosaic of distinct knowledge systems—as a set of indigenous sociologies, indigenous economics, and so on, all functioning independently. The UNESCO document's claim that there are more than 10 000 distinct cultures in the world is helpful in dramatising the diversity of human experience, but may also be misleading, because it reifies the idea of 'a culture' (cf. Friedman 1994).

Georges Balandier's *Sociology of Black Africa* (1955), one of the most important attempts by a metropolitan social scientist to understand the dynamics of colonialism, gives a key reason. A colonised society is a society in crisis. The colonial situation itself puts so much pressure on local social orders as to force radical change. This applies to knowledge systems as well as to labour systems, producing the tensions and uncertainties with which Hountondji and his colleagues grappled in *Endogenous Knowledge*. Even in postcolonial situations, the fragility of the institutional base for social science, the crisis of organicity in Latin America, the failure to establish a coherent social science tradition in Australia all show the unsuitability of a mosaic theory of multiple knowledges.

I will go so far as to say the only possible future for social science on a world scale involves a principle of unification. Shariati, Hopenhayn and the others were acting in a principled way when they constructed arguments using materials from the metropole. But they were not joining a school, they were not being subsumed by metropolitan theory, and they were not entering someone else's monologue.

The relationship with metropolitan knowledge in these cases also involved a critical distance: a willingness to challenge metropolitan formulations (e.g. Shariati on Marx), or to judge when to *leave* a certain theoretical position (e.g. Hopenhayn and García Canclini on postmodernism). It involved an autonomous capacity to make diagnoses of a certain social conjuncture (e.g. Akiwowo on West African social change, Al-e Ahmad on change in Iran). Social science in the periphery also, as I have shown through the book, injects themes that are relatively uncommon in metropolitan thought. These include the social significance of the land, the experience of dispossession and loss, the discontinuities in colonisation, and the metropole-capacity of the global centres.

Engagement, critique, respect and recognition (in Pearson's sense) are bases of mutual learning. The development of social science involves an educational process, which we now need to think about on a world scale. The unification of social science is not a process of propagating the metropole's truth, because the metropole too must learn—at least as actively as the periphery.

Social knowledge as science

We must therefore move beyond the idea of systems of social knowledge as distinct, closed entities, except as a rare limiting case. The moment we ask Hountondji's question about the *truth* in indigenous knowledge, we are obliged to think in a different way. This opens questions about the growth of indigenous knowledge and the transformations of social thought in dialogue and collective learning.

To speak of the knowledge of society as science is to presume, first, that it is corrigible in research. The major professional activity of social scientists (apart from writing grant applications) is investigation. We spend our time collecting information, interpreting what we have collected, and trying to relate it to existing knowledge. This collective practice, mundane as it often is, has a crucial epistemological function. This is how the state of the world is mapped, how errors and distortions are found, how the credibility of theoretical claims is decided.

There is, then, a permanent revolution within social science, based on the empirical dimension in the collective learning process. The idea of dirty theory suggested in Chapter 9 recognises this dimension, and contests Thomas Kuhn's (1970) well-known concept of 'normal science', which reduces most scientific practice to routine problem-solving within an established paradigm. The permanent revolution of corrigibility, in fact, provides one of the best arguments against metropolitan domination. If social science in the periphery is dependent on theory in the metropole, that theory is protected from its rightful vulnerability—since metropolitan theorists rarely pay attention to the research from the periphery, while social scientists in the periphery rarely feel authorised to rewrite the ideas of the metropolitan expert.

To speak of social science is, second, to presume a capacity for generalisation. How generalisation works is a delicate and difficult question, but the fact of generalisation is vital. A drive towards generalisation is constitutive of science, and this is why we need theory, why science can never be simply a heap of facts. Theory is the way we speak beyond the single case. It involves imagination, the search for patterns, the critique of data. It is how we get the criteria for comparisons and the terms of a diagnosis. Theory, too, is organic to the growth of social science. In this sense, I consider Akiwowo's experiment in indigenous sociology (Chapter 5), with its intention of contributing to a 'general body of explanatory principles' in world social science, to be absolutely justified.

To emphasise investigation, corrigibility, generalisation and the growth of knowledge is also to recognise limits to social science. There are some situations where this form of knowledge does not apply, or should not apply. Veena Das in *Critical Events* gives us such cases. With the Bhopal disaster of 1984, she refused to anthropologise among the victims, and turned instead to look at how the state handled the event. With the Partition violence of 1946–48, she recognised events that were outside the reproduction of social relations, that in some ways could not be spoken and could not be interpreted.

I have suggested that colonial conquest itself has such characteristics, as an event of massive incomprehensibility. However well we research and theorise the societies that came into existence in its wake, a thread of that incomprehensibility runs forward to this day. It produces what Noel Pearson called 'the space between the two systems', and the continuing need to make an effort for recognition. We should not worry if that recognition is always partial; there are limits to any system of social knowledge.

In *African Philosophy* and in his later work, Paulin Hountondji argues that there is one discipline of philosophy, not many—though in that discipline, more voices and cultural experiences should be represented. My argument leads to a similar view of social theory.

This point underlies my critique of Northern theory. On close examination, mainstream sociology turns out to be an ethno-sociology of metropolitan society. This is concealed by its language, especially the framing of its theories as universal propositions or universal tools. The models of agency offered by Coleman, Giddens and Bourdieu are excellent examples of this point (Chapter 2). Prebisch made the same observation about mainstream economics: it was based on the experience of the metropole but framed its arguments as if universal (Chapter 7). Regrettably, the same must be said of mainstream economics since Prebisch died, though there are still dissenting voices (Stiglitz 2002).

Metropolitan sociology (to continue with the discipline I know best) is a splendid ethno-sociology. It has profound insights, well-honed methods, well-defined concepts and lots of skilled practitioners, some of whom are my best friends. But its theorising is vitiated whenever it refuses to recognise its ethno-sociological being—or, to put it another way, its situation in the world and its history in the world. The failures of recognition documented in the first part of this book have consequences. They result not in minor omissions but in major incompleteness, and a profound problem about the truthfulness of arguments framed as universal generalisations.

The truthfulness of social science is a question not much discussed nowadays. We have, perhaps, been seduced by the idea of a 'model', which makes a claim only to usefulness not to truth; or we have been intimidated by postmodern philosophy, which is widely assumed to prove an instability in language that undermines any claim of truth. Truth effects reign, not truthfulness. I am sure that few colleagues in the social sciences nowadays would adopt the naive view that: 'A picture agrees with reality or fails to agree; it is correct or incorrect, true or false.'

Yet I would argue—and the everyday *practice* of social scientists seems to support me—that this quotation from Wittgenstein's *Tractatus* (1921: section 2.2) states a principle that social science actually follows. We do try, as researchers, to make our statements agree with realities in other people's lives that are independent of our statements. We do recognise errors in existing knowledge and persistently try to correct them. And thus we participate in a shared, public learning process.

Certainly, this is only one moment in the construction of social-scientific knowledge. And no one with hands-on experience in empirical research will doubt the difficulty of using complex evidence and establishing firm conclusions. Every method in social science has its controversies. Yet even the most controversial methods—oral history, for instance—allow inference from evidence, if not always the kind of inference that naive positivism expects (for illuminating recent examples, see White, Miescher and Cohen 2001).

Without that core of concern for truthfulness, the claim that our discourse is social science, and so entitled to a certain attention and respect, is hollow. Therefore the incompleteness of knowledge in, and problematic truthfulness of, metropolitan theory—given its hegemonic position—represents a structural difficulty in world social science.

Reconfiguring knowledge on a world scale

Any discussion of the future of social science on a world scale must recognise that metropolitan social science is a going enterprise, and that the background conditions for its global predominance will only change in the very long term.

What can change more immediately is the way metropolitan social science operates, to fit it for the global learning process sketched above. We can place what Shariati called a mark of cancellation on the operation of power in this realm of knowledge. Indeed, every principle of science says that we should.

To change the way metropolitan social science operates in the world requires a retooling that will be arduous and perhaps also expensive. Professional self-images, personal stocks of knowledge, affiliations, citation practices, publication strategies both of individuals and of publishing houses, grant-getting and practical applications of social science, are all at stake. So is teaching. When I was studying the history of sociology (Chapter 1), I became aware of how firmly the dominant perspectives of the discipline in the United States were embedded in its pedagogy and curriculum. They were particularly embedded in the graduate programs that produced the academic workforce for the next generation. That curriculum is changing, and now incorporates more feminist and African-American material than before. To make it fully oriented to world social science requires further change.

Equally possible, and equally arduous, is ending the extroversion of social science in the periphery, to fit that too for global dialogue. A key difficulty here is finding non-metropolitan bases of cultural authority. The story of 'African philosophy' shows dramatically both the need for such authority and its problematic character. The strength of al-Afghani and Shariati was having a dynamic rather than a static conception of Islam to launch their social analysis. The emergence of new social identities in the periphery, as traced by Sonia Montecino (2001) in Chile, is one reason why a static cultural formation cannot ground the social sciences.

Does social science need 'grounding'? Here the postmodern critiques of foundationalism are helpful. The brief discussion of science a few pages ago implied a riskiness in social-scientific knowledge. Knowledge is inherently questionable and, when the institutions of social science are working well, is persistently questioned. It is the foreclosing of questions and thus the end of a learning process that defines the moment when science turns into ideology and its ideas become state, corporate or institutional dogmas.

I think it is helpful to think of social science not as a settled system of concepts, methods and findings, but as an interconnected set of intellectual projects that proceed from varied social starting points into an unpredictable future. (If we can predict the outcome of research, we do not need to do that research. The riskiness of science is fundamental.)

The connections among projects may be tight or loose. In the current configuration of knowledge on a world scale, projects of investigation and knowledge production launched in the periphery have, for the most part, a low degree of connection among themselves. A striking example is the gap between the African Renaissance debates (Chapter 5) and the Latin American debates about regional identity and neoliberalism (Chapter 7), though the two literatures have many issues in common.

It is possible to reshape the circuits through which social-scientific knowledge moves, to modify—since we cannot quickly end—the metropolitan focus. The intellectuals of rich peripheral countries such as Australia, and of the privileged classes in countries like Mexico, Chile, India, South Africa and Brazil, have significant resources for intellectual work and the circulation of knowledge. Because of their location in the post-colonial world, they have—or can have—perspectives which overlap with those of the subaltern majorities.

It is, then, possible to conceive of networks of cooperation in the social sciences that run around and across the periphery. In *La globalización imaginada* (1999), García Canclini names a pattern of 'tangential globalisation'. Creating such networks presumes the regional alliances and markets that are central to García Canclini's proposals for a cultural politics in the era of globalisation.

What would support their development? There have been attempts to find common interests among large groups of countries in the periphery, such as the Bandung non-aligned movement in the 1950s and the G77 in the 1960s. The disintegration of these alliances suggests the difficulty of institutionalising the common ground. Smaller groupings such as Mercosur (the economic alliance of southern cone countries in South America) may be more stable. For the most part, however, the material interests of intellectual workers persistently tie them to the metropole.

To a significant extent, then, lateral links among intellectual workers—especially links beyond one's immediate region—will need non-material rationales. These are, in the first place, intellectual. Once an overlapping problem area is defined, a common interest in truth and depth of understanding can be discovered. There are, in the second place, cathectic links, involving respect and friendship. This may sound banal, but in my experience voluntary association, goodwill and mutual liking are not trivial bases for intellectual cooperation. They provide a basis for shared labour that points forward to emerging shared interests, rather than backward to interests founded in structures of inequality.

Among overlapping intellectual interests, I would emphasise those that concern the making of transnational structures and practices. This is, as nearly as I can formulate it, the common ground among writers as different as Nandy, Al-e Ahmad, Hountondji and García Canclini. Earlier in this chapter I discussed 'studying up', and emphasised that the crucial issue was not to describe social life in rich countries but to understand their capacity to act as metropole—that is, the metropole-effect and the metropole-apparatus. The significance of this distinction is increased by the expansion of the metropole-apparatus into transnational space, where it establishes a certain autonomy from the social order of the rich countries, while continuing to function as metropole on a global scale. A whole research frontier is now developing that concerns this mutation and the interplay between this changing apparatus and the dynamics of peripheral societies.

And democracy . . .

I come, finally, to the political significance of these arguments. Any realistic view of intellectual history must acknowledge that social science has a broad anti-democratic heritage, from nineteenth-century justifications of imperialism to modern technocratic management science, corporate-funded market research, and more. It was entirely consistent with this tradition that neoclassical economics justified the 'There is No Alternative' of neoliberalism in the 1980s.

Under neoliberal power since the 1980s, the social sciences—including economics—face a sustained assault on truth. Neoliberal regimes are ruthless with spin and manipulation and, in combination with corporate advertising, have bent popular expectations to the point where deceit is now normalised in the public realm. (Opinion poll data showing rising distrust of politicians are among the disturbing indicators.)

The bases for social science practice independent of corporate interests are shrinking. In Australia, heavy restrictions already apply to the circulation of official knowledge. For instance, the economic modelling that the national government undertakes before making policy decisions is done in secret, and even Freedom of Information law-suits cannot obtain its findings. Census data, once free, is now expensive. The constriction of social knowledge appears quite rational to the dominant powers. Neoliberalism has little use for social science, except for a schematised economics—and even that is subordinated to the imperatives of corporate and government spin.

Considering this heritage and this present situation, it would seem utopian to look for democratic gains through the development of social science on a world scale. Yet we should. Social science also has a democratic heritage, as studies of class, gender and colonialism show; and it survives because it meets a need for the self-understanding of society. That need intensifies as the dominant powers systematically distort our pictures of reality.

I can think of four main ways in which the development of social science serves democratic ends. The first is through the growth of compassion. Veena Das in one way, Ali Shariati in another, show how social science can embody a feeling with, a solidarity with, the despised and rejected. A multi-centred social science has a great capacity to circulate knowledge of social experiences other than those of the global elites, and thus enable mutual learning. This is, indeed, a long-standing goal of UNESCO, and it is one reason why that organisation was bitterly attacked by neoliberals.

The second is social science's function of critique. When researchers investigate topics that are sensitive for neoliberalism, they find themselves contesting a torrent of lies and distortions from governments and corporate-funded think-tanks. A major example is research on poverty (Saunders 2005). Given the restructuring of the world economy and the growth of the global-private, issues of social justice unavoidably have an international dimension. They must, increasingly, be an internationally shared responsibility among social scientists. Projects such as the Latin American 'Indice de compromiso cumplido' (Valdés 2001), the continent-wide project for monitoring gender equality mentioned in Chapter 7, show the way.

The third is simply that social science produces many forms of knowledge that democratic movements need. Research on transnational power structures is a significant example. Knowledge about income distributions, forms of organisation, strategies of resistance and reform, the impact of new media, and new approaches in education and social dimensions of health are all relevant to democratic politics. Knowledge about these issues circulates, in significant part, through social science.

Finally, world social science is relevant to democracy because it is itself a field of democratic action. To contest a privileged minority's control of a field of knowledge is a democratic cause, whether on a local or a world scale. The learning process based on recognition and discussion among many voices—the picture of social-scientific knowledge which the arguments of this book imply—is inherently a democratic process.

Whether this learning transfers to other arenas depends on what audiences the social sciences find. In Chapter 5 I quoted Mamadou Diawara urging social scientists to 'leave the campus and talk to the people face-to-face'. There are moments when that will work, and moments when it will not; but the principle is good. As Al-e Ahmad's *Gharbzadegi* and Shariati's work at Hosseiniyah Ershad show, it is sometimes possible to create new publics. This is not primarily a matter of new media, though they may help. More importantly, it is a matter of responding to needs for knowledge and understanding. There is every reason to think these needs are shared across regions.

It would be nice to end with a rosy image of the future of social science. But a social science worth having must be at times grim, documenting the pain of worldwide transformations. Current alternatives to metropolitan dominance of social science are not particularly stable. Methods for cooperative intellectual work across regions and across traditions of thought are not yet well established. Therefore, the path for social science sketched in this chapter may not be the one actually taken in the next generation. All I can say is that this is a possible path. It is the one that would maximise the intellectual resources of the social sciences and their relevance for global democracy. Both are goals we should pursue.

References

Abell, Peter 1991. 'Review article: James S. Coleman, *Foundations of Social Theory*'. *European Sociological Review*, vol. 7 no. 2, 163–72.

Abrahamian, Ervand 1989. *Radical Islam: The Iranian Mojahedin*. New Haven: Yale University Press.

Acker, Joan 2004. 'Gender, capitalism and globalization'. *Critical Sociology*, vol. 30 no. 1, 17–41.

Agarwal, Bina 1999 [1992]. 'The gender and environment debate: Lessons from India'. In Nivedita Menon, ed., *Gender and Politics in India*. New Delhi: Oxford University Press, 96–142.

Ahluwalia, Pal 2002. 'The struggle for African identity: Thabo Mbeki's African Renaissance'. *African and Asian Studies*, vol. 1 no. 4, 265–77.

Akiwowo, Akinsola A. 1980. 'Sociology in Africa today'. *Current Sociology*, vol. 28 no. 2, 1–73.

—— 1986. 'Contributions to the sociology of knowledge from an African oral poetry'. *International Sociology*, vol. 1 no. 4, 343–58.

—— 1991. 'Responses to Makinde/Lawuyi and Taiwo'. *International Sociology*, vol. 6 no. 2, 243–51.

—— 1999. 'Indigenous sociologies: Extending the scope of the argument'. *International Sociology*, vol. 14 no. 2, 115–38.

Akhavi, Shahrough 1983. 'Shariati's social thought'. In Nikki R. Keddie, ed., *Religion and Politics in Iran*. New Haven: Yale University Press, 125–44.

Al-Afghani, Sayyid Jamal ad-Din 1968. *An Islamic Response to Imperialism: Political and Religious Writings of Sayyid Jamal ad-Din 'al-Afghani'*. Trans. Nikki R. Keddie and Hamid Algar. Berkeley: University of California Press.

Alatas, Syed Hussein 2006. 'The autonomous, the universal and the future of sociology'. *Current Sociology*, vol. 54 no. 1, 7–23.

Albrow, Martin 1996. *The Global Age: State and Society Beyond Modernity*. Cambridge: Polity Press.

Al-e Ahmad, Jalal 1982a [1962 and 1964]. *Gharbzadegi (Weststruckness)*. Trans. John Green and Ahmad Alizadeh. Lexington, KY: Mazda.

—— 1982b. *Iranian Society: An Anthology of Writings*. Ed. Michael C. Hillmann. Lexington KY: Mazda.

Alexander, Jeffrey C. 1982–83. *Theoretical Logic in Sociology*, Vols 2–3. Berkeley: University of California Press.

—— 1987. 'The centrality of the classics'. In Anthony Giddens and Jonathan H. Turner, eds, *Social Theory Today*. Cambridge: Polity Press, 11–57.

Allardt, Erik 1994. 'Scandinavian sociology and its European roots and elements'. In Birgitta Nedelmann and Piotr Sztompka (eds), *Sociology in Europe*. Berlin: Walter de Gruyter, 119–40.

Althusser, Louis and Balibar, Etienne 1970. *Reading Capital*. London: New Left Books.

Amin, Samir 1974. *Accumulation on a World Scale*. New York: Monthly Review Press.

Amin, Shahid and Bhadra, Gautam 1994. 'Ranajit Guha: A biographical sketch'. *Subaltern Studies*, no. 8, 222–5.

Amirshahi, Mahshid 1995. *Suri & Co: Tales of a Persian Teenager*. Trans. J.E. Knörzer. Austin, TX: Center for Middle Eastern Studies, University of Texas.

Ancich, M., Connell, R.W., Fisher, J.A. and Kolff, M. 1969. 'A descriptive bibliography of published research and writing on social stratification in Australia, 1946–1967'. *Australian and New Zealand Journal of Sociology*, vol. 5 no. 1, 48–76; vol. 5 no. 2, 128–52.

Anderson, Francis 1912. *Sociology in Australia: A Plea for its Teaching.* Sydney: Angus & Robertson.

Appadurai, Arjun 1990. 'Disjuncture and difference in the global cultural economy'. *Public Culture*, vol. 2, no. 2, 1–23.

—— ed. 2001. *Globalization.* Durham: Duke University Press.

Applebaum, Richard P. and Robinson, William I., eds 2005. *Critical Globalization Studies.* New York: Routledge.

Archer, Margaret 1983. 'Process without system'. *Archives Européennes de Sociologie,* vol. 24 no. 4, 196–221.

Arndt, H.W. 1968. *A Small Rich Industrial Country.* Melbourne: Cheshire.

Arthur, Bill and Morphy, Frances, ed. 2005. *Macquarie Atlas of Indigenous Australia: Culture and Society Through Space and Time.* Sydney: Macquarie Library.

Asad, Talal, ed. 1973. *Anthropology and the Colonial Encounter.* New York: Humanities Press.

Attenbrow, Val 2002. *Sydney's Aboriginal Past: Investigating the Archaeological and Historical Records.* Sydney: UNSW Press.

Austin, J.L. 1961. *Philosophical Papers.* Oxford: Clarendon Press.

Auyero, Javier 2001. 'Glocal riots'. *International Sociology,* vol. 16 no. 1, 33–53.

Baehr, Peter 2002. *Founders, Classics, Canons: Modern Disputes over the Origins and Appraisal of Sociology's Heritage.* New Brunswick: Transaction.

Baldock, Cora V. and Lally, Jim 1974. *Sociology in Australia and New Zealand: Theory and Methods.* Contributions in Sociology, No. 16. Westport, CN: Greenwood Press.

Bakunin, Mikhail 1973 [1873]. 'Statism and anarchy'. In Sam Dolgoff, ed., *Bakunin on Anarchy.* London: Allen & Unwin, 325–50.

Balandier, Georges 1970 [1955]. *The Sociology of Black Africa: Social Dynamics in Central Africa.* London: André Deutsch.

Bannister, Robert 1987. *Sociology and Scientism: The American Quest for Objectivity, 1880–1940.* Chapel Hill: University of North Carolina Press.

Barbalet, J.M. 1998. *Emotion, Social Theory, and Social Structure: A Macrosociological Approach.* Cambridge: Cambridge University Press.

Bartelson, Jens 2000. 'Three concepts of globalization'. *International Sociology,* vol. 15 no. 2, 180–96.

Bauman, Zygmunt 1998. *Globalization: The Human Consequences*. Cambridge: Polity Press.

Bayat, Assef 1990. 'Shariati and Marx: A critique of an "Islamic" critique of Marxism'. *Alif: Journal of Comparative Poetics*, no. 10, 19–41.

Beck, Ulrich 1992. *Risk Society: Towards a New Modernity*. London: Sage.

—— 1999. *World Risk Society*. Cambridge: Polity Press.

—— 2000. *What is Globalization?* Oxford: Blackwell.

Beck, Ulrich and Sznaider, Natan 2006. 'Unpacking cosmopolitanism for the social sciences: A research agenda'. *British Journal of Sociology*, vol. 57 no. 1, 1–23.

Behdad, Sohrab 1994. 'A disputed utopia: Islamic economics in revolutionary Iran'. *Comparative Studies in Society and History*, vol. 36 no. 4, 775–813.

Bellamy, Richard 1987. *Modern Italian Social Theory*. Cambridge: Polity Press.

Bendix, Reinhard 1960. *Max Weber: An Intellectual Portrait*. New York: Doubleday.

Bennoune, Mahfoud 1988. *The Making of Contemporary Algeria, 1830–1987*. Cambridge: Cambridge University Press.

Berger, Peter L. 1997. 'Four faces of global culture'. *The National Interest*, no. 49, 23–9.

Bernal, Martin 1987. *Black Athena: The Afroasiatic Roots of Classical Civilization*, Vol. 1. London: Free Association Books.

Bernard, L.L. and Bernard, Jessie 1965 [1943]. *Origins of American Sociology: The Social Science Movement in the United States*. New York: Russell & Russell.

Besnard, Philippe, ed. 1983. *The Sociological Domain: The Durkheimians and the Founding of French Sociology*. Cambridge: Cambridge University Press.

Bhadra, Gautam. 1985. 'Four rebels of eighteen-fifty-seven'. *Subaltern Studies*, no. 4, 229–75.

Bhaskaran, Suparna 2004. *Made in India: Decolonizations, Queer Sexualities, Trans/national Projects*. New York: Palgrave Macmillan.

Bitterli, Urs 1989. *Cultures in Conflict: Encounters Between European and Non-European Cultures, 1492–1800*. Stanford: Stanford University Press.

Boroujerdi, Mehrzad 1996. *Iranian Intellectuals and the West: The Tormented Triumph of Nativism*. Syracuse, NY: Syracuse University Press.

Bottomley, Gillian 1992. *From Another Place: Migration and the Politics of Culture*. Melbourne: Cambridge University Press.

Bottomore, Tom 1987. *Sociology: A Guide to Problems and Literature*, 3rd edn. London: Allen & Unwin.

Bottomore, Tom and Nisbet, Robert, eds 1978. *A History of Sociological Analysis*. London: Heinemann.

Bourdieu, Pierre 1977. *Outline of a Theory of Practice*. Cambridge: Cambridge University Press.

—— 1979. *Algeria 1960: Essays*. Cambridge: Cambridge University Press.

—— 1990. *The Logic of Practice*. Stanford: Stanford University Press.

—— 2001. *Masculine Domination*. Stanford, Stanford University Press.

—— 2002. 'Retour sur l'expérience algérienne'. In Franck Poupeau and Thierry Discepolo, eds, *Pierre Bourdieu, Interventions, 1961–2001: Science sociale et action politique*. Marseille: Agone, 37–42.

Bowlby, John 1980. *Loss, Sadness and Depression*. London: Hogarth Press.

Braithwaite, John 1989. *Crime, Shame and Reintegration*. Cambridge: Cambridge University Press.

Branford, Victor 1904. 'The founders of sociology'. *American Journal of Sociology*, vol. 10 no. 1, 94–126.

Brennan, Teresa 2003. *Globalization and its Terrors: Daily Life in the West*. London: Routledge.

Brock-Utne, Birgit 2002. 'Stories of the hunt—who is writing them? The importance of indigenous research in Africa based on local experience'. In Catherine A. Odora Hoppers, ed., *Indigenous Knowledge and the Integration of Knowledge Systems*. Claremont: New Africa Books, 237–56.

Brubaker, Rogers 1993. 'Social theory as habitus'. In Craig Calhoun, Edward Li Puma and Moishe Postone, eds, *Bourdieu: Critical Perspectives*. Chicago: University of Chicago Press, 212–34.

Brünner, José Joaquin 1998. *Globalización cultural y posmodernidad*. Chile: Fondo de cultura económica.

Bukharin, Nikolai 1965 [1925]. *Historical Materialism: A System of Sociology*. New York: Russell & Russell.

Bulbeck, Chilla 1988. *One World Women's Movement*. London: Pluto Press.

—— 1998. *Re-Orienting Western Feminisms: Women's Diversity in a Postcolonial World*. Cambridge: Cambridge University Press.

Burke, Edmund, III 1980. 'The French tradition of the sociology of Islam'. In Malcolm Kerr, ed., *Islamic Studies*. Santa Monica, CA: Undena University Press, 73–88.

Burrow, J.W. 1966. *Evolution and Society: A Study in Victorian Social Theory*. Cambridge: Cambridge University Press.

Burton, Clare 1985. *Subordination: Feminism and Social Theory*. Sydney: George Allen & Unwin.

Bury, J.P.T., ed. 1960. *The Zenith of European Power, 1830–70*. New Cambridge Modern History, vol. X. Cambridge: Cambridge University Press.

Cain, P.J. and Hopkins, A.G. 1993. *British Imperialism: Innovation and Expansion, 1688–1914*. New York: Longman.

Calhoun, Craig, Li Puma, Edward and Postone, Moishe, eds 1993. *Bourdieu: Critical Perspectives*. Chicago: University of Chicago Press.

Camic, Charles 1989. '*Structure* after 50 years: The anatomy of a charter'. *American Journal of Sociology*, vol. 95 no. 1, 38–107.

Camic, Charles and Gross, Neil 1998. 'Contemporary developments in sociological theory: Current projects and conditions of possibility'. *Annual Review of Sociology*, no. 24, 453–76.

Cardoso, Fernando Henrique and Faletto, Enzo 1979 [1971]. *Dependency and Development in Latin America*. Berkeley, CA: University of California Press.

Centeno, Miguel and López-Alves, Fernando, ed. 2001. *The Other Mirror: Grand Theory Through the Lens of Latin America*. Princeton: Princeton University Press.

Chadha, Yogesh 1997. *Rediscovering Gandhi*. London: Century.

Chakrabarty, Dipesh 1983. 'Conditions for knowledge of working-class conditions: Employers, government and the jute workers of Calcutta, 1890–1940'. *Subaltern Studies*, no. 2, 259–310.

Chase-Dunn, Christopher, ed. 1995. *The Historical Evolution of the International Political Economy*. Aldershot: Edward Elgar.

—— 2002. 'Globalization from below: Toward a collectively rational and democratic global commonwealth'. *Annals AAPSS*, no. 581, 48–61.

Chase-Dunn, Christopher and Grimes, Peter 1995. 'World-systems analysis'. *Annual Review of Sociology*, no. 21, 387–417.

Chatterjee, Bankimchandra 1986. *Sociological Essays: Utilitarianism and Positivism in Bengal*. Trans. and ed. S.N. Mukherjee and Marian Maddern. Calcutta: Rddhi-India.

Chatterjee, Partha 1983. 'More on modes of power and the peasantry'. *Subaltern Studies*, no. 2, 311–49.

—— 1993. *The Nation and its Fragments: Colonial and Postcolonial Histories*. Princeton: Princeton University Press.

Chaturvedi, Vinayak, ed. 2000. *Mapping Subaltern Studies and the Postcolonial*. London: Verso and *New Left Review*.

Chow, Esther Ngan-ling 2003. 'Gender matters: Studying globalization and social change in the 21st century'. *International Sociology*, vol. 18, no. 3, 443–60.

Clark, Terry Nichols 1973. *Prophets and Patrons: The French University and the Emergence of the Social Sciences*. Cambridge, MA: Harvard University Press.

Coetzee, J.M. 1991. 'The mind of Apartheid: Geoffrey Cronjé (1907–)'. *Social Dynamics*, vol. 17 no. 1, 1–35.

Cole, Juan R. 1983. 'Imami jurisprudence and the role of the *ulama*: Mortaza Ansari on emulating the supreme exemplar'. In Nikki R. Keddie, ed., *Religion and Politics in Iran*. New Haven: Yale University Press, 33–46.

Coleman, James S. 1982. *The Asymmetric Society*. Syracuse: Syracuse University Press.

—— 1990. *Foundations of Social Theory*. Cambridge: Harvard University Press.

—— 1992. 'The problematics of social theory'. *Theory and Society*, vol. 21, 263–83.

Collins, Randall 1997. 'A sociological guilt trip: Comment on Connell'. *American Journal of Sociology*, vol. 102 no. 6, 1558–64.

Comte, Auguste 1875–77 [1851–54]. *System of Positive Polity, or, Treatise on Sociology*. 4 vols. London: Longmans Green.

Connell, Raewyn 1983. 'The black box of habit on the wings of history: Reflections on the theory of social reproduction'. In *Which Way is Up? Essays on Sex, Class and Culture*. Sydney: Allen & Unwin, 140–61.

—— 1987. *Gender and Power: Society, the Person and Sexual Politics*. Cambridge: Polity Press.

——. 1990. 'Notes on American sociology and American power'. In H. Gans, ed., *Sociology in America*. Thousand Oaks: Sage, 265–71.

—— 1993. 'The big picture: Masculinities in recent world history'. *Theory and Society*, vol. 22, 597–623.

—— 2000. 'Sociology and world market society'. *Contemporary Sociology*, vol. 29, no. 1, 291–6.

—— 2005a. 'Globalization, imperialism, and masculinities'. In Michael S. Kimmel, Jeff Hearn and Raewyn Connell, eds, *Handbook of Studies on Men & Masculinities*, Thousand Oaks: Sage, 71–89.

—— 2005b. 'Empire, domination, autonomy: Antonio Negri as a social theorist'. *Overland*, no. 181, 31–9.

—— 2007. 'The heart of the problem: South African intellectual workers, globalization and social change'. *Sociology*, vol. 41, no. 1, 11–28.

Connell, Raewyn and Irving, T.H. 1980. *Class Structure in Australian History*. Melbourne: Longman Cheshire.

Connell, Raewyn and Wood, Julian 2002. 'Globalization and scientific labour: Patterns in a life-history study of intellectual workers in the periphery'. *Journal of Sociology*, vol. 38 no. 2, 167–90.

Connell, Raewyn, Wood, Julian and Crawford, June 2005. 'The global connections of intellectual workers: An Australian study'. *International Sociology*, vol. 20, no. 1, 5–26.

Connell, W.F., Francis, E.P. and Skilbeck, E.E. 1957. *Growing Up in an Australian City*. Melbourne: Australian Council for Educational Research.

Copans, Jean 1971. 'Pour une histoire et une sociologie des études africaines'. *Cahiers d'études africaines*, vol. 11 no. 3, 422–47.

Coser, Lewis A. 1956. *The Functions of Social Conflict*. Glencoe IL: The Free Press.

Craig, Jean I. 1957. 'Marriage, the family and class'. In A.P. Elkin, ed., *Marriage and the Family in Australia*. Sydney: Angus & Robertson, 24–53.

Cronjé, Geoffrey 1947. *Regverdige Rasse-Apartheid*. Stellenbosch: Christen-Studenteverenigingmaatskappy van Suid-Afrika.

Crook, Stephen, Pakulski, Jan and Waters, Malcolm 1992. *Postmodernization: Change in Advanced Society*. London: Sage.

Crossman, Peter and Devisch, René 2002. 'Endogenous knowledge in anthropological perspective: A plea for a conceptual shift'. In Catherine A. Odora Hoppers, ed., *Indigenous Knowledge and the Integration of Knowledge Systems*, Claremont: New Africa Books, 96–125.

Crozier, John B. 1911. *Sociology Applied to Practical Politics*. London: Longmans Green.

Darby, Phillip 2005. 'The Alternative Horizons of Ashis Nandy'. *Overland*, no. 179, 53–7.

Darwin, Charles n.d. [1839]. *Journal of Researches into the Natural History and Geology of the Countries Visited during the Voyage of H.M.S. 'Beagle' Round the World*. London: Ward, Lock & Co.

Das, Veena 1995. *Critical Events: An Anthropological Perspective on Contemporary India*. New Delhi: Oxford University Press.

Davies, Alan and Encel, Sol, eds 1965. *Australian Society*. Melbourne: Cheshire.

Davis, Mike 1990. *City of Quartz: Excavating the Future in Los Angeles*. London: Verso.

Deegan, Mary Jo 1988. *Jane Addams and the Men of the Chicago School, 1892–1918*. New Brunswick: Transaction.

Desmond, Adrian and Moore, James 1992. *Darwin*. London: Penguin.

Diawara, Mamadou 2000. 'Globalization, development politics and local knowledge'. *International Sociology*, vol. 15 no. 2, 361–71.

Dietrich, Gabriele 1992. *Reflections on the Women's Movement in India: Religion, Ecology, Development*. New Delhi: Horizon India.

Dodson, Michael 1997. 'Land rights and social justice'. In Galarrwuy Yunupingu, ed., *Our Land is Our Life*. Brisbane: University of Queensland Press, 39–51.

Dollard, John 1937. *Caste and Class in a Southern Town*. New Haven: Yale University Press.

Domhoff, William, ed. 1975. *New Directions in Power Structure Research*. Special issue of *Insurgent Sociologist*, vol. 5 no. 3.

Donaldson, Mike and Poynting, Scott 2007. *Ruling Class Men: Money, Sex and Power*. Berne: Peter Lang.

Dorfman, Ariel 1988. *Last Waltz in Santiago, and Other Poems of Exile and Disappearance*. New York: Viking.

——— 1998. *Heading South, Looking North: A Bilingual Journey*. New York: Farrar, Straus and Giroux.

Dorfman, Ariel and Mattelart, Armand 1975 [1971]. *How to Read Donald Duck: Imperialist Ideology in the Disney Comic*. New York: International General.

Dosman, Edgar 2001. 'Markets and the state in the evolution of the "Prebisch manifesto"'. *CEPAL Review*, no. 75, 87–102.

Du Bois, W.E.B. 1899. *The Philadelphia Negro: A Social Study*. Philadelphia:

University of Philadelphia.

—— 1978 [1950]. 'The problem of the twentieth century is the problem of the color line'. In *On Sociology and the Black Community*. Chicago: University of Chicago Press, 281–9.

—— 1968. *Autobiography*. New York: International Publishers.

Dumont, Louis 1966. *Homo hierarchicus: Essai sur le système des castes*. Paris: Gallimard.

Duncan, David 1908. *The Life and Letters of Herbert Spencer*. London: Methuen.

Durkheim, Émile 1964 [1893]. *The Division of Labor in Society*. New York: Free Press.

—— 1964 [1895]. *The Rules of Sociological Method*. Glencoe IL: The Free Press.

—— 1976 [1912]. *The Elementary Forms of the Religious Life*. London: Allen & Unwin.

—— ed. 1898–1913. *L'Année sociologique*, Vols 1–12. Paris: Alcan.

Easthope, Gary 1974. *A History of Social Research Methods*. London: Longman.

Eckstein, Susan 2002. 'Globalization and mobilization: Resistance to neo-liberalism in Latin America'. In Mauro F. Guillén, Randall Collins, Paula England and Marshall Meyer, eds, *The New Economic Sociology*. New York: Russell Sage Foundation, 330–68.

Eide, Ingrid 2006. 'UNESCO—a personal story'. In Ingeborg Breines and Hans d'Orville, eds, *60 Women Contributing to the 60 years of UNESCO: Constructing the Foundations of Peace*. Paris: UNESCO, 83–91.

Encel, S. 1970. *Equality and Authority: A Study of Class, Status and Power in Australia*. Sydney: Cheshire.

Erikson, Erik H. 1950. *Childhood and Society*. London: Imago.

Escobar, Arturo. 1995. *Encountering Development: The Making and Unmaking of the Third World*. Princeton: Princeton University Press.

Evans, Peter 1995. *Embedded Autonomy: States and Industrial Transformation*. Princeton: Princeton University Press.

—— 1997. 'The eclipse of the state? Reflections on stateness in an era of globalization'. *World Politics*, vol. 50, no. 1, 62–87.

Fairbanks, Arthur 1901 [1896]. *Introduction to Sociology*, 7th edn. New York: Scribner.

Fallding, Harold 1962. 'The scope and purpose of sociology'. *Australian Journal of Politics and History*, no. 8, 78–92.

Fanon, Frantz 1970 [1959]. *Studies in a Dying Colonialism [L'An V de la révolution algérienne]*. Harmondsworth: Penguin.

—— 1968 [1961]. *The Wretched of the Earth*. New York: Grove Press.

Fararo, Thomas J. 1991. 'Review of James S. Coleman, Foundations of Social Theory'. *Social Science Quarterly*, vol. 72 no. 1, 189–90.

Featherstone, Mike 1995. *Undoing Culture: Globalization, Postmodernism and Identity*. London: Sage.

Ferdows, Adele K. 1983. 'Women and the Islamic revolution'. *International Journal of Middle East Studies*, vol. 15 no. 2, 283–98.

Fiss, Peer C. and Hirsch, Paul M. 2005. 'The discourse of globalization: Framing and sensemaking of an emerging concept'. *American Sociological Review*, vol. 70 no. 1, 29–52.

Foucault, Michel 1977. *Discipline and Punish: The Birth of the Prison*. New York: Pantheon.

Franzway, Suzanne 1999. '"They see you coming": A comparative study of sexual politics and women union officials in (English) Canada and Australia'. *Labour and Industry*, vol. 10 no. 2, 147–68.

Friedman, Jonathan 1994. *Cultural Identity and Global Process*. London: Sage.

Gaita, Raimond 1998. *Romulus, My Father*. Melbourne: Text.

Gandhi, Nandita and Singh, Nandita 1992. *The Issues at Stake: Theory and Practice in the Contemporary Women's Movement in India*. New Delhi: Kali for Women.

Gane, Nicholas 2001. 'Chasing the "runaway world": The politics of recent globalization theory'. *Acta Sociologica*, vol. 44 no. 1, 81–9.

García Canclini, Néstor 1993 [1982]. *Transforming Modernity: Popular Culture in Mexico*. Austin: University of Texas Press.

—— 1995 [1989]. *Hybrid Cultures: Strategies for Entering and Leaving Modernity*. Minneapolis: University of Minnesota Press.

—— 1999. *La globalización imaginada*. Buenos Aires: Paidós.

—— 2001 [1995]. *Consumers and Citizens: Globalization and Multicultural Conflicts*. Minneapolis: University of Minnesota Press.

—— 2002. *Latinoamericanos buscando lugar en este siglo*. Buenos Aires: Paidós.

Garretón, Manuel Antonio 2000. *La sociedad in que vivi(re)mos: Introducción sociológica al cambio de siglo*. Santiago: LOM.

Gathercole, Peter, Irving, T.H. and Melleuish, Gregory, eds 1995. *Childe and Australia: Archaeology, Politics and Ideas*. Brisbane: University of Queensland Press.

Genovese, Eugene D. 1976. *Roll, Jordan, Roll: The World the Slaves Made*. New York: Vintage.

Ghamari-Tabrizi, Behrooz 2004. 'Contentious public religion: Two conceptions of Islam in revolutionary Iran'. *International Sociology*, vol. 19, no. 4, 504–23.

Giddens, Anthony 1971. *Capitalism and Modern Social Theory*. Cambridge: Cambridge University Press.

—— 1976. *New Rules of Sociological Method*. London: Hutchinson

—— 1979. *Central Problems in Social Theory: Action, Structure and Contradiction in Social Analysis*. London: Macmillan.

—— 1981. *A Contemporary Critique of Historical Materialism. Vol. I: Power, Property, and the State*. London: Macmillan.

—— 1984. *The Constitution of Society: Outline of the Theory of Structuration*. Cambridge: Polity Press.

—— 1990. *The Consequences of Modernity*. Stanford: Stanford University Press.

—— 2002. *Runaway World: How Globalisation is Reshaping Our Lives*. 2nd edn. London: Profile Books.

Giddings, Franklin Henry 1896. *The Principles of Sociology*. New York: Macmillan.

—— 1906. *Readings in Descriptive and Historical Sociology*. New York: Macmillan.

Gilding, Michael 1997. *Australian Families: A Comparative Perspective*. Melbourne: Longman.

Gilomee, Hermann 1994. '"Survival in Justice": An Afrikaner Debate over Apartheid'. *Comparative Studies in Society and History*, vol. 36 no. 3, 527–48.

Gómez, José Maria, ed. 2004. *América Latina y el (des) orden global neoliberal: hegemonía, contrahegemonía, perspectivas*. Buenos Aires: CLACSO.

Goot, Murray and Rowse, Tim, eds 1994. *Make a Better Offer: The Politics of Mabo*. Sydney: Pluto Press.

Gordimer, Nadine 1979. *Burger's Daughter*. London: Jonathan Cape.

Grenville, Kate 2005. *The Secret River*. Melbourne: Text.

Grieder, Jerome 1981. *Intellectuals and the State in Modern China: A Narrative History*. New York: Free Press.

Guha, Ranajit 1982. 'On some aspects of the historiography of colonial India'. *Subaltern Studies*, no. 1, 1–8.

—— 1983. 'The prose of counter-insurgency'. *Subaltern Studies*, no. 2, 1–42.

—— 1987. 'Chandra's death'. *Subaltern Studies*, no. 5, 135–65.

—— 1989. 'Dominance without hegemony and its historiography'. *Subaltern Studies*, no. 6, 210–309.

Guha, Ranajit and Spivak, Gayatri Chakravorty, eds 1988. *Selected Subaltern Studies*. New York: Oxford University Press.

Guillén, Mauro F. 2001a. 'Is globalization civilizing, destructive or feeble? A critique of five key debates in the social science literature'. *Annual Review of Sociology*, no. 27, 235–60.

—— 2001b. *The Limits of Convergence: Globalization and Organizational Change in Argentina, South Korea and Spain.* Princeton: Princeton University Press.

Gulbenkian Commission on the Restructuring of the Social Sciences 1996. *Open the Social Sciences.* Stanford: Stanford University Press.

Gutmann, Matthew C. and Vigoya, Mara Viveros 2005. 'Masculinities in Latin America'. In Michael S. Kimmel, Jeff Hearn and Raewyn Connell, eds, *Handbook of Studies on Men & Masculinities*, Thousand Oaks: Sage, 114–28.

Gyekye, Kwame 1987. *An Essay on African Philosophical Thought: The Akan Conceptual Scheme.* Cambridge: Cambridge University Press.

Hardt, Michael and Negri, Antonio 2000. *Empire.* Cambridge: Harvard University Press.

—— 2004. *Multitude: War and Democracy in the Age of Empire.* London: Hamish Hamilton.

Hearn, William Edward 1878. *The Aryan Household, Its Structure and its Development.* Melbourne: George Robertson.

Hechter, Michael 1992. 'Review of James S. Coleman, *Foundations of Social Theory*'. *Public Choice*, no. 73, 243–7.

Henisz, Witold, Zelner, Bennet A. and Guillén, Mauro F. 2005. 'The worldwide diffusion of market-oriented infrastructure reform, 1977–1999'. *American Sociological Review*, no. 70, 871–97.

Hiller, E.T. 1933. *Principles of Sociology.* New York: Harper & Bros.

Hinkle, Roscoe C. 1994. *Developments in American Sociological Theory, 1915–1950.* Albany: State University of New York Press.

Hobhouse, L.T. 1911. *Liberalism*. London: Williams & Norgate.

—— 1915. *The World in Conflict*. London: Fisher Unwin.

Hobhouse, L.T., Wheeler, G.C. and Ginsberg, M. 1915. *The Material Culture and Social Institutions of the Simpler Peoples*. London: Chapman & Hall.

Hoecker-Drysdale, Susan 1992. *Harriet Martineau: First Woman Sociologist*. New York: St Martin's Press.

Hooper, Charlotte 2001. *Manly States: Masculinities, International Relations, and Gender Politics*. New York: Columbia University Press.

Hopenhayn, Martín 2001. *No Apocalypse, No Integration: Modernism and Postmodernism in Latin America*. Durham: Duke University Press.

Hopkins, Terence K. 1979. 'The study of the capitalist world-economy: Some introductory considerations'. In Walter L. Goldfrank, ed., *The World-System of Capitalism: Past and Present*. Beverly Hills: Sage, 21–52.

Horne, Donald 1964. *The Lucky Country: Australia in the Sixties*. Ringwood: Penguin.

Horowitz, David, ed. 1971. *Radical Sociology: An Introduction*. San Francisco: Canfield.

Hountondji, Paulin J. 1973. *Libertés: Contribution à la Révolution Dahoméen*. Cotonou: Editions Renaissance.

——1983 [1976]. *African Philosophy: Myth and Reality*. Trans. H. Evans and J. Rée. London: Hutchinson.

—— 1990. 'Pour une sociologie des représentations collectives'. In R. Horton et al., *La pensée métisse*. Paris: Presses Universitaires de France, 187–92.

—— ed. 1997 [1994]. *Endogenous Knowledge: Research Trails*. Dakar: CODESRIA.

—— 1995. 'Producing knowledge in Africa today'. *African Studies Review*, vol. 38 no. 3, 1–10.

—— 1996. 'Intellectual responsibility: Implications for thought and action today'. *Proceedings and Addresses of the American Philosophical Association*, vol. 70 no. 2, 77–92.

—— 2002a. *The Struggle for Meaning: Reflections on Philosophy, Culture and Democracy in Africa*. Athens, OH: Ohio University Press.

—— 2002b. 'Knowledge appropriation in a post-colonial context'. In Catherine A. Odora Hoppers, ed., *Indigenous Knowledge and the Integration of Knowledge Systems*, Claremont: New Africa Books, 23–38.

Huber, Evelyne and Fred Solt 2004. 'Successes and failures of neoliberalism'. *Latin American Research Review*, vol. 39 no. 3, 150–64.

Hudson, Liam 1972. *The Cult of the Fact.* London: Jonathan Cape.

Huneeus, Carlos 2003. *Chile, un pais dividido: La actualidad del pasado.* Santiago de Chile: Catalonia.

Hutchinson, Bertram 1954. *Old People in a Modern Australian Community: A Social Survey.* Melbourne: Melbourne University Press.

Jacobs, Sean and Calland, Richard, ed. 2002. *Thabo Mbeki's World: The Politics and Ideology of the South African President.* London: University of Kwazulu-Natal Press and Zed Books.

Johnson, Pauline 2006. *Habermas: Rescuing the Public Sphere.* London: Routledge.

Johnson, Vivien 1990. *Radio Birdman.* Melbourne: Sheldon Booth.

—— 1994. *Aboriginal Artists of the Western Desert: A Biographical Dictionary.* Sydney: Craftsman House.

—— 1996. *Copyrites: Aboriginal Art in the Age of Reproductive Technologies.* Sydney: National Indigenous Arts Advocacy Association and Macquarie University.

Kagamé, Alexis 1956. *La philosophie bantu-rwandaise de l'être.* Brussels: Académie royale des sciences coloniales.

—— 1976. *La philosophie bantu comparée.* Paris: Présence Africaine.

Kalb, Don 2004. 'Shifting conjunctions: Politics and knowledge in the globalization debate'. *Amsterdams Sociologisch Tijdschrift*, vol. 31 no. 2, 147–91.

Kay, Cristóbal 1989. *Latin American Theories of Development and Underdevelopment.* London: Routledge.

—— 1998. 'Estructuralismo y teoría de la dependencia en el periodo neoliberal: Una perspectiva latinoamericana'. *Nueva sociedad* (Venezuela), no. 158, 100–19.

Keddie, Nikki R. 1972. *Sayyid Jamal ad-Din 'al-Afghani': A Political Biography.* Berkeley: University of California Press.

—— 1981. *Roots of Revolution: An Interpretive History of Modern Iran.* New Haven: Yale University Press.

Kellner, Douglas 2002. 'Theorizing globalization'. *Sociological Theory*, vol. 20 no. 3, 285–305.

Kenyatta, Jomo 1938. *Facing Mount Kenya: The Tribal Life of the Gikuyu.* London: Secker & Warburg.

Kidd, Benjamin 1898 [1894]. *Social Evolution*, 3rd edn. London: Macmillan.

Kiernan, V.G. 1969. *The Lords of Human Kind: Black Man, Yellow Man, and White Man in an Age of Empire*. Boston: Little, Brown.

Kishwar, Madhu and Vanita, Ruth, ed. 1984. *In Search of Answers: Indian Women's Voices from* Manushi. London: Zed Books.

Kuhn, Thomas S. 1970. *The Structure of Scientific Revolutions*, 2nd edn. Chicago: University of Chicago Press.

Kumar, Radha 1999. 'From Chipko to Sati: The contemporary Indian women's movement'. In Nivedita Menon, ed., *Gender and Politics in India*. New Delhi: Oxford University Press, 342–69.

Lafitte, Paul 1958. *Social Structure and Personality in the Factory*. London: Routledge and Kegan Paul.

Lal, Vinay 2002. *Empire of Knowledge: Culture and Plurality in the Global Economy*. London: Pluto.

—— 2003. *The History of History: Politics and Scholarship in Modern India*. New Delhi: Oxford University Press.

La Nauze, J.A. 1949. *Political Economy in Australia: Historical Studies*. Melbourne: Melbourne University Press.

Langman, Lauren 2005. 'From virtual public spheres to global justice: A critical theory of internetworked social movements'. *Sociological Theory*, vol. 23, no. 1, 42–74.

Lawuyi, O.B. and Taiwo, Olufemi 1990. 'Towards an African sociological tradition: A rejoinder to Akiwowo and Makinde'. *International Sociology*, vol. 5 no. 1, 57–73.

Lepenies, Wolf 1988. *Between Literature and Science: The Rise of Sociology*. Cambridge: Cambridge University Press.

Letourneau, Charles 1881. *Sociology, Based upon Ethnography*. London: Chapman & Hall.

Levine, Donald N. 1995. *Visions of the Sociological Tradition*. Chicago: University of Chicago Press.

Lévi-Strauss, Claude 1969 [1949]. *The Elementary Structures of Kinship*. Boston: Beacon Press.

—— 1973 [1955]. *Tristes Tropiques*. London: Jonathan Cape.

Levy, Marion J. Jr. 1970. 'Scientific analysis as a subset of comparative analysis.' In J.C. McKinney and E.A. Tiryakian, eds, *Theoretical Sociology*.

New York: Appleton-Century-Crofts, 99–110.

Liebersohn, Harry 1988. *Fate and Utopia in German Sociology, 1870–1923.* Cambridge, MA: MIT Press.

Love, Joseph L. 1986. 'Raúl Prebisch (1901–1986): His Life and Ideas'. British Library Document Supply Centre, 88/29440.

Ludden, David, ed. 2003. *Reading Subaltern Studies: Critical History, Contested Meaning and the Globalization of South Asia.* London: Anthem Press.

Lukács, Gyorgy 1971 [1923]. *History and Class Consciousness: Studies in Marxist Dialectics.* London: Merlin Press.

Lukes, Steven 1985. *Emile Durkheim, His Life and Work: A Historical and Critical Study.* Stanford: Stanford University Press.

Lüschen, Günther 1994. '25 years of German sociology after World War II: Institutionalization and theory'. *Soziologie,* no. 3, S11–32.

Lyman, Stanford M. 1992. *Militarism, Imperialism and Racial Accommodation: An Analysis and Interpretation of the Early Writings of Robert E. Park.* Fayetteville: University of Arkansas Press.

Lyotard, Jean-François 1984. *The Postmodern Condition: A Report on Knowledge.* Minneapolis: University of Minnesota Press.

MacDonald, Robert H. 1994. *The Language of Empire: Myths and Metaphors of Popular Imperialism, 1880–1918.* Manchester: Manchester University Press.

MacIver, R.M. 1937. *Society.* New York: Farrar & Rinehart.

McGee, Reece, ed. 1977. *Sociology.* Hinsdale: Dryden Press.

McGeough, Paul 2006. 'The changing face of Iran'. *Sydney Morning Herald,* 19–20 August, 23–30.

McMichael, Philip 2000. *Development and Social Change: A Global Perspective,* 2nd edn. Thousand Oaks: Pine Forge Press.

Makgoba, Malegapuru William, ed. 1999. *African Renaissance: The New Struggle.* Tafelberg: Mafube.

Makinde, M. Akin 1988. 'Asuwada principle: An analysis of Akiwowo's contributions to the sociology of knowledge from an African perspective'. *International Sociology,* vol. 3 no. 1, 61–76.

Malik, Hafeez 1980. *Sir Sayyid Ahmad Khan and Muslim Modernization in India and Pakistan.* New York: Columbia University Press.

Mallorquín, Carlos 2006. 'Raúl Prebisch before the Ice Age'. In Edgar J. Dosman, ed., *Raúl Prebisch: Power, Principle and the Ethics of Development,* Buenos Aires: IDB-INTAL, 65–106.

Malouf, David 1990. *The Great World*. London: Chatto & Windus.

Mamdani, Mahmood 1999. 'There can be no African renaissance without an Africa-focused intelligentsia'. In M.W. Makgoba, ed., *African Renaissance*, Tafelberg: Mafube, 125–34.

—— 2001. *When Victims Become Killers: Colonialism, Nativism, and the Genocide in Rwanda*. Princeton: Princeton University Press.

Mann, Michael 2001. 'Globalization and September 11'. *New Left Review*, no. 12, 51–72.

Mannheim, Karl 1940 [1935]. *Man and Society in an Age of Reconstruction*. London: Routledge & Kegan Paul.

Martin, William G. and Beittel, Mark 1998. 'Toward a global sociology? Evaluating current conceptions, methods, and practices.' *Sociological Quarterly*, vol. 39, no. 1, 139–61.

Martinelli, Alberto 2003. 'Global order or divided world?' *Current Sociology*, vol. 51, no. 2, 95–100.

Marchand, Marianne H. and Runyan, Anne Sisson, eds 2000. *Gender and Global Restructuring: Sightings, Sites and Resistances*. London: Routledge.

Mbiti, John S. 1969. *African Religions and Philosophy*. London: Heinemann.

Mendez, Jennifer Bickham 2002. 'Transnational organizing for maquila workers' rights in Central America'. In Nancy A. Naples and Manisha Desai, eds, *Women's Activism and Globalization*. New York: Routledge, 121–41.

Merton, Robert K. 1957 [1949]. *Social Theory and Social Structure*, 2nd edn. Glencoe, IL: The Free Press.

Meyer, John W. 2000. 'Globalization: Sources and effects on national states and societies'. *International Sociology*, vol. 15 no. 2, 233–48.

Mill, John Stuart 1891 [1843]. *A System of Logic*. London: Longmans Green.

Mills, C. Wright 1959. *The Sociological Imagination*. New York: Oxford University Press.

—— 1962. *The Marxists*. New York: Dell.

Mingay, G.E. 1963. *English Landed Society in the Eighteenth Century*. London: Routledge and Kegan Paul.

Mirsepassi, Ali 2000. *Intellectual Discourse and the Politics of Modernization: Negotiating Modernity in Iran*. Cambridge: Cambridge University Press.

Mistral, Gabriela 2003. *Selected Poems.* Albuquerque: University of New Mexico Press.

Mittelman, James H. 2004. *Whither Globalization? The Vortex of Knowledge and Ideology.* London: Routledge.

Mkandawire, Thandika 2000. 'Non-organic intellectuals and "learning" in policy-making Africa'. Paper presented to the EGDI seminar on 'What do Aid Agencies and their Co-operating Partners Learn from their Experiences?', 24 August.

Moghadam, Valentine M. 2000. 'Transnational feminist networks: Collective action in an era of globalization'. *International Sociology*, vol. 15, no. 1, 57–85.

Mohanty, Chandra Talpade, Russo, Ann and Torres, Lourdes, eds 1991. *Third World Women and the Politics of Feminism.* Bloomington: Indiana University Press.

Montecino, Sonia 2001. 'Identidades y diversidades en Chile'. In Manuel Antonio Garretón, ed., *Cultura y desarollo en Chile.* Santiago: Andres Bello, 65–98.

Morgan, J. Graham 1983. 'Courses and texts in sociology'. *Journal of the History of Sociology*, vol. 5 no. 1, 42–65.

Moulian, Tomás 2002. *Chile actual: Anatomía de un mito*, 3rd edn. Santiago: LOM.

Mqotsi, Livingstone 2002. 'Science, magic and religion as trajectories of the psychology of projection'. In Catherine A. Odora Hoppers, ed., *Indigenous Knowledge and the Integration of Knowledge Systems*, Claremont: New Africa Books, 158–72.

Mudimbe, V.Y. 1988. *The Invention of Africa: Gnosis, Philosophy, and the Order of Knowledge.* Bloomington: Indiana University Press.

—— 1994. *The Idea of Africa.* Bloomington: Indiana University Press.

Nandy, Ashis. 1980 *Alternative Sciences: Creativity and Authenticity in Two Indian Scientists.* New Delhi: Allied.

—— 1983. *The Intimate Enemy: Loss and Recovery of Self under Colonialism.* New Delhi: Oxford University Press.

—— 1987. *Traditions, Tyranny and Utopias: Essays in the Politics of Awareness.* New Delhi: Oxford University Press.

—— 2001. *An Ambiguous Journey to the City: The Village and the Other Odd Ruins of the Self in the Indian Imagination.* New Delhi: Oxford University Press.

—— 2003. *The Romance of the State, And the Fate of Dissent in the Tropics.* New Delhi: Oxford University Press.

—— 2004. *Bonfire of Creeds: The Essential Ashis Nandy.* New Delhi: Oxford University Press.

National Inquiry into the Separation of Aboriginal and Torres Strait Islander Children from their Families 1997. *Bringing Them Home.* Sydney: Human Rights and Equal Opportunity Commission.

Nedelmann, Birgitta and Sztompka, Piotr, eds 1994. *Sociology in Europe.* Berlin: Walter de Gruyter.

Nederveen Pieterse, Jan 2004. *Globalization & Culture: Global Mélange.* Lanham: Rowman & Littlefield.

Nisbet, Robert A. 1967. *The Sociological Tradition.* London: Heinemann.

Nkrumah, Kwame 1957. *Autobiography.* Edinburgh: Nelson.

Nochteff, Hugo and Abeles, Martin 2000. *Economic Shocks without Vision: Neoliberalism in the Transition of Socio-Economic Systems. Lessons from the Argentine Case.* Madrid: Iberoamericana.

Ntuli, P. Pitika 2002. 'Indigenous knowledge systems and the African Renaissance: Laying a foundation for the creation of counter-hegemonic discourses'. In Catherine A. Odora Hoppers, ed., *Indigenous Knowledge and the Integration of Knowledge Systems.* Claremont: New Africa Books, 53–66.

O'Brian, Patrick 1987. *Joseph Banks: A Life.* London: Collins Harville.

Odora Hoppers, Catherine A., ed. 2002. *Indigenous Knowledge and the Integration of Knowledge Systems: Towards a Philosophy of Articulation.* Claremont: New Africa Books.

Oeser, O.A. and Emery, F.E. 1954. *Social Structure and Personality in a Rural Community.* London: Routledge and Kegan Paul.

Oeser, O.A. and Hammond, S.B. 1954. *Social Structure and Personality in a City.* London: Routledge and Kegan Paul.

O'Hanlon, Rosalind 2002 [1988]. 'Recovering the subject: *Subaltern Studies* and histories of resistance in colonial south Asia'. In David Ludden, ed., *Reading Subaltern Studies.* London: Anthem Press, 135–86.

Olavarría, José and Enrique Moletto, eds 2002. *Hombres: Identidad/es y Sexualidad/es: III Encuentro de Estudios de Masculinidades.* Santiago: FLACSO-Chile.

Orellana, Marjorie Faulstich, Thorne, Barrie, Chee, Anna and Lam, Wan Shun Eva 2001. 'Transnational childhoods: The participation of children in processes of family migration'. *Social Problems,* vol. 48 no. 4, 572–91.

Organization for Social Science Research in Eastern and Southern Africa 2005. 'Publications'. *OSSREA Bulletin,* vol. 2 no. 2, 44–7.

Orwell, George 1968. *In Front of Your Nose: Collected Essays, Journalism and Letters, Volume IV, 1945–1950.* London: Secker and Warburg.

Pandey, Gyanendra 1982. 'Peasant revolt and Indian nationalism: The peasant movement in Awadh, 1919–22'. *Subaltern Studies,* vol. 1, 143–97.

Pareto, Vilfredo 1935 [1916]. *The Mind and Society: A Treatise on General Sociology.* New York: Harcourt Brace.

Park, Robert E. and Burgess, Ernest W. 1924 [1921]. *Introduction to the Science of Sociology.* Chicago: University of Chicago Press.

Parsons, Talcott 1937. *The Structure of Social Action: A Study in Social Theory with Special Reference to a Group of Recent European Writers.* New York: McGraw-Hill.

Partovi, Pedram 1998. 'Authorial intention and illocutionary force in Jalal Ali-I Ahmad's *Gharbzadigi'. Comparative Studies of South Asia, Africa and the Middle East,* vol. 18 no. 2, 73–80.

Paul, Mandy and Geoffrey Gray 2002. *Through a Smoky Mirror: History and Native Title.* Canberra: Aboriginal Studies Press, Australian Institute of Aboriginal and Torres Strait Islander Studies.

Paxton, Nancy L. 1991. *George Eliot and Herbert Spencer: Feminism, Evolutionism, and the Reconstruction of Gender.* Princeton: Princeton University Press.

Payne, M.W. 1992. 'Akiwowo, orature and divination: Approaches to the construction of an emic sociological paradigm of society'. *Sociological Analysis,* vol. 53 no. 2: 175–87.

Paz, Octavio 1990 [1950]. *The Labyrinth of Solitude,* enlarged edn. London: Penguin.

Pearson, Noel 1997. 'The concept of native title at common law'. In Galarrwuy Yunupingu, ed., *Our Land is Our Life,* Brisbane: University of Queensland Press, 150–61.

Peires, J.B. 1979. 'Nxele, Ntsikana and the origins of the Xhosa religious reaction'. *Journal of African History,* vol. 20 no. 1, 53–4.

Phillips, A.A. 1953. 'Australian literature'. In W.V. Aughterson, ed., *Taking Stock: Aspects of Mid-Century Life in Australia.* Melbourne: Cheshire, 79–96.

Plaatje, Sol T. 1982 [1916]. *Native Life in South Africa: Before and Since the European War and the Boer Rebellion.* Braamfontein: Ravan Press.

Platt, Jennifer 1995. 'The United States reception of Durkheim's *The Rules of Sociological Method*'. *Sociological Perspectives*, no. 38, 77–105.

Polillo, Simone and Guillén, Mauro F. 2005. 'Globalization pressures and the state: The worldwide spread of central bank independence'. *American Journal of Sociology*, vol. 110, no. 6, 1764–1805.

Pollock, David, Joseph H. Love and Daniel Kerner 2006. 'Prebisch at UNCTAD'. In Edgar J. Dosman, ed., *Raúl Prebisch: Power, Principle and the Ethics of Development*, Buenos Aires: IDB-INTAL, 37–63.

Prebisch, Raúl 1950. *The Economic Development of Latin America and its Principal Problems.* United Nations, Department of Economic Affairs. Reprinted in David Greenaway and C.W. Morgan, eds, *The Economics of Commodity Markets.* Cheltenham: Elgar, 1999.

—— 1964. *Towards a New Trade Policy for Development: Report by the Secretary-General of the United Nations Conference on Trade and Development.* New York: United Nations.

—— 1981a. 'The Latin American periphery in the global system of capitalism'. *CEPAL Review*, no. 13, 143–50.

—— 1981b. *Capitalismo periférico: crisis y transformación.* Mexico City: Fondo de Cultura Económica.

Pusey, Michael 1991. *Economic Rationalism in Canberra: A Nation-Building State Changes its Mind.* London: Cambridge University Press.

Quijano, Aníbal 2000. 'Coloniality of power and Eurocentrism in Latin America'. *International Sociology*, vol. 15, no. 2, 215–32.

Rahnema, Ali 1998. *An Islamic Utopian: A Political Biography of Ali Shari'ati.* London: I.B. Tauris.

Ray, Raka 1999. *Fields of Protest: Women's Movements in India.* Minneapolis: University of Minnesota Press.

Reuter, E.B. and Hart, C.W. 1933. *Introduction to Sociology.* New York: McGraw-Hill.

Reynolds, Henry 1996. *Aboriginal Sovereignty: Reflections on Race, State and Nation.* Sydney: Allen & Unwin.

Ricardo, David 1996 [1817]. *Principles of Political Economy and Taxation.* Amherst: Prometheus Books.

Robbins, Derek, ed. 2000. *Pierre Bourdieu.* London: Sage.

Roberts, Helen 1981. *Doing Feminist Research*. London: Routledge & Kegan Paul.

Robertson, Roland 1992. *Globalization: Social Theory and Global Culture*. London: Sage.

—— 1995. 'Glocalization: time–space and homogeneity–heterogeneity'. In Mike Featherstone, Scott Lash and Roland Robertson, eds, *Global Modernities*. London: Sage, 25–44.

Robinson, Jennifer 2006. *Ordinary Cities: Between Modernity and Development*. London: Routledge.

Robinson, William I. 2001. 'Social theory and globalization: The rise of a transnational state'. *Theory and Society*, vol. 30 no. 2, 157–200.

Ross, Dorothy 1991. *The Origins of American Social Science*. Cambridge: Cambridge University Press.

Rostow, W.W. 1960. *The Stages of Economic Growth: A Non-Communist Manifesto*. Cambridge: Cambridge University Press.

Roxborough, Ian 2002. 'Globalization, unreason and the dilemmas of American military strategy'. *International Sociology*, vol. 17, no. 3, 339–59.

Sader, Emir 2002. 'Hegemonia e contrahegemonia em tempos de guerra e de recessão'. In Ana Esther Ceceña and Emir Sader, eds, *La guerra infinita: Hegemonia y terror mundial*. Buenos Aires: CLACSO, 143–58.

Said, Edward W. 1993. *Culture and Imperialism*. New York: Vintage.

Santos, Milton 2000. *Por uma outra globalização*. Rio de Janeiro: Editora Record.

Sarkar, Sumit 1997. *Writing Social History*. New Delhi: Oxford University Press.

Sassen, Saskia 1991. *The Global City: New York, London, Tokyo*. Princeton: Princeton University Press.

—— 2000. 'Spatialities and temporalities of the global: Elements for a theorization'. *Public Culture*, vol. 12, no. 1, 215–32.

—— ed. 2002. *Global Networks, Linked Cities*. New York: Routledge.

Saunders, Peter 2005. *The Poverty Wars: Reconnecting Research with Reality*. Sydney: University of New South Wales Press.

Sayad, Abdelmalek 1996. 'Abdelmalek Sayad in Interview'. In Derek Robbins, ed., *Pierre Bourdieu*. London: Sage, 59–77.

Schuerkens, Ulrike 2003. 'The sociological and anthropological study of globalization and localization'. *Current Sociology*, vol. 51 nos 3/4, 209–22.

—— 2005. 'Transnational migrations and social transformations: A theoretical perspective'. *Current Sociology*, vol. 53 no. 4, 535–53.

Schutz, Alfred 1972 [1932]. *The Phenomenology of the Social World*. London: Heinemann.

Scott, David and U'Ren, Robert 1962. *Leisure: A Social Enquiry into Leisure Activities and Needs in an Australian Housing Estate*. Melbourne: Cheshire.

Seidman, Steven 1994. *Contested Knowledge: Social Theory in the Postmodern Era*. Cambridge, MA: Blackwell.

Serequeberhan, Tsenay, ed. 1991. *African Philosophy: The Essential Readings*. New York: Paragon House.

Shariati, Ali 1979. *On the Sociology of Islam*. Trans. Hamid Algar. Berkeley: Mizan Press.

—— 1981. *Man and Islam*. Trans. Fatollah Marjani. Houston: Free Islamic Lit Inc.

—— 1986a. *What is to be Done? The Enlightened Thinkers and an Islamic Renaissance*. Ed. Farhang Rajaee. Houston: Institute for Research and Islamic Studies.

—— 1986b. 'Shahadat'. In Mahmud Taliqani, Murtada Mutahhari and Ali Shariati, *Jihad and Shahadat: Struggle and Martyrdom in Islam*. Houston: Institute for Research and Islamic Studies, 153–229.

Shiva, Vandana 1989. *Staying Alive: Women, Ecology and Development*. London: Zed Books.

Silva, Eduardo 1996. *The State and Capital in Chile: Business Elites, Technocrats, and Market Economics*. Boulder, CO: Westview.

Sinha, Mrinalini 1995. *Colonial Masculinity*. Manchester: Manchester University Press.

Sitas, Ari 2006. 'The African Renaissance challenge and sociological reclamations in the South'. *Current Sociology*, vol. 54 no. 3, 357–80.

Sklair, Leslie 2001. *The Transnational Capitalist Class*. Malden: Blackwell.

—— 2002. *Globalization: Capitalism and its Alternatives*. Oxford: Oxford University Press.

Slater, David 2004. *Geopolitics and the Post-colonial: Rethinking North–South Relations*. Oxford: Blackwell.

Smart, Barry 1994. 'Sociology, globalisation and postmodernity: Comments on the "sociology for one world" thesis'. *International Sociology*, vol. 9, no. 2, 149–59.

Smelser, Neil J. 1990. 'Can individualism yield a sociology?' *Contemporary Sociology*, vol. 19 no. 6, 778–83.

Smith, Adam 1910 [1776]. *An Inquiry into the Nature and Causes of the Wealth of Nations*. London: J. M. Dent.

Smith, Dorothy E. 1987. *The Everyday World as Problematic: A Feminist Sociology*. Toronto: University of Toronto Press.

Smith, T.V. and White, Leonard D., eds 1929. *Chicago: An Experiment in Social Science Research*. Chicago: University of Chicago Press.

Sonntag, Heinz R. 1999. 'How the sociology of the North celebrates itself'. *ISA Bulletin*, no. 80, 21–5.

Sorokin, Pitirim A. 1928. *Contemporary Sociological Theories*. New York: Harper Bros.

—— 1937–41. *Social and Cultural Dynamics*. New York: American Book.

Spencer, Baldwin and Gillen, F.J. 1899. *The Native Tribes of Central Australia*. London: Macmillan.

Spann, R.N. 1966. 'Cliches and other bad habits in political science'. *Politics*, vol. 1 no. 1, 3–16.

Spencer, Herbert 1954 [1850]. *Social Statics*. New York: Robert Schalkenbach Foundation.

—— 1887 [1873]. *The Study of Sociology*, 13th edn. London: Kegan Paul, Trench.

—— 1893–96 [1874–77]. *The Principles of Sociology*. 3 vols. New York: Appleton.

Spengler, Oswald 1932 [1918–22]. *The Decline of the West*. London: Allen & Unwin.

Stauffer, Robert H. 2004. *Kahana: How the Land was Lost*. Honolulu: University of Hawai'i Press.

Stead, Christina 1965 [1934]. *Seven Poor Men of Sydney*. Sydney: Angus & Robertson.

Stiebing, William H. 1993. *Uncovering the Past: A History of Archaeology*. Buffalo: Prometheus Books.

Stiglitz, Joseph E. 2002. *Globalization and its Discontents*. London: Penguin.

Sumner, William Graham 1934 [1906]. *Folkways: A Study of the Sociological Importance of Usages, Manners, Customs, Mores, and Morals*. Boston: Ginn.

Sun Yat-sen 1975 [1927]. *San Min Chu I: The Three Principles of the People*.

Trans. Frank W. Price, ed. L.T. Chen. New York: Da Capo Press.

Suttner, Raymond 2006. 'Talking to the ancestors: National heritage, the Freedom Charter and nation-building in South Africa in 2005'. *Development Southern Africa*, vol. 23 no. 1, 3–27.

Sutton, Peter, ed. 1988. *Dreamings: The Art of Aboriginal Australia*. New York: Asia Society Galleries.

Swartz, David L. and Zolberg, Vera L., eds 2004. *After Bourdieu: Influence, Critique, Elaboration*. Dordrecht: Kluwer Academic.

Swingewood, Alan 2000. *A Short History of Sociological Thought*, 3rd edn. Basingstoke: Palgrave.

Taft, Ronald 1962. 'The myth and migrants'. In P. Coleman, ed., *Australian Civilization*. Melbourne: Cheshire, 191–206.

Taylor, Ian and Williams, Paul 2001. 'South African foreign policy and the Great Lakes crisis: African Renaissance meets *vagabondage politique?*' *African Affairs*, no. 100, 265–86.

Tema, Bothlale Octavia 2002. 'Science education and Africa's rebirth'. In Catherine A. Odora Hoppers, ed., *Indigenous Knowledge and the Integration of Knowledge Systems*. Claremont: New Africa Books, 128–40.

Tempels, Placide 1959 [1945]. *Bantu Philosophy*. Paris: Présence Africaine.

Tharu, Susie and Niranjana, Tejaswini 1996. 'Problems for a contemporary theory of gender'. *Subaltern Studies*, no. 9, 232–60.

Therborn, Göran 1976. *Science, Class, and Society*. London: New Left Books.

—— 2000. 'Globalizations: Dimensions, historical waves, regional effects, normative governance'. *International Sociology*, vol. 15 no. 2, 151–79.

Thomas, Hugh 1997. *The Slave Trade: The History of the Atlantic Slave Trade, 1440–1870*. New York: Simon & Schuster.

Thomas, William I. 1907. *Sex and Society*. Chicago: University of Chicago Press.

Thompson, E.P. 1965. 'The peculiarities of the English'. *Socialist Register*, 1965, 311–62.

Thrift, Nigel 1985. 'Bear and mouse or bear and tree? Anthony Giddens' reconstitution of social theory'. *Sociology*, vol. 19 no. 4, 609–23.

Todd, Arthur James 1918. *Theories of Social Progress: A Critical Study of the*

Attempts to Formulate the Conditions of Human Advance. New York: Macmillan.

Toer, Pramoedya Ananta 1996 [1979]. *Child of All Nations*. New York: Penguin.

Tominaga, Ken'ichi 1994. 'European sociology and the modernisation of Japan'. In Birgitta Nedelmann and Piotr Sztompka, eds, *Sociology in Europe*. Berlin: Walter de Gruyter, 191–212.

Tomlinson, John 1999. *Globalization and Culture*. Cambridge: Polity Press.

Tönnies, Ferdinand 1955 [1887]. *Community and Association*. London: Routledge & Kegan Paul.

Touraine, Alain 1971. *The Post-Industrial Society*. New York: Random House.

Toye, John and Toye, Richard 2004. *The UN and Global Political Economy: Trade, Finance, and Development*. Bloomington: Indiana University Press.

Turner, Bryan S. 1989. 'Research note: From Orientalism to global society'. *Sociology*, no. 23, 629–38.

Turner, Jonathan H. 1986. 'Review essay: The theory of structuration'. *American Journal of Sociology*, vol. 91 no. 4, 969–77.

Turner, Stephen P. and Turner, Jonathan H. 1990. *The Impossible Science: An Institutional Analysis of American Sociology*. Newbury Park: Sage.

Turney, Clifford, Bygott, Ursula and Chippendale, Peter 1991. *Australia's First: A History of the University of Sydney Volume I, 1850–1939*. Sydney: University of Sydney and Hale & Iremonger.

Tylor, Edward B. 1873. *Primitive Culture: Researches into the Development of Mythology, Philosophy, Religion, Language, Art, and Custom*, 2nd edn. London: Murray.

Urry, John 1986. 'Book review: The Constitution of Society', *Sociological Review*, vol. 34 no. 2, 434–37.

Vahdat, Farzin 2002. *God and Juggernaut: Iran's Intellectual Encounter with Modernity*. Syracuse: Syracuse University Press.

Valdés, Teresa, ed. 2001. *El indice de compromiso cumplido—ICC. Una estrategia para el control ciudadano de la equidad de género*. Santiago de Chile: FLACSO-Chile.

Vale, Peter and Sipho Maseko 2002. 'Thabo Mbeki, South Africa, and the idea of an African Renaissance'. In Sean Jacobs and Richard Calland, eds, *Thabo Mbeki's World: The Politics and Ideology of the South African President*. Pietermaritzburg: University of Natal Press, 121–42.

Vansina, Jan 1985. *Oral Tradition as History*. Madison: University of Wisconsin Press.

Vellinga, Menno 2002. 'Globalization and neoliberalism: Economy and society in Latin America'. *Iberoamericana: Nordic Journal of Latin American and Caribbean Studies*, vol. 32 no. 2, 25–43.

Walker, Alan 1945. *Coaltown: A Social Survey of Cessnock, NSW*. Melbourne: Melbourne University Press.

Wallerstein, Immanuel 1974a. *The Modern World-System I: Capitalist Agriculture and the Origins of the European World-Economy in the Sixteenth Century*. New York: Academic Press.

—— 1974b. 'The rise and future demise of the world capitalist system: Concepts for comparative analysis.' *Comparative Studies in Society and History*, vol. 16 no. 4, 387–415.

—— 1979 *The Capitalist World-Economy*. Cambridge: Cambridge University Press.

—— 1999 *The End of the World as We Know It: Social Science for the Twenty-First Century*. Minneapolis: University of Minnesota Press.

Ward, Lester F. 1897. *Dynamic Sociology, or Applied Social Science as Based upon Statical Sociology and the Less Complex Sciences*, 2nd edn. New York: Appleton.

—— 1903. *Pure Sociology*. New York: Macmillan.

Weber, Max 1989 [1894]. 'Developmental tendencies in the situation of East Elbian rural labourers'. In Keith Tribe, ed., *Reading Weber*. London: Routledge, 158–87.

White, Luise, Miescher, Stephan F. and Cohen, David William, eds 2001. *African Words, African Voices: Critical Practices in Oral History*. Bloomington: Indiana University Press.

White, Patrick 1956. *The Tree of Man*. London: Eyre & Spottiswoode.

Williams, Nancy M. 1986. *The Yolngu and their Land: A System of Land Tenure and the Fight for its Recognition*. Canberra: Australian Institute of Aboriginal Studies.

Wiredu, Kwasi 1980. *Philosophy and an African Culture*. Cambridge: Cambridge University Press.

Wittgenstein, Ludwig 1974 [1921]. *Tractatus Logico-Philosophicus*. Trans. D.F. Pears and B.F. McGuinness. London: Routledge.

Yacine, Tassadit 2003. 'L'Algérie, matrice d'une oeuvre'. In Pierre Encrevé and Rose-Marie Lagrave, eds, *Travailler avec Bourdieu*. Paris: Flammarion, 333–45.

—— 2005. 'Pierre Bourdieu, amusnaw Kabyle ou intellectuel organique de l'humanité'. In Gérard Mauger, ed., *Rencontres avec Pierre Bourdieu*. Bellecombe-en-Bauges: Editions de Croquant, 565–74.

Yeo, Eileen Janes 1996. *The Contest for Social Science: Relations and Representations of Gender and Class*. London: Rivers Oram Press.

Yunupingu, Galarrwuy, ed. 1997. *Our Land is Our Life: Land Rights—Past, Present and Future*. Brisbane: University of Queensland Press.

Zhang, Zhen 2001. 'Mediating time: The "rice bowl of youth" in *fin de siecle* urban China'. In Arjun Appadurai, ed., *Globalization*. Durham: Duke University Press, 131–54.

Zacharin, Robert Fyfe 1976. *Emigrant Eucalypts: Gum Trees as Exotics*. Cape Schanck, Victoria: the author.

Zubrzycki, Jerzy 1960. *Immigrants in Australia: A Demographic Survey Based on the 1954 Census*. Melbourne: Melbourne University Press.

Index